PROCESSING WORDS

PROCESSING WORDS

Writing and Revising on a Microcomputer

Bruce L. Edwards, Jr.

Bowling Green State University

PRENTICE-HALL, INC., Englewood Cliffs, New Jersey   07632

Library of Congress Cataloging-in-Publication Data

EDWARDS, BRUCE L.
  Processing words.

  Includes index.
  1. English language—Rhetoric—Data processing.
2. Word processing. 3. Microcomputers—Programming.
I. Title.
PE1408.E344 1987   808′.02′0285   86-25234
ISBN 0-13-723636-0

Editorial/production supervision
  and interior design: F. Hubert
Cover design: Photo Plus Art
Manufacturing buyer: Ray Keating

Printed in the United States of America

10 9 8 7 6 5 4 3 2 1

ISBN 0-13-723636-0   01

PRENTICE-HALL INTERNATIONAL (UK) LIMITED, *London*
PRENTICE-HALL OF AUSTRALIA PTY. LIMITED, *Sydney*
PRENTICE-HALL CANADA INC., *Toronto*
PRENTICE-HALL HISPANOAMERICANA, S.A., *Mexico*
PRENTICE-HALL OF INDIA PRIVATE LIMITED, *New Delhi*
PRENTICE-HALL OF JAPAN, INC., *Tokyo*
PRENTICE-HALL OF SOUTHEAST ASIA PTE. LTD., *Singapore*
EDITORA PRENTICE-HALL DO BRASIL, LTDA., *Rio de Janeiro*

For Joan, my Beatrice and my Gloriana.
Whatever good thing I may accomplish here or elsewhere,
it is only through and for you that it comes to be.

Contents

CHAPTER 3
Writing to Understand   *34*

CHAPTER 4
Writing to Communicate   *44*

CHAPTER 5
Writing to Develop and Organize   *54*

CHAPTER 6
Revising on a Microcomputer: An Overview   *69*

CHAPTER 11
Editing: Polishing the Final Draft   *152*

CHAPTER 12
Writing for Self-expression   *168*

CHAPTER 13
Writing to Explain, Analyze, and Persuade   *193*

A Word About Processing Words

Processing Words is a book about writing and revising effectively on a microcomputer. You need not worry about the "compatibility" of this textbook with the particular computer or word processor you are using. The practical writing strategies, writing assignments, and variety of exercises in this text can be performed with any computer or software, whether your computer is expensive or inexpensive, portable, desktop, or mainframe!

Processing Words is not, however, a general introduction to computing or even a guide to word processing per se. At its core, it is a textbook about writing and revising and it is based upon the most recent and useful research in composition. In writing *Processing Words*, I have assumed that your instructor will provide you with the necessary information (or, in computer lingo, "documentation") to operate your computer and software. Your instructor has, perhaps, also provided you with a list of commands or operating steps to get you started.

In discussing various word processing operations in this text I have been careful to use generic, easy-to-understand terminology that will be applicable to whatever software you'll be using in your writing course. (Appendix II contains a glossary to help you keep track of the meaning of terms along the way, and, of course, your instructor will be glad to clarify or explain anything else you need to know in order to use *Processing Words* in the most effective way.)

AN OVERVIEW

Chapters 1 through 5 serve two main functions. First, they explain and illustrate how using the microcomputer can assist you in becoming a more effective writer. Second, they introduce the key components in the composing process: getting and exploring ideas, forging and focusing a thesis and intention, analyzing the intended audience, and creating the early drafts of a text.

Chapter 1 introduces you to the microcomputer *as a composing medium*, that is, as an electronic stylus for writing, revising, and printing your writing assignments. Chapter 2 suggests how you can write to discover what to write about in a text, offering four different strategies for getting started in exploring what you know and don't know about a topic. Chapter 3 helps you learn how to write to understand, that is, write the first draft of your text, and determine your main point and the overall intention of your text. Chapter 4 teaches you how to analyze your audience and anticipate their needs as you draft your text. Chapter 5 discusses and illustrates four different strategies for developing and organizing your draft: narration, description, exposition, and argumentation.

Three possible writing tasks are introduced in Chapter 2: a personal narrative, an explanatory text, or a persuasive text. In this assignment you will practice the strategies for discovering, understanding, and communicating your ideas that you will later use in the writing tasks of Chapters 12 and 13. Throughout Chapters 2 through 4 you will follow the work of my student, John Bebb, as he works toward his own first draft.

While the first five chapters of *Processing Words* show you how to move from prewriting to the creation of your first draft, Chapters 6 through 10 are designed to help you use the microcomputer to select and apply appropriate revision strategies for making your text clear, coherent, economical, suitably developed, and stylistically graceful.

Chapter 6 presents an overview of the revising process, suggesting strategies you can use on the microcomputer to plan and execute a revision that will make your text more effective. Chapter 7 focuses on the paragraph, offering strategies for revising your paragraphs so they are clear, unified, coherent, and complete. Chapter 8 provides strategies for making your prose more lean and economical by eliminating passiveness and redundancy in sentences and word choice. Chapter 9 focuses on two components of effective prose, fullness and grace, providing strategies for remedying both under- and over-developed prose, that is, saying too little about too much and saying too much about too little, and for creating sentence patterns in your text that will make your prose more graceful and appealing to your reader.

Chapter 10 puts all of these revising components together in a case study of John Bebb's revision of his explanatory text introduced first in Chapter 2. Here you will see how John applied the strategies presented in Chapters 6 through 9 to create a finished, effective version of his explanatory text. Chapter 11 completes the discussion of preparing a text for one's readers, focusing on the final component of successful writing—editing—and how the microcomputer can facilitate this process. This chapter, while not a substitute for a handbook, surveys the basic proofreading and editing problems apprentice writers face.

The final three chapters round out *Processing Words* with a focus on the particular kinds of writing tasks most college writers face. Chapter 12 presents three expressive writing assignments—the journal, the personal narrative, and the opinion text—offering both professional and student texts for discussion and example. Chapter 13 follows with three transactional writing tasks—the explanatory text, the analytical text, and the persuasive text—accompanied again by professional and student examples.

Chapter 14 presents effective strategies you can use to write a research paper on a microcomputer. The basic components of researching and writing a research paper are exemplified in the work of Sarah Scheinblum as she constructs a research paper about her favorite author, C. S. Lewis.

ACKNOWLEDGMENTS

No textbook is produced without the assistance of a great many colleagues and associates, and *Processing Words* is no exception in this regard. I offer my thanks to the editorial and production staff at Prentice-Hall, Inc., especially Phil Miller, who believed in this textbook from the start, Jane Baumann, his cheerful and helpful assistant, and Frank Hubert, my resourceful and patient production editor.

I express my gratitude as well to the reviewers of the various versions of this manuscript: Thomas T. Barker, Texas Tech University; Francis Hodgins, University of Illinois–Urbana; Sylvia A. Holladay, St. Petersburg Junior College; William Ingram, University of Michigan; Stephen Marcus, University of California, Santa Barbara; W. Dean Memering, Central Michigan University; James R. Nicholl, Western Carolina University; Audrey J. Roth, Miami-Dade Community College; and William Wresch, University of Wisconsin–Stevens Point. They should not be held accountable, of course, for the final version of this textbook, as I have in some cases stubbornly resisted their well-intended suggestions.

In conceiving and composing *Processing Words*, I have been influenced by many an article, theorist, and teacher during my years as a professor of English, active in the lively and fulfilling profession of teaching composition. Certainly my mentors, Donald Stewart and Robert Grindell of Kansas State University, and Maxine Hairston, James Kinneavy, Steve Witte, and Lester Faigley of the University of Texas at Austin, deserve some credit for sowing any seeds of solid composition pedagogy which may sprout here.

Beyond these general influences in writing *Processing Words*, I owe a few individuals special recognition here. First, I owe an incalculable debt to my colleague at Bowling Green State University, Alice Heim Calderonello, with whom I collaborated on a previous textbook (*Roughdrafts: The Process of Writing*, Houghton Mifflin, 1986). Alice has taught me many things about my profession, not the least of which include how to plan and write a textbook, how to communicate rhetorical ideas effectively to students, and how to translate theory into practice. *Processing Words* would not exist without my exposure to her innovative conceptualizations about the revising and editing process.

Secondly, I, along with a generation of other composition teachers and textbook writers, owe a large debt to the pioneering work of such researchers as Linda Flower, Nancy Sommers, Richard Lanham, and Joseph Williams. Flower's explorations of the writing process have helped me understand how writers make sense of their ideas in order to translate them for their readers. Sommers' research into the revising behavior of professional and student writers has informed much of what I suggest to students about rewriting their texts on a microcomputer. Both Lanham and Williams have offered the profession dozens of insights into how to control wordiness and sprawl in student prose, and I am specifically indebted to them for much of the advice I offer in Chapters 8 and 9 for rewriting a text for clarity, economy, fullness, and grace.

While acknowledging my debt to these important contributors to contemporary composition theory and pedagogy, I must also acknowledge other colleagues here at Bowling Green State University who have supported and influenced the writing of *Processing Words*. Les Barber, chair of the Department of English, Tom Wymer, assistant chair, Kathy Hart, director of the General Studies Writing program, and Kendall Baker, Dean of Arts and Sciences, have each been enthusiastically supportive of my inquiry into computer-based composition pedagogy. At each turn, they have offered me the freedom and the institutional support I needed for my research and writing.

Other colleagues and friends also deserve mention. Tom Klein has been an unfailing encouragement to me in my professional career and exemplifies to me all the qualities I hope to communicate to my students as a writing teacher, and human being. Jim Karpen, now of Maharishi International University, provoked my thinking about about the impact of computers on literacy while I directed his dissertation here at BGSU and he continues to challenge my thinking on these matters. Three graduate students, Brenda Green, Craig Hergert, and Mark DelMaramo, worked with me on a pilot project using the microcomputer in freshman English and taught me a great deal about what composing principles can and should be employed in the composition classroom of 2001.

I offer my special gratitude to the undergraduate students whose work appears in various forms in *Processing Words*: Chris Abels, Pam Day, Selena Campbell, John Bebb, and Sarah Scheinblum. In addition, Lynnette Porter, a Ph.D. candidate in rhetoric and composition here at Bowling Green, provided valuable help to me in preparing several sections of the instructor's manual that accompanies this text.

The support staff in the department of English at BGSU is immeasurably helpful to anyone trying to complete a manuscript of any kind. My warm thanks to: Suzanne Andrews, department administrative assistant during the birth of *Processing Words*, who always made sure my computer supplies and my reimbursements were in order and on time; and Jessica Wade, Karen Bernhardt, and Joanne Lohr, secretaries and receptionists extraordinaire, who make working in the department a delight and a privilege.

To a special few friends and confidants who continue to encourage my efforts to write and make sense of my life, I extend my continuing appreciation: The Abels family, the Alexanders, the Davises, the Doughertys, and the Days. To Bruce and Betty Edwards and Mary Klever, my always understanding dad, mom, and grandmother. I convey my deep love and gratitude for their support of my love of words.

Finally, I must acknowledge what is without question the most significant contribution to this project, that of my wife and children. They have kept me (mostly) sane during the ordeal that textbook writing represents. For those who know Joan, the dedication at the front of this book is self-explanatory. And to my four gifts of grace, Matthew, Mary Elizabeth, Justin, and Michael: I can finally answer your oft-asked question, "When are you going to be done, Daddy?" *Now*.

BRUCE L. EDWARDS, JR.

CHAPTER 1

The Microcomputer as Composing Medium

MEET FUTUREWRITER: COMPOSING VERSUS TRANSCRIBING

Shirley Biagi, writing in her book *A Writer's Guide to Word Processors,* describes the person she calls *FutureWriter:*

> The writer will be able to move large blocks of copy from page one to page sixteen flawlessly, while the word processor (at the writer's discretion) rearranges the new edited version and renumbers the pages. This writer will be able to insert words whenever necessary without retyping the entire manuscript, and without drawing careful insertions into typewritten text.
>
> FutureWriter will be able to type without ever having to hit a carriage return or worry about whether the copy should be single- or double-spaced because the word processor will format the copy automatically. With a single command, this writer can justify copy so that the right margin is completely even all the way down the page.
>
> By pushing another key, FutureWriter can correct misspellings throughout an article. And the writer who wants to change the name of a central character in a story, for instance, can tell the word processor to find that character's name throughout the text and change it. This writer also will be able to print flawlessly correct final copy at a rate of one page every four seconds.[1]

The amazing thing about Biagi's "FutureWriter" is that such a writer exists right now! All the features of writing that she describes as futuristic are available today—for almost any microcomputer, and any writer. The microcomputer used as a writing and revising tool is sometimes called a "word processor," and we will use these two terms somewhat

---

[1]Shirley Biagi, *A Writer's Guide to Word Processors* (Englewood Cliffs, N.J.: Prentice-Hall, Inc., 1984), pp. 4–5. © 1984 by Prentice-Hall, Inc., Englewood Cliffs, N.J.

1

interchangeably in *Processing Words*. If you are enrolled in a course using this textbook, congratulations—you have just joined the revolution! This composition text is designed to help apprentice writers like you take advantage of these advances in computer technology.

By far, one of the most dramatic effects of the influx of computers into business, industry, scientific research, and education has been how it has changed the way many people *write*. Even the invention of the typewriter did not alter the way the majority of writers and editors actually did their work because the typewriter still dealt with the single page, one page after another. It was simply a tool for formatting the composition created with pen or pencil or dictated into a tape recorder of some kind.

With the advent of video display terminals, VDTs, in most newsrooms across the country, "word processing" became a reality. Writers wrote their stories on the screen and sent them electronically to their editors, who edited their stories "on-line" and then sent them to the composing room to be printed as the next morning's newspaper. Following the journalists' lead, the modern composition classroom has begun to reap the advantages of the new technology.

There are two separate components in the writing process for most writers: writers *compose*, then they *transcribe*. In the past, the writer's options in performing these steps were limited. Typically writers would compose their texts with paper and pen—or on a typewriter—and then transcribe their "final" versions. They would then either recopy their texts neatly for their intended reader or transfer their handwritten texts to the typewriter, which was designed to create readable, "clean" copy ready for a reader.

The problem with this composition/transcription division is that hardly any writer recopies or types without making mistakes. And if writers make mistakes, they have to be corrected somehow, often by recopying or retyping an entire page or manuscript. Even at its best, typing restricts the motivation and the ability to revise. The fact is, most writers, no matter how accomplished as typists they may be, spend more time transcribing the final draft of a paper than they do in creating it in the first place.

The word processor is not, however, just a super typewriter, a tool for *transcribing*. When you write with a word processor, the medium is not the familiar paper and pen, but VDT and cursor. The video display terminal, or computer monitor, is your work space, your blank tablet; the cursor, the blinking light on your VDT, is your writing stylus, your electronic pencil. The characters entered from the computer keyboard appear on the screen and may be added to, moved, deleted, or rearranged at the command of the writer. The text on the VDT is alive, dynamic, malleable. Nothing is permanently fixed. All options are open.

In effect, the medium for composing and the medium for transcribing *merge* on a word processor. The text you the writer have composed may be printed directly from the version you have created electronically. Writing with a word processor combines typing with composing, revising, and editing; the only separate operation is printing, and this is done with the pressing of a few keys. By merging these formerly separate processes—composing a text and transcribing it—into one, you the writer are freed to attend to the most important issue in the writing process: the communication of ideas and experience.

WHAT A MICROCOMPUTER CAN
AND CANNOT DO FOR YOUR WRITING

Learning to write with pen and paper, you discovered a great deal about the writing process. You would get ideas, explore them, write a draft, revise it, write another, do more revision . . . Oh those revisions! Hardly anyone likes to revise because it means rewriting and, worse, recopying. Even if you have learned how to type, revising is still a chore: you finish a page and find you've consistently misspelled "separate"—that means messy corrections; you are about to hand a paper in and discover you need to change the introduction—that means troublesome cutting and pasting; you complete that fifteen-page research paper and discover that your footnotes and bibliography are not in the proper form—that means retyping the whole thing.

The very technology of writing—pen, erasable paper, typewriters, scissors, paste, correction fluid—discourages the writer from serious, extensive revising and rewriting, since even a few minor changes can make a text look messy or ugly. Proofreading, that neglected art, is forbidding if for no other reason than this: you fear that you *will find* something to change! Simply put, who has the time to rethink, change, or fix everything that should be revised in a writing task?

The good news about the computing revolution then, is that it has freed writers from most of their former excuses for hating revision. Writing with a microcomputer, or word processor, makes revision and editing easier, faster, and just more "do-able." It enhances all the skills a writer already has. While brainstorming, outlining, and discovery drafts are helpful components of even a paper-and-pen writing process, they become even more versatile and productive on a word processor.

The other side of the coin, the not-so-good-news, is that while writing with a word processor makes composing, revising, and editing easier and more pleasurable tasks, no technique, no technological advance by itself will make a poor writer a good writer. Composing is a complex cognitive and physiological skill, and your own writing process is affected by a number of individual factors. Learning to write is still a matter of learning and using language, rhetoric, and logic effectively.

Would-be housebuilders who do not know how to read blueprints or select quality building materials will hardly be successful—even if they have state-of-the-art tools. Similarly, having tools to accomplish a writing task faster and more easily is no consolation to those who still need to learn how to generate ideas, find a thesis and intention, draft a text, and revise it appropriately in the first place.

Consequently, *Processing Words* is not primarily a book about computers. It is a book about learning to write and revise—and how to do it more effectively *with the use* of a word processor.

Even though *Processing Words* is not designed per se to introduce you to computing or to the software employed in your writing course, it *will* teach you how to use them both more productively in writing your texts. It assumes that most word processing software programs have common features, and that these can be discussed and illustrated by their generic names: SEARCH/FIND, BLOCK COPY, INSERT, CURSOR MOVE-

MENT, and the like.[2] (In Appendix I you will find a tutorial that will help you chart the basic functions of your word processing software so you can be on-line and working on your first writing task in no time.)

The manual, or documentation, that comes with your computer and word processing software will tell you what you need to know to use it for writing tasks. Answers to specific questions about how your software operates, how to open a file, enter text, save a file, print a text, and so on, can be found by referring to the appropriate sections in such material. (Your instructor may also have prepared a special tutorial for the particular software you will be using as well.)

A TYPICAL WRITING SESSION:
SOME COMPUTER BASICS

The easiest way to understand what writing with a microcomputer is like is to look over the shoulder of a writer at work. Here is a description of a typical writing session on a microcomputer. Any unfamiliar terms you encounter will be explained as you read through various portions of this text—or they may be found in the glossary in Appendix II.

Judy Robinson checked her watch. She had several minutes to get to the computer lab before it opened at 8 A.M. She planned to begin work on her next freshman writing assignment: a personal experience essay about her family. Judy gathered up her writing tools: her textbook, a notebook in which she had jotted some ideas for the assignment, and a blank diskette on which she would store her text at the end of the session.

After she arrived at the lab, she showed the operator her student ID and requested a copy of the word processing software she would be using. She then selected a microcomputer station that wasn't being used. The first thing she did was turn on the microcomputer. Since the one she was using had two disk drives, she opened the top drive and inserted the word processing disk and then closed the door of the drive. In the bottom drive, she inserted her own blank diskette. The disk drive whirred for a few seconds and then a menu came up on the VDT, or screen, giving her several options for starting the session.

Since the blank diskette she brought with her had not been initialized, or prepared to receive data, Judy selected the INITIALIZE DISK option. The disk drive whirred a bit more and then returned Judy to the menu. Her diskette had been initialized and was ready to receive any texts she would later wish to save. Next, Judy selected EDIT A FILE from the menu and the menu was replaced with a blank screen, ready for Judy to enter text. At the top of her screen was a line of information which told her such things

---

[2]*Software* is a term that refers to the actual programs, stored on diskettes, that you will use in operating the microcomputer. In order to write with a microcomputer you will need not only the computer itself but also a program, called a *word processing program* (or, word processor), that will be entered into the computer's memory and permit you to begin writing. (The term ''word processor'' can sometimes also refer to a kind of computer whose only purpose is the creation and editing of texts. In those computers the software is ''built-in.'' We will not usually be using the term in this sense, however.)

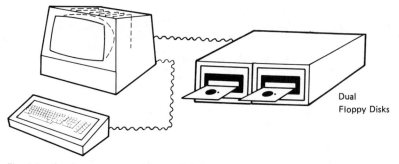

Fig. 1.1   A microcomputer with two disk drives.

as what page she was on (in this case, page 1), whether she was in single- or double-spaced mode, and where her left and right margins were.

From here, Judy began to type as she might on a regular typewriter, except that whenever she made a mistake, that is, entered a character, word, or block of text she decided to change, she simply moved the cursor to the appropriate point(s), deleted the error or unwanted text, and then replaced it with something more appropriate. After she had created about two pages of material, she scrolled back through the text, using the cursor control keys on her keyboard, looking at her ideas and deciding which ones had the most promise. She decided that her second paragraph worked better as an introduction, so she marked the beginning and ending of the text she wanted to move and, with the appropriate keystrokes, ''cut'' it and relocated, or, ''pasted,'' it to the beginning of her text.

After inserting a few more lines here and there in her text she decided to end the session, since she had to make it to a 9:00 class across campus. She pressed a series of keys which saved her text, but not before being asked to name the file she was working on. She named it FIRST TEXT. After she typed in this name, the disk drive whirred again, and she was returned to her opening menu. She selected the CHECK DIREC-

Fig. 1.2   Two sizes of diskettes: $5\frac{1}{4}$ and $3\frac{1}{2}$ inch diskettes.

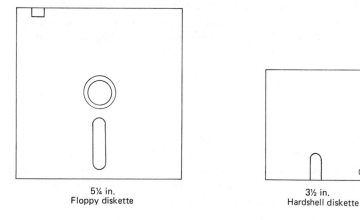

5¼ in.
Floppy diskette

3½ in.
Hardshell diskette

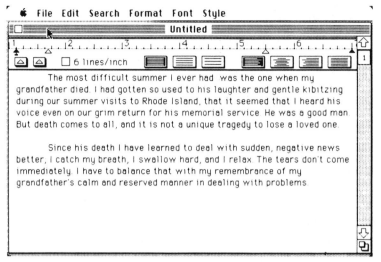

Fig. 1.3   Text being edited on a VDT.

TORY option to see if her text had been properly saved. When the directory on her disk drive came up on the screen, she noted that FIRST TEXT appeared. She opened the bottom disk drive door and removed her diskette. She then removed the word processing diskette from the top drive and turned off the computer. She returned the word processing diskette to the operator and headed for her 9:00 class.

In this scenario, you should understand that Judy did not walk into the computer lab without any preparation or previous experience. She had spent several days just getting acquainted with the operation of the computer and the word processing software required for the course. When she finally entered the lab for serious writing, she was ready. When you begin to use the microcomputer, you will want to set aside some time just to learn the basic operations involved, long before you begin any serious writing. You'll be surprised to find, nevertheless, that but a little practice will make it easy to use the word processing software designated for your course. The more you use your microcomputer and software, the more comfortable you will become with it.

GETTING STARTED WITH YOUR COMPUTER AND SOFTWARE

As you learn the various commands that operate your software, *jot them down on the chart in the inside cover of this book;* this chart will help you organize and remember what you need to know to begin and complete a writing session successfully. If your instructor has provided you with a manual or documentation that explains how to get started using your microcomputer and word processing software, you should study it carefully before going to your microcomputer station. There is no substitute, though, for hands-on practice. Take your time in practicing and mastering the various functions that you will be using the most.

Here are some of the basic commands and functions of computers and word processing software that you will need to know in order to use *Processing Words* effectively:

1. How to turn on the computer and insert the appropriate software disk to start a writing session
2. How to open or call up the word processing software you will be using
3. How to prepare a blank disk to receive information and, depending upon your computer's operating system, how to name the diskette
4. How to read and select operations from the "menu" that your word processing software provides
5. How to move the cursor and scroll the text up and down and from left to right
6. How to set margins and tabs, how to select the appropriate spacing for your text, and how to select format options, such as ragged right, right justification, or centered text
7. How to enter text and save, merge, and retrieve files from storage
8. How to perform such operations as entering text, inserting text, deleting text, block-copying text, block-moving text, and searching for and replacing text
9. How to print a text and select such options as underlining, italics, typeface (font), and typesize (pitch) for special effects.

Don't panic! You don't need to learn all these things the first time you sit down in front of your computer. You will gradually add word processing operations to your repertoire as you practice composing. Take heart! Like learning to drive a car, word processing at first seems like an impossible task since you have to remember how to do several different things simultaneously or in special sequence. But after only a few sessions you will feel comfortable with both the jargon and the operation of your word processor. By learning one step at a time you can avoid a great deal of frustration.

The tutorial in Appendix I which I mentioned earlier will help you ferret out most of the intricacies of your word processor in a more elaborate way; however, we will conclude this chapter with a basic tutorial in how to get going on your system plus a discussion of one particular kind of file you will be asked to create and use in *Processing Words*.

Most microcomputer systems consist of three components: the computer itself, including the keyboard; a VDT (or monitor); and a storage device known as a **disk drive.** In addition to these components, known as **hardware,** you will need a copy of the word processing program disk (known as **software**) you will be using, plus your own blank diskette(s), on which you will store texts you are creating and editing.

The first things you will need to know *include*: how to turn your computer on, how and when to insert a disk, how to initialize a blank diskette, and whether or not you must access the word processing software with a special keystroke or command or whether this software is self-starting, providing you with a menu. A **keystroke** refers to any time a particular key is pressed on the keyboard. To prepare youself for using your word processor, answer the following questions; some require a simple yes or no, others require that you identify a particular operation, command, or keystroke.

1. What brand of computer do you have? _____ (Some well-known brands include, Radio Shack TRS-80, Apple IIe, Apple Macintosh, IBM PC, Kaypro, Atari, and Commodore.)

2. How many disk drives are built in or attached to the computer? _____ If you have two, which is Drive A? _____ Which is Drive B? _____

3. Will there be a printer attached to your microcomputer? _____ Or, will you need to compose on one system and then print on another? _____

4. What word processing software will you be using? _____ (Some popular programs include Bank Street Writer, Scripsit, WordStar, MacWrite, WordPerfect, and Microsoft Word.)

5. What size or format of blank diskettes will you need to purchase to use your particular microcomputer? (Diskettes come in two sizes, $3\frac{1}{2}$ inch and $5\frac{1}{4}$ inch, and come single-sided and double-sided.) _____

6. Where do you turn the computer on? _____ Will you need to turn the monitor on separately? _____

7. Should your program diskette (the diskette containing the program with which you will begin a writing session) be inserted *before* you turn it on, or *after*? _____

8. What diskette needs to be inserted first: an operating system disk? the word processing disk? or, something else? _____

9. Once your program disk is up and running, what commands or keystrokes, if any, do you need to enter in order to call up the word processing menu? _____

10. Once your program disk is up and running, what are the steps in initializing a blank diskette, that is, formatting a blank diskette to receive data? (Some microcomputers, such as the Apple Macintosh, ask you if you wish to initialize a diskette when you insert a blank, unformatted diskette.)
    Step 1: _____   Step 2: _____
    Step 3: _____   Step 4: _____

11. How do you save a file and quit a program? By pressing a certain key or pressing a combination of keys? _____ How do you exit from the system itself? By removing the diskettes and turning it off, or by some other step(s)? _____

Trying It Out

At your microcomputer, follow these steps to begin a session:

1. Turn on your computer and/or monitor.

2. Insert the appropriate start-up disk (either a system diskette or word processing diskette).

3. Select the appropriate option for initializing your blank diskette.

4. Initialize your blank diskette by inserting it into the appropriate disk drive and performing the appropriate command. If required, select a name for the diskette which distinguishes it from others you may eventually be using.

5. Insert your word processing software (if you haven't already) and call up the menu. Select the option required to create or edit a file and type in a few lines. Save your work and look for it in the directory of your files.

6. Quit the program you are presently in, remove the diskette, and end the session.

USING TEMPLATE FILES

Interspersed through the book are special files referred to as **template files,** one of the unique features of *Processing Words.* These are text files you will be asked to create to assist you in finding ideas, analyzing your own prose, and stimulating your investigative powers as you work through a writing task.

Basically, you will create these files as you would any other file or text you create with your word processing software (WPS). When you are asked in a chapter discussion to create such a file, simply begin an editing session the way you would any other task and type the appropriate information on the screen and save it under the name suggested. (Appendix I provides you with help in setting up these files, or you can consult your instructor.)

The purpose of the template files is to give you a consistent and systematic tool for moving through the various stages implied in a writing task. For instance, an audience template file will help you specify certain aspects of your intended audience so you can draft your text with this audience in mind. A revision template file will help you look for distinctive features of your text that need special attention and rethinking.

The first step in using the template file is to create a workable version, following the instructions supplied in Appendix I. The template file is designed to be used by itself or to be called up within another active file you are working with. When you use the template file by itself you will open the file and answer the questions appropriately. Since you will want to use a fresh version of the file each time, you should be careful to save both the ''master'' template file as well as the new template file that contains the answers you have provided to the file's questions. Save the new file under another name whenever closing a particular session. For instance, you may open the AUDIENCE template file, answer its questions about the audience for the particular assignment you are working on, and then save the whole file—including both questions and answers—as ''Text #1 Aud.'' That way the original template file will remain ''blank'' and available for your next session under its own name, ''AUDIENCE.''

FINAL TIPS

Here are a few more tips for learning how to use your computer and word processing software:

- If you have access to the manual or documentation for the word processing software you are using, take it to the lab with you. Pace yourself in reading through the basic commands, practicing each one separately until you understand how it works and what it is for. At first it will seem as if there are a dozen things to learn (and there are), but be patient: the only way to learn how to use it is to "play" with it, making mistakes and learning from them.

- Start with some of the basic word processing operations and commands—starting a session, inserting a diskette, opening a file, entering text, saving a text, and printing a text—before trying out anything too fancy or complex.

- Allow yourself a block of uninterrupted time for learning how to use your computer and the word processing software. Don't panic if you get stuck. Use the menus that your software provides within the program itself. Consult the manual, consult the operator on duty—or even another student in the lab. Most students are taught as much by listening to their peers as they are by receiving formal instruction.

- Use the inside cover of this book to record the various commands which operate your word processing software. If your manual has a "quick card," or summary of basic commands, it will also be a handy guide to refer to when you are learning how to use your software.

- *Unlearn* some habits you may have picked up in using a typewriter:

    1. Your word processing software probably has "word wrap," a feature that automatically returns the cursor to the next line when you exceed the right margin. Try to avoid pressing the carriage return except when you want to insert a blank line after a portion of text, for instance, after a paragraph. If you operate the keyboard as you would a conventional typewriter, you will lose some of the advantages that the word processing software allows.

    2. Note whether your word processor uses the backspace key to *delete* text. If so, you must not use this key to move backwards through your text. Most likely you will use another set of keys (indicated by directional arrows), or a "mouse" (a device which allows you to move through text by rolling a specially sensitive ball on your desk top), to control cursor movement and scrolling.

WRITERS AT WORK:
AN OVERVIEW

One way to learn how to compose effectively is to observe the behavior of successful writers. When you follow the behavior of a successful writer, step-by-step, you can discover insights into your own writing process which thereby enable you to apply fresh approaches to your own prose. Throughout Chapters 2 through 4 and in Chapter 10, you will follow the writing process of one of my students, John Bebb, as he works through the various components of the writing process. Later, in Chapter 14, I will present the work of Sarah Scheinblum as she moves through the various stages of constructing an effective research paper. The work of these two writers will help make the components of writing which *Processing Words* presents more concrete.

As you watch John and Sarah move toward their final drafts, you will have viewed the evolution of two successful texts from beginning to end. Nevertheless, in one sense, any depiction of a writer's composing process is a fiction. That is, it is a recreation based upon the writer's all too faulty recollection and the evidence gleaned from looking at various drafts. A great deal of what happens in the writing process never gets on the VDT or paper; we capture what we can. Total explicitness is impossible. Textbooks like this one always seem to make the process look neat, compact, and infallible. Of course, this is not the case. If the composing process could be reduced to, say, fifteen or twenty "rules," then indeed one might teach writing merely by having students memorize formulae.

In presenting these student texts, I want to enable you to witness, perhaps for the first time in your experience as a writer, the evolution of another writer's text. In so doing, you will likely learn more about yourself as a writer and, perhaps, some new things about what works and what doesn't in drafting and revising a text.

CHAPTER 2

Writing
to Discover

THE ELEMENTS OF SUCCESSFUL COMPOSING

Successful writers don't always know what it is they want to say when they sit down to write. And during their composing process, their texts pass through several stages on the way to becoming final drafts. But it is safe to generalize that experienced writers have learned that the writing process is *recursive,* that is, they have learned that they must double back and forth among the components of the writing process, writing and rewriting their texts as they discover what they want to say and how to say it to their intended readers.

Experienced writers begin a writing task by *writing to discover,* that is, they find, explore, and pursue their ideas using various brainstorming tools. Once they have discovered a subject matter they wish to write about, they *write to understand,* that is, they probe their ideas, groping to explain them to themselves while fashioning a focused thesis and forging a specific intention. Finally, they *write to communicate,* transforming ideas that make sense only to them into a text that conveys their meaning clearly and directly. In this chapter and in Chapters 3 through 5, we will consider the strategies successful writers use to begin a writing task, explore, develop, and organize their ideas, and communicate those ideas in a draft suitable for its intended audience.

While textbook writers are always tempted to describe the composing process in terms of four or five "infallible," discrete steps or stages, such a linear view of composing will not do. The microcomputer makes the recursiveness of writing quite concrete. The possibilities for changing your text by adding to it, rearranging it, or deleting from it, are unlimited. This flexibility can, of course, be good and bad news, since it can sometimes multiply the choices a writer faces indefinitely, temporarily freezing the process in its tracks. But the benefits of composing with a word processor far outweigh the potential hazards. As you practice the various writing strategies found here and in later sections, however, remember that each writer's composing strategy is a little different.

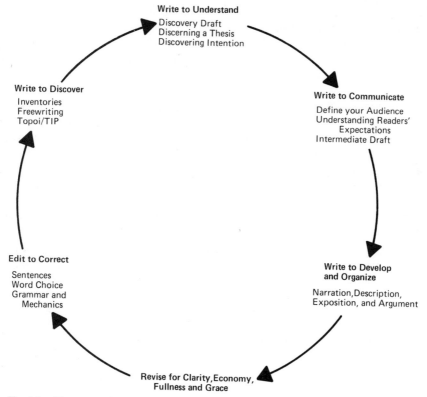

Write to Understand
Discovery Draft
Discerning a Thesis
Discovering Intention

Write to Discover
Inventories
Freewriting
Topoi/TIP

Write to Communicate
Define your Audience
Understanding Readers'
Expectations
Intermediate Draft

Edit to Correct
Sentences
Word Choice
Grammar and
Mechanics

**Write to Develop
and Organize**
Narration, Description,
Exposition, and Argument

Revise for Clarity, Economy,
Fullness and Grace

Fig. 2.1   The composing process.

You may combine some of these functions or perform some of them in a different order than presented here. Still, many writers have no discernible pattern in the way they compose and find that by adopting or adapting the patterns presented in this textbook they gain a helpful starting point for developing their own composing strategies.

WRITING TO DISCOVER

How do you begin to write after you are given a particular writing task? Do you make an outline? Read a particular set of magazines? Take a walk in the park? Start writing random ideas down? One way or another, a writer must begin. This beginning component is sometimes called ''prewriting,'' or writing to discover what it is you want to write about and what you wish to say about your chosen topic. For many writers this takes place in the mind; for others, it must all be explored graphically on paper or on a VDT. In this chapter you will be presented with four prewriting strategies to help you search for a subject to write about.

Prewriting, however, is not just for beginnings; as you work through a draft of a text, you may discover that you have not said enough to explain something; or, you may realize that you need to add more specific detail about a particular topic. At these junctures you may turn again to these prewriting strategies to help you develop your text. Before looking at some specific strategies for generating ideas for your writing tasks, here are a few general tips for prewriting on a microcomputer:

• Use the microcomputer as an electronic notebook in which you can record ideas and associations as fast as you think of them. Since the text in a word processor is so ''malleable,'' you will be able to expand it, alter it, move it, rework it, with the flash of a few keystrokes.

• You may find it useful in responding to a writing task to create one file just for prewriting, another file for analyzing your audience, and another one for your first draft. If your word processor has features which allow you to merge files or call up one file while you are working with another, you can have your prewriting materials before you any time you want. If you don't have this option, you can still make a hard copy (a paper printout) of these notes for your use while you are drafting.

• You may, if you like, think of the screen before you as a blank sheet of paper—but one whose spacing can be altered and that can be scrolled up or down, depending on what the writer wants to see at any particular moment. You may find it helpful to press the carriage return a few times after each grouping of ideas so you can create a sense of open space that may encourage your further expansion of those ideas. You can always remove the carriage returns later or move any part of your text where you want it. The extra space will also help you distinguish different sections of the text from each other as you develop them.

EXERCISES

Use your VDT as an electronic notebook to jot down your ideas about one or more of the following situations:

a. Jot down the qualities you want in a best friend or an ideal roommate. At the end of your list, write a brief ''advertisement'' for publication in the campus newspaper which presents these qualities and appeals for an applicant.

b. You have an unexpected inheritance from a rich aunt. Jot down the uses to which you will put the money. After making the list, write a letter back home to your parents, describing how you'll use this newfound gold mine.

c. As a famous textbook writer, you've just begun your tenth book on writing. Spend a few minutes jotting down possible titles for your latest creation—a book about writing with the aid of computers. Then write a letter to your publisher explaining the features of your new text.

FOUR PREWRITING STRATEGIES

In the rest of this chapter I want to present four different prewriting strategies that will help you get started with any writing task. As they are presented here, they move from the relatively simple strategies of inventories and freewriting to the more complex and highly structured strategies of the Classical Topoi and the Tagmemic Invention Procedure.

Inventories

An *inventory* is a list of items which a writer separates into different classifications and categories. Inventories are used to "take stock," to determine what our possessions are. Our minds marvelously categorize experiences and ideas, but as writers we sometimes forget what we know about a topic or idea, and we need something to prompt our discovery or retrieval of these ideas. Creating an inventory, a list of "known" facts, can help us discover a subject to write about or assist us in exploring a subject that we have already settled upon. When writers survey their ideas in an inventory, they thus increase their options for choosing a topic.

EXERCISE

Making inventories at the VDT is a matter of entering some lists under different headings. Later in this chapter and in other writing tasks throughout *Processing Words,* you will use inventories to get started on a writing task. To discover something about yourself as a writer, and to practice making inventories, respond to the following prompts. First, type in a heading, such as "Things I like to write about," then insert a carriage return space and begin entering as many responses as you can think of. Then move on to the next one.

a. Things I like to write about
b. Things I don't like to write about
c. Things I find most interesting about the items in List a
d. Things I find difficult about writing itself
e. Things I find most helpful to do when I get stuck while I am writing
f. My most successful writing experiences
g. My least successful writing experiences
h. The most important strengths in my writing process
i. The most troublesome weaknesses in my writing process
j. The most useful revising strategies in my writing process

What did you discover about yourself as a writer? Be sure to save this inventory on a disk, and make a hard copy for future reference. You will be using this information for a writing assignment at the end of the chapter.

Freewriting

Freewriting is writing you do for yourself as you ponder a topic and record your ideas as quickly as possible. While freewriting has been used traditionally as a way to fill up a blank sheet of paper with words, the microcomputer is the perfect medium for it. Freewriting on a microcomputer allows you maximum freedom for sparking the imagination; such features as word wrap and automatic scrolling allow you to proceed unencumbered by pencil breaks or even turning a piece of paper over. Freewriting is quite simple to do. Here is how to get started:

1. Find an idea to explore.
2. Write for at least ten to fifteen minutes without stopping.
3. Type whatever comes to mind.
4. If you draw a blank, just type again the word or sentence you last wrote until something clicks.
5. Don't stop to edit or delete anything.

Here is an excerpt from five minutes of my own freewriting complete with my uncorrected typos:

Sometimes I panick when i am facing a blankk piece of paper but I always seem to be able to generate ideas on a VDT. Exceptt now I amm freezing up about it because i know that the textbook reader willl be looking over this when I'm through. Ahhhhhhh. What do/would I really like to be writing about here? Baseball. Baseball. The pennant races, the smell of hot dogs, the weak soft drinks at the ballparks. Anything about baseball. Certain players: Rose, Thornton, Parker, Valenzuela, Brett. And the old players: Banks, Mantle, Mays, Berra, Howard, Cobb. And listening to baseball when I was growing up—Akron, Ohio, hot summer nights listening to the even-then hapless Indians fall behind in early June and collapse by August. Those summer nights, long ago, all sorts of associations with growing up, dreams, sentimental nonsense I guess.

Now you try it. Select one of the items from your inventory and begin. Start at the top of your screen and start filling it with whatever comes to mind.

FREEWRITING AND GHOSTWRITING

Are you still too much of an editor to be completely free in freewriting? Try this: Turn the brightness down on your monitor so that you can't see the VDT screen in front of you and write for ten minutes. The microcomputer will still be storing your text, just not in front of you. Some composition teachers call this ''ghostwriting'' because it allows you to ''spill out'' what's in your head without feeling any compulsion to stop and edit.

Freewriting in the ghostwriting mode will allow you to write without your editing ''censor'' interfering. After you've ghostwritten for about ten minutes, turn the monitor back on and see what you have. Be sure to save this freewriting episode on your diskette or make a hard copy for future reference.

TIPS FOR USING FREEWRITING

• You may want to have several freewriting episodes during a prewriting session, none of them longer than ten minutes each, as you begin a writing task. After each episode, read over what you have written and write a brief summary sentence which capsules or nutshells your main idea(s). Then scroll below it and begin again.

• When you name this freewriting file, choose a name that will indicate the kind of file it is, for instance, ''Free Text #1''; or, if you are using word processing software such as *Wordstar* that asks for an extension in the file name, you might choose something like ''Free.TX1'' representing ''freewriting for text #1.''

• You may want to call up the same freewriting file later to use with other prewriting strategies. For instance, as you begin TOPOI (see next section), you may want to use your freewriting file as the starting point. Thus, you would call up your freewriting file by name and then scroll below it to use the TOPOI template. At the end of such a session you may or may not want to save the file under a different name, depending upon whether you want to keep your prewriting documents separate.

• *Reminders.* Before you close any work session, check these operations:

1. Have you saved work you may wish to consult later?

2. Have you printed a hard copy of any text you wish to take with you for further examination, elaboration, or revision?

3. Have you checked your disk space available to see if you have enough memory left for future use?

The Classical Topoi

The classical topoi have long been used by writers to generate information and ideas for their writing and speaking tasks. The word *topoi* is a plural Greek word which refers to ''places'' where these ideas and information may be ''found.'' These ''places'' were comprised of questions whose answers assisted the inquirer in discovering or remembering important information about the topic under scrutiny. The topoi are thus a more elaborate way to explore and generate information about a topic than inventories and freewriting.

Aristotle's original list of topoi included twenty-eight; for our purposes, we will concentrate on just five of them, each accompanied by four questions. **Definition** topoi help you to define the terms important to your topic and place it in a particular context. **Comparison/contrast** topoi help you to compare the topic with others like it and determine its unique qualities as well as its similarities to other items/ideas like it. **Relationship** topoi explore the causes, effects, and destiny of the topic, helping you think about the historical origin and present context for its existence. **Testimony** topoi assist you in surveying common and expert thinking about the topic, suggesting areas for further inquiry and research. **Circumstance** topoi help you use your imagination to consider the factors which make something possible or impossible, or which could cause the topic under consideration to change or alter its present form.

How to Use the TOPOI Template

First, you will need to create a template file like the one presented here. Second, you will need to perform the appropriate file operations to call it up on your screen. (See ''Using Template Files,'' Chapter 1.) Here is the TOPOI template:

TOPOI Template
X = Topic Under Consideration

1. Definition
   a. How is X defined?
   b. How are you defining X differently?
   c. With what other kinds of things may X be grouped?
   d. How may X be divided into component parts?

2. Composition/Contrast
   a. What is X similar to?
   b. What is X different from?
   c. What is most unlike X? How?
   d. What is most like X? How?

3. Relationships
   a. What is the origin of X?
   b. What are the effects of X?
   c. What is the purpose of X?
   d. What comes before and after X?

4. Testimony
   a. What do most people think of X?
   b. What do experts think of X?
   c. What is my experience with X?
   d. What are current stereotypes about X?
5. Circumstance
   a. Is X possible or impossible?
   b. What circumstances make X possible or impossible?
   c. Should X exist in its present form? Why?
   d. What could happen to X to make it change?

Call up a fresh TOPOI template on your VDT. For a reminder of the topic you are exploring, use the SEARCH/REPLACE command at your disposal to replace "X" with the topic you are exploring. Then, at your VDT, answer each question as best you can, inserting a carriage return space after each answer, then scrolling down to the next question. Here's how I used TOPOI to explore my emerging topic, "writing about baseball":

TOPOI Template
X = Topic Under Consideration (Writing About Baseball)

1. Definition

    a. How is writing about baseball defined?

For my purposes, it will mean writing about listening to baseball during my boyhood. Baseball was a game that was heard more than seen when I was growing up. Those announcers were my eyes.

    b. How are you defining writing about baseball differently?

One could write about baseball in the contemporary scene: high salaries, drug abuse, failing franchises, and so forth. I want to write about baseball in the ideal—as it was for me, growing up.

    c. With what other kinds of things may writing about baseball be grouped?

I suppose it's like writing about any American sport, football or basketball. But then no game lends itself to broadcast (as opposed to telecast) as well as baseball does. Baseball is slow-paced and leaves announcers time to set the scene.

    d. How may writing about baseball be divided into component parts?

I want to write about (1) how the announcers brought the game home to me; (2) their effect on me and my dreams of playing major league baseball; (3) how, in time, I lost interest in my early dreams; (4) how I still love baseball but for different reasons.

2. Comparison/Contrast

    a. What is writing about baseball similar to?

Well, it's similar to writing about other sports: football and basketball, for example, use a ball, are team sports, generate fan interest, and are played by millions of professional and amateur athletes.

    b. What is writing about baseball different from?

Well, it's different in that writing about baseball seems to call up all sorts of images and ideas that other sports don't. And the individual players have a more specific role in the outcome of a game. Most football players are really anonymous, especially if they are not offensive players.

    c. What is most unlike writing about baseball? How?

Writing about almost anything else: politics, social problems, you name it. You can take baseball as seriously as you want, but it's not life or death. However, it has the feel of a religious conviction.

    d. What is most like writing about baseball? How?

As mentioned above, I suppose writing about religion would be close to writing about baseball because it can generate so much fervor.

3. Relationships

    a. What is the origin of writing about baseball?

People have been writing about baseball since it became a major American attraction. Some names come to mind: Tom Boswell, Red Smith, Dick Young. In my own case, I have always loved baseball and writing about it seems as natural as anything. There are some great baseball novels by Mark Harris.

    b. What are the effects of writing about baseball?

It is exhilarating. It is a recalling of great days, great names, wonderful, delightful experiences; it is almost as real as actually being a time machine.

    c. What is the purpose of writing about baseball?

For one thing it will help remind me what I once was and what I have become. It will also help me articulate what it is that I love about the sport and what I like about writing about it.

    d. What comes before and after writing about baseball?

Much thinking, daydreaming, recalling. Not a few tears. A recapturing of that old feeling of awe and mystery. Writing about baseball will be refreshing and depressing at the same time. I will know what I miss and also know that I may never recover the same enthusiasm I once had.

4. Testimony

    a. What do most people think of writing about baseball?

They probably associate with the sports pages, that is, current baseball news—who's in the lead, who is leading the league in hitting, home runs, and the like. They probably don't think of it as something to philosophize about.

    b. What do experts think of writing about baseball?

By experts, I guess I would think of baseball writers who do it for a living. They probably share my reverence for the game and treasure a really well-done treatment of some baseball themes. *Sports Illustrated* devotes a column in each issue to "Reminiscence." That's my inspiration I guess.

    c. What is my experience with writing about baseball?

I have written some but not much. I've never kept a journal, but it would come in handy now. I still remember one game several years ago after I had moved to Texas from Kansas. I could just barely pick up the signals of WIBW in Topeka, which carried the Royals' games. I was homesick for Kansas and heard the Royals score eight or nine runs in the ninth inning to beat the Milwaukee Brewers 13–12. Old George Scott had a key hit for the Royals.

    d. What are current stereotypes about writing about baseball?

I don't know that there are any, but there sure are plenty about baseball itself—that it is too slow, that it has been overtaken by football in fan support, and so on. It's still the best sport to watch—and read about.

5. Circumstance

a. Is writing about baseball possible or impossible?

Possible! That's what I am doing right now. On the other hand, perhaps it is futile to expect to capture the excitement, tension, pacing of a game in mere words.

b. What circumstances make writing about baseball possible or impossible?

Well, I grew up with baseball as the center of my summers, the dream of winters, the hope of spring. Then, I guess because I have become a writer and a writing teacher, I naturally turn to my favorite subjects to write about. That's baseball.

c. Should writing about baseball exist in its present form? Why?

I would certainly read more about baseball if I could. That is, if there were more writers like Tom Boswell of the *Washington Post* and more periodicals like the *Sporting News*.

d. What could happen to writing about baseball to make it change?

I suppose if baseball became a political issue, more people would write about it and more people would want to read about it. Since the Commissioner of Baseball was the chair of the Olympic Committee, I'm sure he has brought a lot of attention to the sport that it might not have otherwise gotten.

As I scrolled back through my answers to the TOPOI questions I was surprised to discover a great deal of "stuff" that I hadn't previously thought about. My topic, "writing about baseball," led me through a number of unexpected corridors and stimulated my thinking about a number of items, including my motives for writing, how I thought an audience might respond to the topic of baseball, and even which memories were strongest for me. In some of the questions, I even went beyond the boundaries of the question to add seemingly extraneous information. (I had no idea how much of that Royals game I remembered—over six years ago!)

Now that you have read about TOPOI and have seen an example of it at work, it is your turn to try your hand at it. Choose one of the following topics and work through each of the five TOPOI sections.

The effect of cable-TV on network programming
Tougher drunk-driving laws
The fate of the U.S. space program
The morality of abortion
The effect of computerization on society
Declining college entrance exam scores
The brutality of football
Celebrity newscasters overshadowing the news
The nuclear arms race

TIPS FOR USING TOPOI

• If your word processor permits file-merging you may find it helpful to open a previous prewriting file, scroll down to the end of the file and call up the TOPOI template, exploring key ideas further.

• If you get stuck trying to answer one of the questions, move ahead to something else and scroll back later. And don't worry about trying to address the question in a very specific way: type in whatever occurs to you, even if at the moment it seems irrelevant or uninteresting. It may be valuable later!

• *Reminders:* Before you close any work session, check these operations:

1. Have you saved work you may wish to consult later?

2. Have you printed a hard copy of any text you wish to take with you for further examination, elaboration, or revision?

3. Have you checked your disk space available to see if you have enough memory left for future use?

The Tagmemic Inventing Procedure (TIP)

The **tagmemic inventing procedure** (TIP) is a tool of inquiry which consists of three two-part questions which help you explore and generate information about your topic. It works like TOPOI as a very focused brainstorming tool, but it is more compact and, perhaps, systematic. Instead of answering a list of twenty questions, TIP asks you to perform six kinds of analyses of the item you are investigating. It works best with a narrowed topic and specific items within the topic to analyze.

How to Use TIP

First, create the following template file and name it "TIP." Next—depending upon how your word processor manages files—you will either open up a file to work with (perhaps one of your previous inventing files), or call up the TIP template itself.

After TIP is in place on your VDT, determine what item "X" will represent (that is, what aspect of your emerging topic or thesis you wish to explore) and work through each set of questions. You may start with a large, broadly based item ("writing about baseball") or with a more narrow aspect within the topic ("summer baseball nights"). To remind yourself of your topic, use the SEARCH/REPLACE command to replace X with your topic. "X" may be something as abstract as a concept (love, honor, failure) or something as concrete as a specific event (the Kentucky Derby of 1957; the January 22, 1973 Supreme Court decision on abortion; the 1983 U.S. invasion of Grenada).

TIP Template
X = Item to Be Explored

1. In itself
DEFINE X

      a. As it is now:

      b. As it was or might be:

2. As a system
DIVIDE X

      a. As it is now:

      b. As it was or might be:

3. In a system
CONTEXTUALIZE X

      a. As it is now:

      b. As it was or might be:

As a guide to the kind of information TIP generates, note this:

DEFINE X: Question 1A generates information about the item as it is, frozen in time, defining it by comparing and contrasting it with other items like it. Question 1B generates information about the item's origin—how it has behaved or existed in the past and how it might behave or exist in the future—and information about how its past or future status compares and contrasts with that of other items like it.

DIVIDE X: Question 2A generates information about the item as a system, frozen in time, dividing it into its component parts, focusing on the parts and how they relate to one another. Question 2B generates information about the item's behavior or existence as a system in the past and in the future, and explores the relationships within its component parts and how they have or might change.

CONTEXTUALIZE X: Question 3A generates information about the item within a system, frozen in time, placing it in context in a larger system or hierarchy of relationships. Question 3B generates information about the item's past or future role in a larger system or hierarchy of relationships and how its role has changed or might change.

Here is my session with TIP:

TIP Template
X = Summer Baseball Nights

1. In itself
DEFINE X

    a. As it is now:

Summer baseball nights mean to me watching a game on TV or maybe a trip to the little league diamonds to watch my son and daughter play. It means getting with other parents to tone done the volume of other parents who yell too much at games. It means waiting up for the 11:00 news to see the results and highlights of the day's schedule.

    b. As it was or might be:

Summer baseball nights used to mean a magical radio broadcast of Cleveland Indians games. The announcers were Jimmy Dudley and Bob Neal or Harry Jones. I would sit at home in my room, the window fan droning on, while I rooted for my star-crossed heroes, the Indians. I doubt if it could ever be the same again. My youthful fantasies of becoming a major league player have been dashed in the bright light of morning. Not another day at the ball park, but at my desk grading papers.

2. As a system
DIVIDE X

    a. As it is now:

What makes up a summer baseball night now? Flicking on the set to see if there's a game, any game, no matter who is playing, on television. Since ABC took over Monday Night Baseball, they only show games in June and July anyway. It's a feeling of warmth, the sun beginning to set, a secure feeling, baseball is being played—somewhere. And, it is thrilling to know that even at 11:00 P.M. EST, somewhere on the west coast they are just beginning a game. It is tainted too: stories of drug abuse, outrageous salaries, watered down teams because of expansion. Baseball was a game. Now it is merely a business.

    b. As it was or might be:

In my boyhood, a summer baseball night was the Cleveland Indians. Maybe a transistor radio as loud as I could get it, blaring the game while I bounced a rubber ball off the garage, digging out hot grounders and flinging them to an imaginary first baseman. The game—the game was everything. Even a loss by the Indians was not too crushing. There would be another night like this one, another summer night to dream and dream. Perhaps my son is dreaming the same dream.

3. In a system
CONTEXTUALIZE X

   a. As it is now:

A summer baseball night must now become a rare instance. There are too many distractions: meetings to attend, paper work to attend to, shuffling kids around. Once all the time in the world was mine to drink and eat baseball. Now it is, as they say, a "pastime"—not a religion. It must be "fitted into" a schedule, planned for, in order to exist. I get few summer baseball nights now.

   b. As it was or might be:

Summer baseball nights, long ago, seemed endless. Only the advent of another school year (the return to school destroys the summer) could dampen my spirits and expectations. But one didn't have to schedule anything. There was no "system" into which it "fit." An eleven-year-old boy had no schedule. He only needed to think of baseball. Today an eleven-year-old boy is already choosing a career for goodness sakes. His summers are being robbed from him by an early adulthood. Too sad.

TIPS FOR USING TIP

• As you can see, TIP generates information similar to that generated by TOPOI, but it also helps you to clarify even more the relationships between your ideas. After exploring your selected "item" as extensively as you think it is necessary and fruitful, scroll through your generated information carefully, looking for recurring ideas, key terms, or notions which will need further exploration and definition. Insert an asterisk in front of each of these items for easy identification later, either on-line or on a hard copy.

• If your word processor permits file merging you may want to call up one of your earlier inventing files, and scroll through it, looking for aspects of your topic to explore with TIP. After you have identified several of these items, scroll to the end of the file, call up the TIP template, and begin exploring!

• Move through the TIP questions freely; if you get stuck in one, move on to the next. You can always scroll up or down when something else hits you.

• Don't worry about connections or correctness at this point; turn the editor and the censor off. Type in everything and anything that the questions bring to your mind. The data you generate will be raw material waiting to be shaped and focused during the drafting of your text.

• *Reminders:* Before you close any work session, check these operations:

   1. Have you saved work you may wish to consult later?

2. Have you printed a hard copy of any text you wish to take with you for further examination, elaboration, or revision?

3. Have you checked your disk space available to see if you have enough memory left for future use?

Now it's time for you to put TIP in action:

1. Choose a topic to explore with TIP, perhaps something you have already explored in previous prewriting sessions. Or, consult the list of topics you examined in practicing TOPOI and choose one you have not previously explored to examine with TIP.
2. If you've worked with a broad topic, narrow your focus and choose three items within it which seem worth pursuing and explore them, using TIP.

ONE WRITER WRITING:
JOHN BEBB'S EXPLANATORY TEXT

In this and in several of the following chapters of *Processing Words* you will examine John Bebb's writing process at work. Before we look at John's prewriting sessions, however, I want to explain a few of the details of John's assignment and how he went about completing it.

John and his class members were assigned an explanatory writing task. An explanatory text explains something thoroughly, accurately, and clearly for a reader, describing its features, its effects, its origins, and so on, the specifics always depending upon the writer's intentions and the writer's sense of audience. (For a fuller explanation of explanatory texts, see Chapter 13.) Specifically, John was asked to write about something he knew well—how to do something, a historical event, a favorite vacation spot, for example—which he was interested in explaining to a group of readers.

Some in-class time was devoted to the initial prewriting for the writing task, but John did most of his early composing using a microcomputer. He didn't know immediately what he wanted to write about, but he began to toy with the idea of composing a text about computers and computer printers, since he had recently purchased a personal computer and a printer himself. Here are some excerpts from the printout of John's initial freewriting session.

FREEWRITING:

```
     dot-matrix printers: fast, lines and word made of
dots. How do they do that anyway? I remember the first time
I printed with one of those things. I see a lot of my
teachers are using them. The lab has letter-quality
printers too, the kind that look like a typewriter but work
```

```
when the computer tells them to. They are alot slower than
the dot-matrix ones. Dot-matrix; ribbons; cloth; using a
print head that can burn out; businesses use them for memos
and data bases but they use the letter-q ones for
correspondence. a friend of mine has a dot-matrix printer
for doing programs. That frogger game he made up was on
dot-matrix print. dot-matrix: faster, less quality, used
by business and programmers; less expensive than letter-
quality printers. Dot matrix printers = impact, something
''hits'' dots onto a paper. letter-quality: uses daisy-
wheel, typewriter-like font; different typestyles are
available. They are slower. More expensive. Used for
correspondence and typesetting. Noisy . . . clap-track.
     a computer user needs to weigh: cost; speed; quality
needed; long-range goals; kind of interface needed; kind
of software; before buying.
```

John printed a hard copy of these sessions and took them back to his room where he began looking for a "hook" which would interest a group of readers and spur his own composing process. At his next computer session he used the TOPOI template to further explore his ideas. Here are some excerpts from that afternoon's prewriting session:

TOPOI TEMPLATE
X = TOPIC UNDER CONSIDERATION (COMPUTER PRINTERS)

```
1.  Definition
     a.   How is computer printer defined?
          They are printers--as opposed to typewriters--
designed to do high-speed printing for computers and word
processors.
     b.   How are you defining computer printers
differently?
The only difference is in the word ''printer.'' Most of us
think of printing presses or typewriters.
     c.   With what other kinds of things may computer
printers be grouped?
As I said, they're like typewriters but don't have their
own keyboard. They're much faster than typewriters,
usually.
     d.   How may computer printers be divided into
component parts?
They consist of a power source, a platen (like a
```

typewriter), a ribbon or ink source, a paper feeder
(friction/tractor), a print head (dot-matrix/daisy wheel/
other font types), and a connection port to receive data.

2.   Comparison/Contrast

    a.   What are computer printers similar to?

    Well, they're similar to typewriters, and like other
high-speed equipment, designed to run a long time without
failure.

    b.   What are computer printers different from?

Well, they're different from most typewriters, since you
can use printers to print single pages or the whole text.

    c.   What are most unlike computer printers? How?

Having to hire people to type for you or depending upon
your own typing skills. Since you can correct on the screen
before printing, computer printers make it easy to revise
and retype at the push of a few keys.

    d.   What are most like computer printers? How?

A printer's compositor that lets you print in different
fonts and sizes without actually doing a lot of work.

3.   Relationships

    a.   What is the origin of computer printers?

    They came out of the same revolution that produced
microcomputers. Developers saw a market for high-speed
printers that could work comparatively as fast as
computers do.

    b.   What are the effects of computer printers?

They free people to do lots of other things. They probably
are ruining the typing business on campus for freelancers.
Or, maybe they have just created a new kind of
entrepreneur.

    c.   What is the purpose of computer printers?

They are designed to handle lots of data and to print it
very quickly.

    d.   What comes before and after computer printers?

There would be no computer printers without computers. I
suppose information just gets out to people that much more
quickly now.

4.   Testimony

    a.   What do most people think of computer printers?

Well, computer users think they're great and others probably think how useful they are.

    b. What do experts think of computer printers?
They're indispensible to nearly any industry or business.

    c. What is my experience with computer printers?
I own a Star Micronics 10x which dropped in price $100 since I bought mine. I know how it works and I can repair it myself. I've already replaced the print head and learned how to program it to print in any font I want.

    d. What are current stereotypes about the printers?
That if you wait long enough they'll keep coming down in price and getting more features.

5. Circumstance

    a. Are computer printers possible or impossible?
Possible!

    b. What circumstances make computer printers possible or impossible?
Well, as above, computers created the necessity for them.

    c. Should computer printers exist in their present form? Why?
Yes, and they're on their way to becoming better and better.

    d. What could happen to computer printers to make it change?
Well, people could just stop using computers and printers, I guess, but they won't!

As John scrolled back through his answers on this template file, he discovered several things he needed to know before drafting his text. First, he realized that he needed to be especially careful in setting up a frame of reference that would enable his readers—novice computer buyers—to follow his discussion. Plus, he discovered that there were a lot of potential vague words—that is, obscure or jargon words—involved in his topic and he would need to decode these for the reader. He made a few notes on the hard copy of his prewriting materials about these matters. After John worked through TOPOI the first time, he thought of other topics within his main topic that should be usefully examined, and he pursued several of them.

The next day, fresh from examining the hard copies of his prewriting materials, he turned to the TIP procedure to explore aspects of his narrowing topic. Here is an excerpt from the printout of his TIP materials:

TIP TEMPLATE
X = COMPUTER PRINTERS

1.   In itself
DEFINE Computer Printer

   a.   As it is now:

Computer printers typically are dot-matrix or letter-
quality daisy wheel printers. They are used in conjunction
with microcomputers to provide high-speed reproduction of
data from numbers to text.

   b.   As it was or might be:

Computer printers evolved to accompany the revolution in
high-speed computing. They handle data fast and free the
user to perform other functions. Future printers will be
faster and more versatile.

2.   As a system
DIVIDE Computer Printer

   a.   As it is now:

Printers are made up of a platen, connection port cover,
paper feeder, power source, and print head. They usually
come with a manual which shows how they're used and how to
change their features (such as font, font size).

   b.   As it was or might be:

Before computer printers, typewriters were the main
handlers of business data; after that came large, bulky
printers the used large rolls of green and white ''number
cruncher'' paper. Future models will have multiple font
and fontsize controls and other features.

3.   In a system
CONTEXTUALIZE Computer Printer

   a.   As it is now:

Printers are connected with the computer via a port,
either parallel or serial. A printer may be customized to
match the kind of computer you have or the particular kind
of software being used.

   b.   As it was or might be:

In the future the computer and the printer may be one unit.
There are a few like that now. It used to be that the
printer was as large, bulky and ''un-versatile'' and ''un-
portable'' as the computers were.

As we've seen, after his initial freewriting sessions John used the TOPOI and TIP template files to elaborate his topic, helping him decide what territory should be covered. We have not presented all of the prewriting that John did here, nor would it all be instructive. The key thing is that John's writing process was primed and motivated by early prewriting sessions which paved the way for his later drafting work.

EXERCISES

1. As you look through John's initial freewriting session, what seem to be the most promising topics or ideas for pursuing? What are some specific points that emerge from these rough notes?
2. Which of the TOPOI questions seem to have given John the most help on his topic, Computer Printers? Which seemed to give him the least help? What relationships or ideas did he discover that you think would be helpful in later planning and drafting?
3. What information did the TIP questions help him discover? How did TIP work differently than TOPOI in surveying specific features or relationships, that is, what did TIP uncover that TOPOI didn't about John's topic?
4. If you were John, where would you go from here in developing your topic? Would you feel "ready" to try a draft of the text, or would you do more prewriting?

WRITING TASK:
YOU, THE WRITER

Following is your first writing task. At your VDT work through the various prewriting tools you have learned in this chapter to explore the topic suggested. You will be using these tools and others in Chapters 3 through 5 to plan and draft your text. Be sure to save each prewriting session appropriately and print a hard copy for your use later when you begin drafting your text.

Look carefully at the inventories you created at the beginning of this chapter about your writing behavior. What did you discover about yourself as a writer? What has been the character of your previous experiences as a writer? Who have been your best teachers? Under what circumstances did you learn to write? What is the most important thing you have learned about writing?

Select several of the items you generated for your inventories and explore them, using the freewriting, TOPOI, and TIP procedures you learned in this chapter. As you work through them, begin looking for a topic that you think is worth pursuing.

As you do further prewriting about your topic, consider the *kind* of text you might write. As you work through the other planning and drafting strategies in Chapters 3 through 5, you will be asked to write one of three kinds of texts: a personal narrative, an explanatory text, or a persuasive text. A personal narrative based on this topic might relate your experiences as a writer, telling the reader the "story" of how you learned to write. An explanatory text might explore and explain what you remember about the teaching methods—both good and poor—your instructors used in grade school through high school. A persuasive text might argue that writing skills are an important and crucial aspect of education and any future career, offering evidence that will convince a group of skeptical students.

Whichever kind of text you decide to write, you will find that the best place to start is with a solid prewriting session in which possible topics and approaches to your writing task are discovered and explored.

CHAPTER 3

Writing
to Understand

After spending time in prewriting and discovering a topic, a writer is ready to compose a quick draft of a text, bringing an organization and texture to its ideas in the form of sentences and paragraphs. This initial draft is often called a *discovery draft,* since in it you are writing to *understand,* that is, writing to discover how best to develop and organize your text so that it clearly communicates to your reader. In writing a discovery draft your mission is to identify your true thesis and intention in writing a text; it serves as a trial run of your ideas that can later be harvested for a more developed, reader-oriented draft.

WRITING A DISCOVERY DRAFT

How do writers begin a discovery draft? They pursue a topic, beginning with the pre-writing materials they have created earlier. Note that while the discovery draft is usually written very quickly, it is not merely freewriting. Freewriting is a somewhat random search for ideas; composing a discovery draft is a search for the specific points and organization of a text. In some ways, it is simply a "spilling over" of the writer's mind. Your discovery draft may ramble a bit as you are finding your way. You may present information that is not well connected to what precedes it or comes after, and that may be deleted before the final editing is done. The connections may still be in your head. Sentence structure may be sloppy, convoluted, or fragmented; you are still working out the best form of what you want to say. Words may be vague or imprecise—you are leaving "markers" behind that will later be clarified and elaborated.

Because you are writing the discovery draft to *explore and understand* what you have to say, you should rarely stop to edit anything (unless you decide to alter the information you are presenting or get a brainstorm that is too fruitful to pass up). While writing the discovery draft, you should try to cover all the ground you think the text should cover, in the order you think it should be covered. Remember: your main concern is to get all of your ideas out onto the VDT, whether or not you can stop to develop them all as fully as they will eventually need to be developed for your reader. Quite often the writer of a *discovery* draft ends up pursuing more than one thesis and eventually must eliminate those which cannot be coherently addressed in a single text.

Here's an example of a discovery draft a student wrote about how she felt after John Lennon, the late pop music star and former member of the Beatles, was assassinated. Selena Campbell took several hard copy pages of prewriting with her to the computer lab to guide her discovery draft.

At the top of her screen she typed,

> I want my readers to understand that I took his death very personally and that John Lennon's death was more than one more senseless killing; it was the end of an era in music.

Her overall intention, therefore, was to craft a personal narrative which involved her readers in her emotions and persuaded them that the event she related was a significant one that they should reflect upon with her.

No Man Is an Island:
America and John Lennon's Death[1]
Selena Campbell

(1) There is no simple way to describe how I felt the night John Lennon was shot. (2) I heard my parents talk about where they were when they heard that President Kennedy had been killed but it was little more than a childhood bedtime story to me. (3) It doesn't mean any more to me than hearing that President Lincoln is shot. (4) My sister feels differently because she is older and closer to the Kennedy era than I am. (5) But John Lennon is different. (6) He meant a lot to my generation since he was an original Beatle. (7) They were the first foreign group to come to America and make it big, especially on TV.

(8) But there I was, sitting in my room with the radio on, finishing some homework, when the report comes on. (9) The DJ said that Lennon had been shot and killed in front of his apartment in New York. (10) I was devastated and couldn't quit crying. (11) The next day at school I am sitting in first period class and I notice that quite a few others are sort of out of it too. (12) It wasn't just a rock star who died last night; it was the end of an era, the death of a whole generation. (13) Even the success of John's son Julian will not take away the sting of that event and no TV movie about him and Yoko will keep me from remembering how shocking that news was.

Selena composed her draft very quickly at the VDT. Note that in this draft she did not concern herself with proper grammar, but only with a flow of ideas. The first thing she did was to think of a title to capture her intention and to give her a landmark to scroll back to when she got stuck. This familiar strategy helped her get started with the

---

[1]Reprinted by author's permission.

draft. She knew the draft would be much shorter than a later draft, but she was satisfied that she got the main ideas she wanted to cover:

1. She had heard her parents talk about John F. Kennedy's assassination and it had meant little to her.
2. John Lennon's death had, in contrast, moved her deeply.
3. Hearing the report had been an experience she would never forget.
4. Sorting out her feelings and those of others with whom she discussed it, she decided that Lennon's death represented more than the death of one man; it meant the end of a particular era in history.

You can see in this draft that Selena was basically trying to get her ideas out and in some order. She wrote to herself, not to her readers. Most of her ideas are undeveloped and some of the sentence structure is quite convoluted. In evaluating her draft, she knew that it still needed a great deal of development and better organization to eventually be effective for another reader. For instance, her last two sentences seem to be the most important in the whole draft, yet only Selena knew at this point in her writing process what these sentences meant. She would later have to explain to the reader more elaborately how Lennon's death "was the end of an era" and that his son's musical success did not help her forget that fateful night. She would have to work further on such matters as voice, grammar, stance toward audience, and proper tone.

Nevertheless, her draft did help her discover what else needed to be said about her topic and how and where she could make the appropriate connections and transitions betwen her ideas. She used this discovery draft as a basis for an intermediate draft; she knew how to move from it to a draft which directly engaged her readers. A discovery draft thus helps writers test their ideas before they settle down to write a more developed draft. In crafting a discovery draft, you should keep in mind the following principles.

TIPS ON WRITING A DISCOVERY DRAFT

1. Remember that the discovery draft is written for your own benefit. While your task is to pursue the ideas you've discovered in prewriting sessions, don't be short-circuited by editing matters which can be taken up in a later draft.

2. Pursue all the key ideas which surfaced in your original prewriting. If you are writing a personal narrative, you should mention as many aspects of the experience you are writing about as possible. If you are writing an explanatory text, any terms which you find in your inventing and planning should be mentioned and elaborated upon in your discovery draft. If you are writing a persuasive text, you should gather together as many arguments, chunks of evidence, and important data in the draft that will help your case.

3. Some writers develop their own shorthand in composing a discovery draft, placing an ''X'' or ''*'' near a sentence, term, or idea which they intend to come back to for further development later. Rather than lose your flow of thought, use one of these markers to indicate a place where you plan to return and move on to the next idea you wish to explore. Later, you can examine a hard copy of the draft or use your microcomputer's

SEARCH/REPLACE function to look at each of these junctures carefully and decide what to do.

4. The discovery draft is not only an opportunity to discover what you want to say, it can also help you discover *how* to say it. Some writers find it helpful to "talk to themselves" in the draft by bracketing [   ] comments about how to produce the text that is emerging. For instance, this writer paused to remind herself about how to handle the structure of her argument in a persuasive text:

> The fact is, few people realize that prostitution is not a "victimless" [define] crime. [Fill in with specific examples of broken marriages, child abuse victims.] Because TV glorifies the life of the call girl [maybe start a new paragraph?], too many younger women are drawn to the streets. The figures [add later] are startling.

5. In your discovery draft, you should express any private feelings you have about your topic, even if later you decide to delete them as irrelevant to your intentions or distracting to your reader. Some ideas need to be expressed as you write so you can "get them out of your system"; if these notions don't surface, they sometimes stall your composing process or, later, *block* you from making some explicit connections for your reader that remain implicit in an earlier draft.

In our earlier example, for instance, Selena needed to describe how she felt the next day at school in order to remember certain other details of the experience that she would incorporate later. If she had not included these in her discovery draft, she may not have been able to tie certain strands of her narrative together. You may find yourself saying in a later draft, "It was important for me to write this, but it is now important for me to delete it; it's in the way now."

6. After you have completed a discovery draft, take a break and spend some time in planning the rest of the text, using the strategies discussed in the rest of this chapter. Don't begin a second draft until after some time has passed. This will make the text more fresh the next time you look at it and allow you to be more objective about how to proceed.

WRITING TASK

Write a discovery draft of the text you were assigned at the end of Chapter 2.

DISCERNING A THESIS

The prewriting techniques you learned in Chapter 2 and the process of writing a discovery draft you just considered are primarily scouting activities for writers which helps them discover what they want to say. Successful writers move from these components of the process to planning, which is primarily a *reader-oriented* activity. It is important that writers not try to take their readers into account too soon—before they have fleshed out the main ideas they wish to explore. But once they have spent an adequate amount of time in thinking through their ideas, it is important for them to plan the rest of their development and organization. Our discussion in the rest of Chapter 3 will focus on two key planning issues: thesis and intention.

The thesis of a text is the main point a writer wishes to convey to a reader. A thesis statement answers the question, "What do I want to say in this essay?" A well-written essay has only one, clear thesis. Such a thesis can be supported responsibly with concrete evidence and examples and will be plausible to its audience. As you examine your discovery draft, create the following template file and scroll below each question and answer it. Be sure to print a hard copy of this file to guide your later development in an intermediate draft.

Discovery Draft Thesis Template

1. What main points emerge in your discovery draft? List them.

2. Which points are most interesting to you? Why?

3. Which points would be most interesting to your potential readers? Why?

4. Which points might require further elaboration or defense for your readers? What might they want to know more about? What might they question? Brainstorm.

5. Which point seems to be the most important one, that is, which point is really central to the meaning of your draft as it stands? Paraphrase this thesis below in answer to this question: "What I really want to say is . . . "

6. Is this thesis a clearly focused statement of what you want your readers to understand when they finish your text? If not, examine your discovery draft and find a more appropriate thesis by starting again at #1 above.

7. Will this thesis be believable to your potential readers? Will it seem original and relevant to your potential readers? That is, does it make a meaningful and useful contribution to a discussion of your topic? Or is it just a rehash of typical wisdom on the topic? How can you refine your thesis to make it more plausible and interesting to your readers? Explain.

8. Can you expand upon this point or build your whole essay around it? That is, is there enough to say about this issue or topic that will allow you to develop a worthwhile text about it? List examples, illustrations, or further elaboration that would develop or clarify this point.

EXERCISES

1. Review the discovery draft you have developed for the writing task at the end of Chapter 2 using the above template file. What aspects of your education and experience as a writer did you explore and/or uncover? What kind of text (personal narrative; explanatory text; persuasive text) seems to be suggested by the material you've generated? Answer the template questions and begin now to form an effective thesis.

2. Consider the following theses and judge them according to these criteria: (a) clarity; (b) originality; (c) believability; (d) promise of development. If you find any one to be inadequate, write a note to its writer, offering a description of a revised version which might present a more effective thesis.

 a. Competitive handball is a sport with many healthful advantages. (audience: group of physical education majors)
 b. America would have won the Vietnam War if it had used nuclear weapons. (general audience)
 c. Drinking while driving is dangerous to the health of men and women. (general audience)
 d. Between 1970 and 1980, the rock-and-roll group with the biggest impact on American music was Chicago. (young adults, aged 21–30)
 e. The farming community is the backbone of American commerce. (readers of a small-town newpaper)
 f. Raising this state's drinking age to 21 would decrease homicide by at least 30 per cent. (readers of a campus newspaper)
 g. Stephen King writes very suspenseful novels. (general audience)
 h. The old saw about "Red sky at night, sailor's delight, Red sky at morning, sailor take warning" has, in fact, a quite scientific basis. (readers of a scientific newsletter written for the interested non-scientist)
 i. The Olympic Games after the 1980's will be marred by further boycotts by Eastern bloc nations. (general audience)
 j. The product being returned in this box was defective. (letter to a manufacturer of a portable cassette player)

DISCOVERING INTENTION

Writing to understand not only involves identifying a useful thesis, it also involves determining an *intention* for your text. In this section you will learn how thesis and intention interact to give you a clear plan for proceeding through the drafting and eventual revising of your text. Many apprentice writers think about writing in this way:

> "I know what I want to say: 'computers are essential tools in modern society.' So, I'll just find as many things as I can that say *that* to my readers."

But finding a thesis is not enough. A writer is accountable for more than just "saying" something to a reader, that is, her task is something more than just "expressing" her thesis. A writer must discover a *reason* for writing about that thesis for an audience. Too many apprentice writers conceive a writing task as an invitation to write an auto-biography or merely to "express." As a result they usually produce a text which is neither cohesive nor informative. Writers must not only try to *express* themselves; they must be guided by an overall *intention*.

What is intention? In drafting a text, a writer proceeds from certain purposes that guide its development and organization. In other words, at some point in the evolution of a text, as a writer you must determine what you want your text to *do*. In thinking about his thesis about computers, John Bebb might have chosen to do one of the following things in his text:

1. convince a skeptical audience that computers are essential tools in modern society
2. report to a committee on the advisability of acquiring computers as tools in a particular business application
3. satirize the computer phobia that exists among a particular segment of society.
4. explain the development of computers and document the inroads they have made into various institutions in modern society.

John's task was not just to "say something" about computers, but to develop and organize his text out of a central intention that would have to be clear to his readers. John eventually chose to develop his thesis in an explanatory text about how to purchase computer printers wisely.

Building on the preceding list above, here is a catalogue of some of the intentions a writer may have in drafting a text:

1. tell a story to entertain
2. analyze the consequences of an event so it can be avoided in the furture
3. provide information to an audience so it can make a decision about a purchase
4. explain the nature of something for a reader so that it may be repaired
5. persuade a reader of the validity of a particular ethical principle
6. instruct a reader in a particular skill so he or she can perform it

This list of intentions suggests the range of options open to the writer searching for a reason to create a text. Each of these intentions results in a certain kind of text.

When John Bebb examined his thesis, he modified it to match his emerging sense of what kind of text he wanted to write. He then came up with this purpose statement:

> My thesis is that a person buying a computer will want to buy a printer as well; he or she should choose wisely. My intention will be to explain how to go about purchasing a computer printer that is suitable to the buyer's needs.

EXERCISES

1. Using the discovery draft and thesis you've generated for the writing task at the end of Chapter 2, fashion some purpose statements of your own which include an adequate thesis and clear intention for your text. Ask yourself what you want your text to *do*. For instance, your intention may be to relate your experiences as a writer in order to *persuade* the reader that it is important for high school students to prepare themselves well for college composition courses; or you may wish to explore your junior high teacher's writing assignments to *inform* the reader about how writing practice can be made more enjoyable.

A purpose statement might take this form:

"The thesis of my text is . . . "
"What I want to do with my thesis is . . . "

2. To help you understand further the idea of intention and to illustrate how different texts may be crafted from the same thesis, consider the following theses with which a writer might begin the search for intention. Look at each one carefully and think about the different kinds of intentions a writer might have in writing with these theses. Make some inventories at the VDT, describing at least two or three different texts that might be created from each thesis. Here is an example:

Thesis: "Teddy bears are a big fad for collectors."

Possible Texts:

A text which *analyzes* the phenomenon of teddy bear collecting—how it started, what kinds of people are involved, what reasons move them to collect them.

A text which *persuades* someone who thinks collecting is a bogus and meaningless hobby that it is, instead, a fulfilling avocation which brings happiness and financial gain to many, using teddy bear collecting as a key example.

A text which *tells the story* of how the writer began to collect teddy bears and why it is an enjoyable hobby.

Describe the kinds of texts which might be created from these theses:

  a. The department of Education was created during Jimmy Carter's presidency.
  b. The council's proposal for a downtown mall will revitalize the city.
  c. The NCAA basketball tournament has grown from 24 to 64 teams in less than a decade.
  d. In modern society, cancer is a more devastating disease psychologically than TB ever was.
  e. The conservativism on college campuses in the early 1980's was a great contrast to the 1960's liberal activism.

JOHN'S TEXT:
WRITING TO DISCOVER AND UNDERSTAND

You have already observed how John Bebb prepared for his first draft with an extensive prewriting period. After reviewing his materials, John began his drafting session by typing his thesis and intention at the top of the screen, scrolling back to it every once in a while to keep himself focused on the task at hand. After a few false starts in which he typed a sentence or two and then deleted them, John launched into a discovery draft of his text which is reprinted below, just as he created it, without revisions.

How to Buy a Computer Printer

John Bebb

(1)   The computer revolution has affected every corner of
our society today. Especially in education, computers are
more and more prominent. If one doesn't know how to use
them, then he is just about out of luck. Therefore, it is
important for each and every individual student to become
cognizant of the features of computers and printers.

(2)   The purpose of this essay is to help the reader
understand how computer printers assist in the
accumulation and dissemination of data for business,
school, and home. A computer without a printer is like a
car without gasoline. Unless there is a way to store and
transmit the information that a computer assists the user
in accumulating, there is no way for it to become as
resourceful a tool as it should be.

(3)   If you are in the market for a printer, then the
information I am about to present will be of interest to
you. But there is good news and bad news. First, the good
news: printers have more and more features these days,
are compatible with almost any computer, and users can
count on a greater speed than before. But the buyer should
beware: there is also some bad news too. There are a
bewildering array of models and choices. And the retail
stores are usually full of high-pressure salespeople who
want to sell you whatever they can, whether it is what you
need or not. Finally, if you decide to order through the
mail, there are the hassles of dealing with companies in
which you don't know anyone and far away.

(4)   The first thing to decide when you are ready to buy a
printer is what kind of print quality you will need. There
are three general descriptions of computer printer
quality: letter quality, which is the best, near-
letter-quality, which is faster but not as good, and
draft-quality, which is for the writer's eyes only. The
second thing to decide is how fast you need your data
printed. If you are going to write only a few letters or
reports a day or week, then a letter-quality printer will
suffice. On the other hand, if you will be producing
hundreds of letters and reports you may want a dot-matrix
one. Finally, cost is a big factor. How much do you want
to spend? The letter-quality ones are slow and expensive;

the dot-matrix ones are fast and cheap. Only you can
determine this.

(5)   The following chart will help you decide what
features, speed and price you need: [note to me: supply
chart]

          I myself recently bought a computer and printer and I
can say that I am glad that I read a lot about them before
entering the store. Since I was well-informed I was not
bamboozled by a high-pressure salesperson. I knew the
right questions to ask and knew what models would be
suitable, the only catch was coming up with the money to
pay for it!

John made a hard copy of this first draft and returned to his desk to evaluate it. His verdict was that it contained many features that he would need to "translate" so that his reader could understand his point. He could see a clear thesis and intention emerging— "here's how to buy a computer printer"—but he knew a number of personal quirks and anecdotes had crept into his draft that needed to be removed. Further, he had not yet hit upon the right stance and tone to take, since he seemed to alternate between formality and casualness that would no doubt unnerve the reader. John's prewriting and discovery draft had served him well, and he was confident that he knew how to make his intermediate draft more sensitive to the needs of his audience.

EXERCISES

1. What is John's organizing principle in this draft? Does he reveal it to the reader clearly?
2. What ambiguous elements do you find in John's first draft? Is his thesis clear?
3. John is attempting to write an explanatory text. Is this intention clear? What concepts and terms will he need to be especially careful about explaining to his readers?
4. If you were advising John on his next draft, what changes would you suggest he make in organization or development?

CHAPTER 4

Writing
to Communicate

The writer's ultimate goal is to communicate and not merely express a viewpoint. At some point successful writers must analyze the needs and expectations of their eventual audience to guide their final organization and development of their texts. The drafting process is replete with choices and options, false starts and false leads—a persistent looking behind one's shoulder to see where one has been and ought to be headed. As you begin to move toward an advanced draft of your text you should thus analyze the characteristics of your audience, since it can increase your control of subject matter and its development. The following template file will assist you in focusing your text. Use it as a series of freewriting prompts to get you to think about your audience and their needs:

Audience Template

1. My general topic is:
   This is what my audience knows about it:
   This is what my audience doesn't know about it:
   This is what I must not leave out:
   This is what I can leave out:

2. My audience's attitude toward my topic and thesis will be (a) sympathetic; (b) indifferent; (c) skeptical; (d) antagonistic, because:

3. These facts about my audience's age, gender, and/or educational and cultural background are particularly relevant to the organization and development of my text:

4. My real purpose in asking my audience to consider my thesis is:

5. What I want them to do or think after they have read my text is:

6. The role I am playing in the text is: (a) advocate; (b) storyteller; (c) reporter; or (d) instructor; and it will affect the way I organize and develop my text in this way:

Let's examine each prompt and how it can help you in addressing the audience you've selected for your text:

Prompt 1 raises questions about the content of your text and how well it will communicate to your readers. How familiar will your readers be with the kind of information or argument you are making in your text? Will they be overly familiar, so that your material or approach may seem trite or predictable? If so, that will help determine, in part, the way you will proceed in organizing and developing your text. Is the topic or subject matter fairly new to your audience? If so, you will need to proceed more methodically, carefully defining terms and setting contexts for their understanding.

Prompts 2 and 3 uncover the important characteristics of your audience in light of their own needs and outlooks. Once you make clear your text's thesis, what will your audience find most challenging, interesting, controversial, troublesome, etc., about it? What aspects of your thesis will need special defense or explanation? When you think of the readers to which your text is directed, who comes to mind? Are they uniformly part of a particular group, such as, machinists in a trade union? Do they have in common a particular educational, social or cultural background, such as, a group of dentists who attended school in the midwest? Are they predominantly women? Or divorced fathers? Or children of mixed race? By asking these questions about your audience you can plan and, later, revise more effectively.

Prompts 4 and 5 get at the heart of your text, its intentions, and the overall impact you want it to have. What motives do you have for writing it? For instance, you may be drafting a text which explains the alarming growth in lung cancer victims among women. Do you want your readers to be merely aware of the appropriate statistics, or is it your real concern that they stop smoking? If so, you will need to plan and revise your draft accordingly as you work through the drafting of it.

Prompt 6 helps you reexamine and focus your personal role as the writer of your text: what organization (ways of sequencing and ordering the information I am presenting), what diction (choice of words), voice (first person? familiar? formal?) and tone (authoritative? matter-of-fact? urgent?) will best serve my goals in the text I am drafting? If I am an "advocate," I will need to provide ample documentation and support for my position and perhaps explain my credentials for arguing the point. If I am a "storyteller," my main task is to narrate my tale as coherently as possible, including all important details in an appropriate order. If I am a "reporter," I want to remain objective and distant from my subject matter and convey a sense of deliberate neutrality. If I am an "instructor," I must be careful to explain key concepts clearly, address the level and expertise of my readers, and make sure that my ideas are presented in a sequence that fits the phenomenon I am trying to teach.

Consider how John Bebb responded to these freewriting prompts concerning his text about computer printers:

Audience Template

1. My general topic is: computer printers

This is what my audience knows about it:
This is what my audience doesn't know about it:
This is what I must not leave out:
This is what I can leave out:

While most of them have probably been exposed to computers a little bit, they may not know any of the intricacies of how a printer is attached or why a computer and printer are anything more than a glorified typewriter. I will have to define my terms carefully and be sure to build in enough context to help them follow my explanation about which printers would work best for them.

2. My audience's attitude toward my topic and thesis will be (a) sympathetic; (b) indifferent; (c) skeptical; or (d) antagonistic, because:

Many of them will be enthusiastic about computers, but I know a lot of them will have that technophobia that keeps them from being completely sympathetic to my thesis.

3. These facts about my audience's age, gender, and/or educational and cultural background are particularly relevant to the organization and development of my text:

Since I am writing to my peers, they are generally my age; about half of them are male and half female. They are freshmen in college, mainly from an urban environment. Quite a few of

them are business majors, with a few majoring in phys ed, biology, and elementary education. There are two English majors and one journalism major.

4. My real purpose in asking my audience to consider my thesis is:

I want them to be informed about their options in buying printers. In the next few years nearly all college graduates will own or need computers and will need to make choices wisely. Except in rare instances, the purchase of a computer doesn't include a printer. Yet, a computer is not as useful without one. Therefore, I must make them aware of their buying options and necessities.

5. What I want them to do or think after they have read my text is:

To make an intelligent buying choice when they decide to purchase a printer.

6. The role am I playing in the text is: (a) advocate; (b) storyteller; (c) reporter; or (d) instructor; and it will affect the way I organize and develop my text in this way:

I am trying to be a disinterested reporter of information. I will need to keep technical terms to a minimum for sure. In addition, I will have to structure my text so that the concepts and ideas proceed logically from my opening paragraph. I will probably use some graphic devices (headers; paragraph labels) to signal the organization of the text explicitly and devise some kind of pricing and model chart to help them compare their options. The reader should see my text as a reporting of facts and not merely some personal experience.

As you can see, John's careful analysis of his audience has helped him plan the very organization and development of his text even before he has begun his intermediate draft. This will not only save him some time later, it will also make it easier for him to chart his progress and plan a revision later in his writing process.

EXERCISE

Do a thorough audience analysis for the text you are drafting for the writing task at the end of Chapter 2.

1. Create and call up the Audience Template.
2. Respond to each prompt on the screen as you brainstorm about your audience for this text, inserting a carriage return after each of your responses.
3. Don't leave anything out which you think would be profitable for tailoring your text to this audience.

INTENTION AND READER'S EXPECTATIONS

If you are unsure of your intentions when you begin to write a second draft, you should not be troubled. A tentative intention can be clarified in the act of drafting itself if you proceed with the reader in mind. Therefore, the next task for the writer after establishing a workable thesis and intention, and analyzing the audience is to anticipate—as well as possible—the expectations of your audience.

Writers have both *global* and *local* intentions. Global intentions, such as choice of subject matter and thesis, the kind of text one intends to write, what audience the text is directed to, and what voice or tone to employ, provide the writer with boundaries for evaluating a text, that is, a framework to determine if the text has met the writer's original goals. Local intentions, such as the length of a particular sentence, what verb to use in a given clause, whether to underline a key term, or how to make a paragraph more coherent, arise in the actual drafting of a text. Global intentions, by and large, are made before a draft is begun—though they can be adjusted to match the writer's evolving notion of what the text should be. Local intentions, on the other hand, manifest themselves line by line, word by word as the writer thinks through the meaning and shape of the text.

More will be said later in *Processing Words* about both kinds of intentions, but it is useful to keep the two kinds distinct. You cannot plan *everything* in advance; ideas, words, phrasings, and specific adjustments to your audience will occur to you as you draft.

Just as writers have *intentions,* readers have certain *expectations* for the texts they read. Different kinds of texts have different conventions associated with them, and readers come to rely upon these conventions to help them interpret what they are reading. For instance, a *report* to a student committee on parking problems at a university might be expected to have as simple and as informal a structure as this:

    I. Discussion of the existing parking space available
    II. Discussion of the need for more parking
  III. Recommended action of the committee

On the other hand, a major proposal to the president of the university to increase parking by building a large parking tower might have as formal a structure as this:

      I. Summary of proposal
    II. Presentation of committee's credentials and research
  III. Summary of previous activity upon which the proposal is built
  IV. Discussion of the need the proposal addresses
   V. Discussion of objectives of the proposal
  VI. Discussion of means by which the proposal will meet these needs
 VII. Presentation of the construction costs involved
VIII. Concluding appeal

As you can see, different kinds of texts represent different intentions for writers and different expectations for readers. To be successful as a writer then, you must consider and control such matters as audience, tone, and voice in your planning since global intentions such as these deal with the text as a whole and affect the end you wish to achieve. You must ask yourself about such global choices as:

1. In what order am I going to draft the text, that is, will I start with the introduction and work through to the conclusion, or will I start somewhere in the middle?
2. Will I stop now to tinker with sentences or sections which aren't quite the way I want them to be, or will I press on and get the next draft done quickly?
3. Should I begin with a formal statement of thesis and intention, or should I move into my subject matter more subtly and draw the reader in with a less obvious approach?
4. What is the best voice and stance in this text? Should I remain objective, matter-of-fact, and distant or should I present myself as a concerned individual, revealing my own subjective responses to the issue or proposition discussed in my text?

As I suggested, you may eventually change your intentions as you interact with what you actually discover in the writing process, but it is important to set a plan for proceeding through your drafting activity in order to have a barometer or guide for later revision and rewriting. While a writer's global intentions for writing are never "pure"—one can hardly *explain* without attempting to *persuade* or present a compelling *personal story* without doing a great deal of *analyzing* of the situations involved—by choosing a primary intention, a writer's planning will be more effective and efficient.

LOOKING FOR INTENTION

Outlining

Writing teachers have traditionally emphasized the importance of outlining a text before producing it. Some writers, however, are more successful than others in producing outlines. Thankfully, the word processor has made outlining much less of a chore since the writer can move items around so easily. Outlining can help you visualize the intention for your text as you imagine it evolving out of your prewriting. No outline should be a straitjacket; you should depart from any outline if your thesis and intention lead you in another direction in the drafting of a text. But an outline can help keep you on the right path as you draft. There are basically three sorts of outlines that a writer can use early in the drafting process to guide the production of a text: (1) the topic outline; (2) the sentence outline; and (3) the paragraph outline.

The **topic outline** works as a tool for creating a quick overview of the territory the writer wishes to cover in a text. Details are listed, basically in the order the writer expects to use them, but the purpose of the outline is to help the writer come to some early notion of the shape of the text. The **sentence outline** is a more elaborate outline which attempts to put flesh and blood on the bare bones that a topic outline provides. The writer uses complete sentences to explore the specific facts, propositions, and ideas that will be examined in the drafting of the text. The **paragraph outline** assists the writer in planning the larger units of a text by describing the basic content, direction, and order of the paragraphs that will appear in the text. Here are some examples of the three outlines John Bebb used to explore his intention:

Topic Outline

I. Buying a computer printer: the good news
   A. How printers assist in accumulating and disseminating data and information
      1. Business
      2. School
      3. Home
   B. The features of the new printers
      1. Font and font size
      2. Speed and programmability
II. Buying a computer printer: the bad news
   A. The bewildering array of models and choices
   B. The pressure of retail stores
   C. The uncertainty of mail order purchase
III. A how-to guide to buying a computer printer
   A. Assessing the print quality you need
   B. Assessing the speed you need
   C. Assessing the features and price range you need
      1. A comparative chart of features
      2. A comparative chart of prices

Sentence Outline

I. The good news about printers is their versatility and speed.
   A. Printers assist business, school, and home in accumulating and disseminating data and information.
   B. These printers can be programmed to change font, font size, and special graphics.
   C. These printers print fast.
II. The bad news about printers is the array of choices and the experience of purchasing them.
   A. There are a bewildering number of manufacturers and features represented in the printer market.
   B. The buyer must then decide whether to buy it in a retail store and perhaps face high-pressure tactics, or take a chance on a mail order purchase at a reduced cost.
III. What do you do when you decide to buy a computer printer?
   A. You must determine what kind of print quality you need for your application: dot-matrix or letter-quality.
   B. You must decide how much speed you need in processing the information you want to disseminate.
   C. You determine which of the many features that printers offer are essential to your application and your price range.
      1. Here is a chart which depicts the range of features and options.
      2. Here is a chart which depicts the price range of various computer printers and manufacturers.

Paragraph Outline

   1. Computer printers facilitate the accumulation and dissemination of data and have become an essential add-on to today's computer.

   2. Because of the wide range of options a purchaser has in selection and in vendor, the decision is often a difficult one.

   3. There are a number of factors which must be weighed in order to make a wise choice in purchasing a computer printer.

Nutshelling

Nutshelling helps you distinguish major ideas from minor ones by helping you to decide how those major ideas are related to one another. Nutshelling is helpful both early in the planning process and later in the revising process.

Nutshelling asks "So what?" at each juncture of your text, that is, what is this part of the text supposed to accomplish for the reader? At your VDT—with hard copies of your inventing and planning activities to date beside you—anticipate how many "parts" your text will have (probably at least three and, depending upon its complexity, perhaps as many as ten or fifteen). The exact number of parts at this juncture is unimportant—only that you can begin to see the whole text emerging. For each "part" describe what you think should happen in that section.

Here's a sample of the nutshelling John Bebb did for planning his text on computer printers:

Part I: This part introduces and sets up the whole text. I describe the revolution in computers and printers and show how they have altered the way people think about data and information.

Part II: Here I want to display the number of features available in a printer, say something about how they work, and describe how they interact with computers.

Part III: In this midsection, I want to talk about the perils of trying to select one out of the many available and how to avoid the pressure of salespeople and the uncertainty of mail order buying.

Part IV: Nearing the climax, I want to begin tying everything together with specific information about printers, comparing them in various ways.

Part V: Here I will present charts comparing features, price, and manufacturers.

Part VI: In this concluding section, I will sum up appropriately my main advice in selecting a printer.

EXERCISES

1. You may find it useful to exchange your drafts and planning material with one of your peers to see how clearly your thesis and intention are shaping up. Ask your partner to explain in his or her own words what your main points and intention seem to be in your text. This "peer review" will become even more helpful after you complete a first draft, and later you may wish to use the final draft checklist in Chapter 6 to gauge the effectiveness of your texts.
2. Review the materials you have generated for the writing task you have been working on. Use one or more of the outlining or nutshelling techniques you have learned in this chapter to examine your purpose statement and to explore a possible organization for the content of your text.

THE INTERMEDIATE DRAFT: WRITING TO COMMUNICATE

Perhaps you are not the kind of writer who needs to write a discovery draft to proceed successfully through the composing process. Perhaps your first draft is usually an "intermediate draft," by which I mean a draft whose thesis and intention are clear from the start, whose organization and development are well-conceived, and whose sense of audience is already evident. An intermediate draft is a draft that is organized and developed with the reader's needs in mind.

In some ways it is difficult to describe what writers do to produce an intermediate draft in discrete terms. An intermediate draft is begun much the way a writer begins a discovery draft. The main difference is that when you begin an intermediate draft you already have produced a trial run of your ideas and you are trying to take the audience into account directly, organizing paragraphs and constructing sentences which will be clear not only to you but to your readers as well. It is much easier to watch writers in action, considering the moves they make, than to offer an abstract description, and in Chapter 10 you will see how John Bebb produced an intermediate draft from his discovery draft. But there are a few generalities about drafting a reader-oriented text on a micro-computer that can be helpful:

1. You should gather together all of your prewriting materials and your discovery draft and give them a thorough reading before beginning the next draft. Work through your hard copy of the discovery draft, circling or marking in some other way the key points you want to develop further in this draft.

2. Consult your audience analysis, plotting a strategy for writing clearly and directly to it. What sections of the discovery draft need the most work to be truly accessible to your audience? Are there particular sentences or words that need to be rewritten to be clear and direct? Note these parts of your text with a line in one of the margins.

3. If you have used outlining or nutshelling, proceed to draft paragraphs that match your plan, guarding against wandering off into territory that is irrelevant to the points you wish to make. If you don't have a specific plan of attack, you may alternate between different sections of the text, writing an opening or a conclusion, then moving to the middle paragraphs. Or you may double back many times within and between sections of the text, composing sentences which progressively add information, clarify meaning, and take the reader into more direct account.

4. At the end of this process, your minimum goal is to have created a suitable opening and conclusion. Check the opening and closing sections to determine if you have fairly introduced your subject matter and thesis, and have concluded without being abrupt or merely regurgitative.

Chapter 5 will provide you with more specific advice about developing different kinds of texts further, while Chapters 6 through 9 provide you with specific advice for analyzing your draft and determining how to proceed with the revision of your intermediate draft as you work toward a final draft.

EXERCISE

Write the next draft of your text based upon the writing task at the end of Chapter 2, guided by your prewriting materials, your discovery draft, and any of the other analytical tools you have learned in Chapters 3 and 4. After you have completed this draft, examine it carefully. What will your next steps be in composing a more reader-centered draft?

JOHN'S TEXT:
MOVING TOWARD THE INTERMEDIATE DRAFT

As soon as John determined his main point, he began to explore it: "Buyers of computer printers must choose between speed and print quality." His initial analysis of the thesis he made convinced him that this was too narrow a topic. "My text is really about how to buy a computer printer intelligently and not just about the differences between kinds of printers," he told himself.

As he began to consider his intention for writing the text, his thesis became more clear to him: "My thesis is that a person buying a computer will want to buy a printer as well; he or she should choose wisely. My intention in writing a text about this thesis will be to explain how to go about purchasing a computer printer that is suitable to the buyer's needs."

Next, John considered his audience. He already had a pretty good idea of his audience, but the audience template helped him visualize even more concretely those to whom he would address his text.

With his purpose statement in mind, John was optimistic that his prewriting and previous experience with the topic prepared him well for drafting this explanatory text, but he wanted to explore this intention a bit further. Thus, John went to his VDT and began sketching his intermediate draft using the tools of outlining and nutshelling presented in this chapter.

He first tried a topic outline. Wanting to expand these thoughts, he gave the outline some depth by creating sentences to point to the information he would be presenting, creating a sentence outline. Finally, to see how the draft itself might take shape, he described various paragraphs in an outline format.

After experimenting with these outlining forms, John determined that his intention was to explain to his audience the basic choices involved in computer printers and to assist them in making an appropriate choice. This stated intention was to help him plan the rest of his text in his selection of detail, order of information, and his voice, stance, and tone.

In addition to outlining, John spent a few minutes nutshelling the various parts of his text as he imagined it would develop. John's nutshelling helped him distinguish his major ideas from minor ones and before ending his session he used it to plan the actual construction of the text. John looked at his outline and asked "So what?" at each juncture as he described in his own words what each section of the text was supposed to do.

After three sessions of prewriting and drafting, John felt ready to attempt an intermediate draft of his text. Armed with hard copies of his various planning materials he began with the blank screen in front of him. In Chapter 10 you will have a chance to see what John's next draft looked like.

EXERCISES

1. As you examine John's prewriting activities, which seemed to be the most helpful to him?

2. What are the special problems John will face in drafting an explanatory text about his topic? If you were advising him, what would you urge him to pay special attention to in writing his next draft?

CHAPTER 5

Writing to Develop and Organize

As you work toward the next draft of your text you will eventually need to make some decisions about how to develop and organize the material you have generated thus far. This chapter moves us far from the technology of microcomputers in the composing process to some more traditional rhetorical notions about how prose evolves and develops into a coherent, readable text. I have no tricks up my sleeve in this chapter—just straightforward discussion of ways you can develop your text effectively. This section of *Processing Words* should serve as a reference chapter for you as you make decisions about how to make your intention clear in the development and organization of your text.

Whether you are working with your prewriting materials or your discovery draft, you must at some point create texture in your draft, that is, give your ideas a substance and structure that communicate your intention clearly in the text. This chapter will consider four traditional ways to proceed in organizing and developing the thesis and intention of your text: narration, description, exposition, and argumentation. Consideration of these modes of discourse will help you decide how to order your information, and how you can best reveal the intentions of your text.

As we illustrate the nature and use of each mode in this section, be aware that you will probably use two or more of these modes in any text you write. Regardless of your intention in writing your text, you will need to become proficient in using all four modes of development.

NARRATION: ORDERING TIME

Narration orders time, tells a story. Typically, a writer chooses a point in time and moves forward from that point to a point closer to the present, relating events and selecting details to convey the significance of those events to the reader. What details you choose to report and the order in which you report them determine the meaning the reader discerns in your narrative. Here are two sample narrative paragraphs:

(1) As we were going back, our route took us through Grand Rapids, Michigan, on a Saturday night. That was to be the last of my personal driving career. Since I had passed my driver's test in Philadelphia under a tough policeman and had been congratulated, Fran let me take the wheel during this five-mile-an-hour Saturday night traffic. As we crawled along, I suddenly called out, "Oh Fran, look at the pretty fountain . . . colored lights . . ." And crunch—we had locked bumpers with the car ahead.[1]

(2) Used car lots were scattered among the blocks of old buildings that separated the business section from the railroad yards. He wandered around in a few of them before they were open. He could tell from the outside of the lot if it would have a fifty-dollar car in it. When they began to be open for business, he went through them quickly, paying no attention to anyone who tried to show him the stock. His black hat sat on his head with a careful, placed expression and his face had a fragile look as if it might have been broken and stuck together again, or like a gun no one knows is loaded.[2]

In these two examples, the purpose of the paragraph is to get the reader from one past event to another point nearer the present. The first is from the personal experience of the writer, recounting an incident in first person. The second is written in third person and is a fictional narrative piece taken from a novel. If you intend to tell a story or write a biographical sketch, you may employ the narrative mode almost exclusively throughout your text. Keep in mind, though, that a mode is not a particular kind of text, but simply a way of expressing organization and development to reveal your overall purpose to your reader.

DESCRIPTION:
ORDERING THE READER'S SENSES

Description *orders the reader's senses* by vividly depicting a place, an object, a person, a setting, or mood. Effective description allows a reader to see, hear, feel, smell, and taste the object of the writer's description. Since your readers depend upon you to *show* and not just *tell* them what you are attempting to convey, you should strive to use concrete rather than abstract language and to employ specific rather than general word choice. Concrete language confronts readers' senses, presenting them not with abstractions ("The coffee was strong."), but vivid images ("That coffee would have burned a hole through plate glass."). Specific language avoids generality and vagueness ("The crowd was enthusiastic.") and instead aims for precision ("The delegates interrupted the speaker

[1]Edith Schaeffer, *The Tapestry*. (Waco, Texas: Word Books, 1981), 183.
[2]Flannery O'Connor, *Three by Flannery O'Connor*. (New York: New American Library, 1962), 40.

more than a dozen times with deafening applause.''). To see specific and concrete language used in context, examine the following descriptive paragraphs:

(1) Tom grasped a heavy oaken chair that stood ornamentally in the hall and, elevating it above his head, ran madly at the four men. When he was almost upon them, he let the chair fly. It seemed to strike all of them. A heavy oak chair of the Old English type is one of the most destructive of weapons. Still, there seemed to be enough of the men left, for they flew at him from all sides like dragons.[3]

(2) Dorothy Leigh Sayers was an energetic and enthusiastic person at home in many worlds. She liked riding a motorcycle, making up crossword puzzles, and writing plays about the New Testament. She had a miraculous gift for languages and a fantastic sense of humor. She wrote chatty, amusing letters to her friends, while she also gave lectures on intellectual subjects that were both clear and entertaining. Reading them today makes her seem to be here in person—a big, impressive woman, her spectacles perched on her nose before her blue, nearsighted eyes, her short gray hair shoved back in the mannish style of the 1920's, talking with you in her deep, attractive voice and making occasional, emphatic gestures with her beautiful hands.[4]

These two examples demonstrate the source and power of effective description: well-chosen, concrete and specific diction which paints the scene (an action sequence) or renders an abstraction (the essence of a writer's personality and appearance) for the reader in bold, clear strokes.

EXERCISES

1. At your VDT, write a primarily narrative paragraph for one of the following topics which traces chronologically a series of events. Print a copy for class discussion.

    a. An important or special experience from your childhood
    b. An event during your first week on campus as a freshman
    c. How you prepare for a major exam in a course you dislike
    d. One episode in a memorable vacation trip
    e. What you did yesterday as soon as classes were over

2. At your VDT, write a vividly descriptive paragraph for one of these objects or situations, avoid mere ''telling,'' and employ concrete and specific word choice. Print a copy for class discussion.

    a. The first time you drove a car
    b. The physical appearance of a relative or close friend

[3]Stephen Crane, ''A Christmas Dinner Won in Battle.'' *A Christmas Treasury,* Ed. Jack Newcombe. (New York: Viking Press, 1982), 95.

[4]Alzina Stone Dale, *Dorothy L. Sayers: Maker and Craftsman.* (Grand Rapids: Eerdmans Pub. Co., 1978), xiii.

c. The inside of a local fast-food restaurant you visit frequently

d. A child awaiting a doctor's appointment in an office full of adults

e. The feelings associated with seeing a police car with flashing lights in your rear-view mirror.

f. The album cover of a favorite recording artist

g. Halftime at a high-school football game

h. Your least favorite instructor

EXPOSITION: ORDERING INFORMATION

Exposition covers six distinct ways of selecting and ordering information: (1) division; (2) illustration; (3) comparison and contrast; (4) definition; (5) process analysis; and (6) cause/effect analysis. Writers employ exposition to *explain* phenomena for their readers.

Division

Division analyzes an object or phenomenon into its component parts. Each division within a text should meet certain logical criteria:

1. Each division should further the writer's intention in discussing the item. If a writer will be considering four types of computer printers in a section of the text, it will make sense to divide the appropriate discussion into four parts.

2. The divisions within a text should not overlap. That is, the divisions should be clear and distinct; if they are not, perhaps the division should not be made in the first place. For example, if ink-jet printers and dot-matrix printers can be best discussed within one classification of printers with similar functions, then no division should be made.

3. The set of divisions the writer makes should be complete. No important part should be left out. An essay explaining how to buy a computer printer that left out an entire category, such as letter-quality printers, would be ineffective.

4. The divisions should be consistent, that is, each division should be based on the same principle of division. A discussion of computer printers would not be effective if divided into inconsistent classifications such as these: (1) letter-quality printers; (2) dot-matrix printers; (3) printers which use multi-colored ribbons. The first two classifications are based upon the *kind* of printer each is; the third classification is a variation *within* different kinds of printers and not a classification of printers, and is thus inconsistent with the other two.

Writers use division to indicate the scope or coverage of a topic in their texts and to indicate a particular organizational principle they intend to use in their texts. Here are two examples:

1. *Indicating coverage:* The sports figures that I am mainly concerned with I have divided into three major categories: Aging Superstar, Demoralized Has-been, and Hopeful Rookie. They do not cover all the types but they each manifest two essential characteristics, bravado and self-pity, that reveal a great deal about the modern hero.

2. *Indicating an organizational principle:* One can readily distinguish four varieties of sentence errors among freshman students: fragments, dangling modifiers, fused sentences, and faulty equation. I will take up each of them in order, indicating how they may be corrected.

EXERCISES

1. At your VDT, divide one of the following topics into appropriate subtopics as they might be covered in an expository text. Be sure to follow the four principles for dividing topics and ideas we have discussed.

> *Example:* Abortion and the question of rights
>
> the rights of a woman to control her own body
> the rights of the father
> the rights of the unborn
> the rights of government to legislate moral principles

   a. The qualities most important for an effective teacher
   b. The modes of transportation most accessible to students on your campus
   c. The ethical issues which leaders of the 21st century will face
   d. The options open to athletes who participate in sports which have no professional leagues to support them
   e. The kinds of movies Hollywood tends to make during the 1980's

2. At your VDT, move your cursor under the divisions you have created for exercise #1 and compose an opening paragraph for an expository text which might discuss the topic under consideration. Print a copy for class discussion.

3. Examine the principle of division employed in the following two paragraphs. Determine the effectiveness of each division and, where appropriate, compose a new division which is more suitable at your VDT. Print a copy for class discussion.

   a. In this essay I will attempt to demonstrate that, contrary to popular opinion, baldness is not a hereditary trait. In order to persuade you of this fact, I will examine (1) my family; (2) what medical science says about baldness; (3) famous bald men; (4) the right conditions for losing one's hair.
   b. Essentially there are four ingredients for a successful political campaign. Two of them can be bought; two of them cannot. A candidate must be seen by the public as attractive, caring, smart and experienced. A candidate lacking any one of these qualities will not win.

Illustration

Illustration provides readers with practical examples of the assertions that writers make. Writers illustrate in order to convey a sense of fullness and deliberation in their texts. To be taken seriously, a writer must support statements with carefully chosen examples and relevant details. A thin text, full of assertions without illustrative examples conveys a sense of irresponsibility to readers. On the other hand, details for their own sake, irrelevant to the purpose at hand can be equally off-putting to readers.

In the following paragraph, the writer has supplied plenty of examples and details, but it is not clear to the reader what these are examples and details *of.* That is, the reader does not have a context for understanding what it is the writer is trying to illustrate, since the basic point of the passage is unclear:

> As romantic fiction such as *Love's Crimson Ardor* has grown in popularity, the appearance of these paperbacks at local garage sales has increased as well. I attended such a sale the other day and found no less than two hundred of these paperbacks, some tattered and torn, others whose pages were hardly creased. It is apparent that some people buy the books to put on shelves and not for reading. Most of the buyers I talked with, however, go to these garage sales to find reading material, not wall decorations. I suspect it is the same even at the commercial booksellers.

It is difficult to determine whether the writer intends to "illustrate" the popularity of romantic fiction, the surprising number available at garage sales, or the reading habits of those who buy such fiction. A revision of the paragraph would select and focus the illustrative material so that it became more apparent to the reader *what* was being elaborated:

> The popularity of romantic fiction such as *Love's Crimson Ardor* is confirmed even by a visit to the local garage sale. Not only do commercial booksellers make a profit on such novels, so do our neighbors and friends. At the sale I attended several days ago, housewives and college students were carrying away armloads of these books. Whether or not they were buying them for reading pleasure or to fill in some empty shelves in their living rooms, the publishers will not mind. The profits are just as green.

EXERCISES

1. At your VDT, generate appropriate illustrative material for one of the indicated topics. Print a copy for class discussion.

> *Example:* Crime is rampant in this city.
> Residents of Halcomb City are well aware of the rampant crime which has recently plagued us. The police blotter reads like a *TV Guide* listing of cop show plots: two breaking-and-enterings, four stolen cars, one attempted assault, and six disorderly conducts, all within a twelve-hour period over the weekend. Just two years ago, Halcomb City received national recognition for its safe streets. In those intervening two years, crime has increased by 200% and three out of five of us have been touched by theft, arson, or assault.

a. The arts on this campus nearly always suffer from underfunding.
b. In recent years the Miss America pageant has become less racist and sexist.
c. Refusing to register for the draft is tantamount to denying one's citizenship.

   d. Freshman English tends to be the least favorite course for new college students.

   e. After its experience in Iran, it is unlikely that the American public will ever again support a Middle Eastern tyrant.

2. Analyze one of the following paragraphs, evaluating the relevance and effectiveness of the illustrative material provided. At your VDT, rewrite the paragraph where appropriate to provide greater elaboration, to make the passage more coherent, or to clarify the point the writer seems to be making. Print a copy for class discussion.

   a. When America boycotted the Olympics in 1980, most of us were in support of the boycott. Looking back, it is hard to say that it was a success. The next time it happens, more of us will protest the boycott and argue for participation.

   b. If there was ever a dominant soft-rock group in America's turbulent 1970s it was Bread. David Gates' melodic voice led millions of us to buy single after single. Remember "Make It With You," "Diary," and "If"? No recording group of the period sold more records or filled more auditoriums. Where did they go? What happened to them? David Gates had a brief solo career which was climaxed by his "Goodbye Girl" single from the movie of the same name. Bread went the way of many other soft-sounding groups of the 1970's: into the chasm of disco and acid-rock, never to return.

Comparison and Contrast

Writers compare and contrast items in order to bring similarities and differences into sharper relief. As you learned in using the prewriting tool, TIP, in Chapter 2, discerning the similarities and differences between two or more ideas, persons, institutions, or events can assist you and your readers in understanding better the relationships between them. Comparison and contrast are not, however, a kind of text in themselves; they are a means to an end. The writer chooses to compare and contrast something in order to further some other goal in a text—to prove that one quarterback is more capable than another or to establish that Vietnamese refugees have suffered more than Cambodian refugees in the aftermath of the Indo-China war, for instance.

   In this comparison/contrast package, civil war historian, Bruce Catton, examines the similarities and differences between Ulysses S. Grant and Robert E. Lee in order to underscore the different philosophies of life each represented:

   . . . Grant and Lee were in complete contrast, representing two diametrically opposed elements in American life. Grant was the modern man emerging; beyond him, ready to come on the stage, was the great age of steel and machinery, of crowded cities and a restless, burgeoning vitality. Lee might have ridden down from the old age of chivalry, lance in hand, silken banner fluttering over his head. Each man was the perfect champion of his cause, drawing both his strengths and his weaknesses from the people he led.

   Yet it was not all contrast, after all. Different as they were—in background, in personality, on underlying aspiration—these two great soldiers had much in common.

Under everything else, they were marvelous fighters. Furthermore, their fighting qualities were really very much alike.[5]

EXERCISE

At your VDT, write a comparison/contrast paragraph, using one of the topics listed below with the stated purpose. Print a copy for class discussion.

  a. Compare/contrast comedienne Joan Rivers with another talk show host establishing that Ms. Rivers or the host you have chosen is more entertaining.
  b. Compare/contrast the American League and the National League, demonstrating that one of them plays superior major league baseball.
  c. Compare/contrast two fast-food chains, establishing that one has a more palatable menu than the other.

Definition

To define something, writers aim to identify those distinctive features that set the item apart from other things like it, explaining both what it *is* and what it is *not*. That is to say, writers both "classify" and "differentiate" the item from other items similar to it. Here are two samples of this definition mode.

> *Soccer:* the American name for European football, a game in which two opposing teams try to kick or head a soccer ball into the opponents' goal. With the exception of the goal keeper, no team members may use their hands in moving the ball up and down the field.

Note that the term is first *classified* ("a game . . .") and then further *differentiated* (". . . in which two opposing teams try to kick . . .") from other games like, perhaps, American football.

> *Browning automatic rifle:* an air-cooled, automatic or semi-automatic, gas operated rifle used in World Wars I and II.

Note that this definition is almost entirely *differentiation*, since the "class" of the item ("rifle") is already included in the term being defined ("Browning automatic *rifle*"). The rifle is specifically contrasted with other weapons by mode of firing, mode of operation, time period of usage, etc.

Writers sometimes clumsily employ definition in a text in this abrupt and somewhat unnatural way:

---

[5]Bruce Catton, "Grant and Lee: A Study in Contrasts," in *The Bedford Reader.* Eds. X. J. Kennedy and Dorothy M. Kennedy (New York: St. Martin's Press, 1985), 177.

The dictionary defines "myth" as "any ancient narrative containing fantastic events, whether true or false." In discussing Tolkien's work this definition is very important.

In contrast, the following definition is skillfully woven into the texture of the writer's prose:

> To call Tolkien's works "myths" is not to degrade them. Myths are primarily stories—stories with a long history, containing fantastic events, whether believed or not by the people who repeat them. In this sense, much of the Old Testament is full of "myths." But this does not mean that the stories are not true or are unhistorical. It simply means that the Old Testament stories fit into a pattern which modern critics label "myth."

Notice that "myth" is indeed defined in this passage, but only as a means to an end—to elaborate a discussion of a particular author's work. The term is not only classified ("Myths are stories . . .") and differentiated ("containing fantastic events"), but also is illustrated with an example (". . . much of the Old Testament is full of 'myths'"). The reader thus understands the term myth and its significance for the work of Tolkien.

EXERCISES

1. At your VDT, compose a definition for each of the following terms which effectively (1) classifies it and (2) differentiates it from other similar terms. Print a copy for class discussion.

a. taxi	f. mustard
b. designated hitter	g. pancreas
c. starlet	h. idiosyncratic
d. Rosetta Stone	i. totalitarian
e. theology	j. calendar

2. Examine one of the following paragraphs. Each employs either an inadequate definition or a vague term (in quotation marks) which needs a more explicit definition than has been supplied by the writer. Refashion the paragraph you have chosen by supplying a definition which more effectively classifies and differentiates the term under consideration. Print a copy for class discussion.

a. As most seniors know, to graduate from any university is no small achievement. There are countless "required courses" which plague even the most adventurous and persevering souls. "Geography," the study of places, and "psychology," the study of human behavior, both tax the patience of the unwary undergraduate beyond endurance.

b. Many recent commentators have mistakenly viewed "meekness" as a negative personality trait, forgetting that meekness is not the same as timidity. Whereas the latter term implies shrinking from authority and being unable to take charge of one's affairs, meekness is the quality of remaining cool under pressure and of remaining modest in the face of achievement. The greatest men and women of history have been meek, but not timid.

c. ''Baseball,'' the American sport played with a bat and four bases, has become popular of late in Europe for reasons not entirely clear. Perhaps it is because it is a game of finesse and subtlety, unlike American football which prizes brute strength and reckless violence.

Process Analysis

A process analysis explains how something is done or how something has come to be the thing it is. Process analysis may be *an end in itself,* as in the case of a writer who wants to explain how to write a computer program, or may be *used to further another purpose the writer has,* as in the case of a writer who explains how a nuclear weapon is constructed not to teach readers how to make one, but to express outrage at the threat of nuclear war itself. To be effective, a process analysis should present all the essential stages in a process, properly ordered and accurately and unambiguously explained.

The following process analysis is intended to explain how to obtain a library card:

Those who wish to obtain a library card at the Poteau City Library must comply with the following rules and procedures. First, you must be at least six years old and be able to write your own name. Secondly, you must apply in person, Monday through Friday between 9 A.M. and 3 P.M. When you come in, you or your parents will need to supply some form of identification with a local address on it. We will then ask you to fill out a brief questionnaire and to read a pamphlet about library use. Following this, we will ask you to sign a form pledging that you will be a responsible user of library materials. We will then issue a temporary card to be used until your permanent plastic card is mailed to you. Your permanent card is usually ready within six working days.

EXERCISES

1. At your VDT, write a brief process analysis for one of the following procedures or phenomena, carefully including all essential steps or stages in their proper order, clearly and accurately. Print a copy for class discussion.
  a. How to purchase a personal computer
  b. How to break up with a girlfriend/boyfriend with little pain
  c. How to save money while at college
  d. How to study for an exam in a difficult subject area
  e. How to choose a roommate
  f. The process of combustion in an automobile engine
  g. The process of photosynthesis
  h. The process of free agency in major league baseball
  i. The process of becoming a residential supervisor in a dorm
  j. The process of getting a record by a new artist played on radio

2. Examine the following process analysis. How effective is it in terms of being (a) inclusive of all essential stages or steps; (b) sequenced in the proper order; (c) accurate, clear and free of ambiguity? At your VDT, rewrite it if you find it to be faulty in any of these three categories. Print a copy for class discussion.

Revising a Draft

The first thing any writer should do in revising a text is to check to see if all the words have been spelled correctly. Nothing ruins a paper more quickly than a misspelled word. Next, a writer should examine each paragraph, looking for sentence fragments. All English teachers will fail a student who uses fragments. Next, the writer should make sure that the punctuation is correct, especially those commas! Finally, check to be sure that you have put your name on each sheet. If the teacher should lose your cover sheet you can rest easy that he'll be able to find all of your paper eventually.

Cause/Effect Analysis

Cause/effect analysis differs from process analysis in the kind of phenomena each typically considers. To explain an effect, one must usually refer to a number of complex, interrelated factors instead of one linear series of steps. While process analysis generally focuses on how something may be done or how something works, cause/effect analysis inquires into how and why something has occurred, that is, cause/effect analysis attempts to account for the reasons behind or the sources of a particular event or state of affairs.

This cause/effect analysis examines the reasons behind the success of a local business:

> How did Joan's Typing Service become central Florida's best known and most lucrative word processing firm? Her story is well-known. When she began her business, Joan herself was the only employee. Setting up shop in her basement, she purchased a new computer, some typesetting software, and a laser printer, and began to advertise her word processing service. Her first customers were faculty and students from Florida College in Temple Terrace, who appreciated her reasonable prices and quick service. Within a few short months, customers from all over Tampa's central business district were clamoring for Joan's expertise, and she was soon in a position to hire two part-time employees and add two extra word processing stations. Within two years, Joan had begun two other word processing outlets and no longer had to work out of her family's cramped basement.
>
> The chief buildingblocks of her three-site word processing empire are easy to identify: low overhead, quick turnaround, and marketing savvy. Joan's initial outlay of $5000.00 for word processing equipment was offset by her having virtually no office rent or utilities during the first year of operation. While she was establishing an identity for her service on campus and in the business community, she had only part-time employees to pay and only small maintenance costs. This enabled her to invest her early profits in better equipment and more office space as she needed it. Because she prided herself on the fast, accurate completion of each job, customers returned with their business and sold others on Joan's reliability. With little direct advertising after her first eighteen months of operation, Joan had built a reputation for quality work at

fair prices. Her well-chosen radio spots and newspaper ads—which focus on the qualities which have made her legendary in Tampa Bay business circles—provide her with the ongoing clientele she needs to maintain the level of success to which she has become accustomed.

EXERCISES

1. Consider some habit or disposition you have developed since your childhood or adolescence. At your VDT, compose a cause/effect analysis of this habit/disposition; attempt to account for its presence in your life. Print a copy for class discussion.

2. Imagine some dramatic change which could occur on campus. Write a cause/probable effect analysis which speculates on the ramifications of this change if it did occur.

3. Examine the following cause/effect analysis, noting the claims which the author makes in attributing causes to the effect under consideration. How plausible is the author's case? How would you alter the analysis to make it more plausible? Write a revised version of this text. At your VDT, write a note to its writer explaining what changes you would make to improve this text. Print a copy for class discussion.

Explaining the A-Team's Success

Most cultured TV viewers are stunned by the popularity of NBC's "A-Team." It had been NBC's top-rated primetime show for more than two years, despite the fact that each week the plot is basically a repetition of previous episodes and contains more gratuitous violence than any other show on network TV. How does one explain it? The answer, I believe, is three-fold.

First of all, most of "A-Team's" viewers are under twelve years old and kids twelve-and-under command the selection of TV shows at 8:00 in every American household. Neither dad nor mom better dare to watch Masterpiece Theatre or Placido Domingo while the kids are still up.

Secondly, after ten years of "sensitive" shows like MASH, the American viewing public seems to be in the mood for something more ragged, gruff, and primitive like "A-Team." The show certainly has no finesse or tenderness. The cast of characters is basically a quartet of macho males, led by the ever-present Mr. T, the villain in *Rocky III,* but hero *par excellence* in this weekly slugfest. America seems to want a hero who says little and wears fifty pounds of jewelry—a far cry from the sleeve-surface cynicism of Hawkeye and B.J.

Finally, producer Stephen J. Cannell, who has given us *The Rockford Files, Stingray, Hunter,* and *Riptide,* knows how to package character and combat in a most cartoonish way, overcoming our abhorrence of violence with broad humor and unlikely pairings. Mr. T and George Peppard in the same show? Machine gun rat-a-tat-tat and *no one* gets killed? Trucks overturn, planes crash, fists fly, and *no one* gets so much as a broken fingernail?

No, the success is not really surprising when one looks at the ingredients present in the show. The only mystery is how we can keep the other networks from borrowing this formula and filling our evenings with B-teams, C-teams and D-teams . . .

ARGUMENTATION: ORDERING EVIDENCE

A fourth mode of development is argumentation. Writers construct arguments in order to persuade their readers that a particular viewpoint or stance is valid and worthy of their acceptance and support. To argue in discourse means to present ''good reasons'' to your readers—facts, evidence, statistics, and so on—that will permit them to justify their acceptance of your claim or proposition. Argumentation implies there is something to argue about, so the writer anticipates that there will be objections to meet and terms to define, and that special attention must be paid to the kind of appeals he or she makes to the audience. Argumentation resembles exposition in some ways, since it requires the writer to present ''information'' about a topic. However, in arguing a point, writers are interested not only in explaining something clearly, but in convincing their readers that their point of view is correct.

This difference in intention—writing to *prove* something valid and not just explain what something is—is at the heart of much writing you will do in college and in the work place as you write proposals and argue the merits of different courses of action. Much could be said about the challenges and issues involved in argumentation, and you will find a fuller discussion of persuasive writing in Chapter 13, but here are a few principles to guide you in developing an argument in your text.

1. *Respect your audience and understand them well.* Address them with the proper mix of reason and emotional appeal. Some arguments require an intricate chain of linking propositions, each defended by a wealth of detail and example. If you were writing an essay to establish that electric power is cheaper than gas, you would need to discuss and debate a number of issues before centering on the main proposition. An audience would likely expect you to marshall data about the sources and cost of both kinds of power and how nuclear energy enters into the discussion. Other arguments focus on more personal issues and involve you in appealing to the character and emotions of the reader, such as in an appeal to stop drunk driving among teen-agers or an end to high unemployment. Determine the proper tone and stance toward your audience and the issue you are discussing. Anticipate their objections.

2. *Define your proposition or claim clearly.* Make sure your reader knows what it is you are trying to prove, and what kinds of evidence will be appropriate to establish its validity or truth. You should select facts, figures, and expert testimony that speak to the issues you are considering. Avoid overloading your reader with irrelevant or inaccurate information that undermines the sincerity or credibility of what you wish to prove.

3. *Define your terms unambiguously.* You may lose your readers early in an argumentative text by using terms loosely or inconsistently, especially if they are part of the proposition at issue. Make sure that any terms you use are precisely expressed and are used unequivocally as you proceed through your argument.

4. *Deductive arguments apply generalizations to individual situations to arrive at other generalizations, while inductive arguments proceed from specific observations and collected evidence to general conclusions.* For example, if you did not know the make-up of your college chorus, you might investigate the backgrounds and experiences of each member, discovering that a majority of them had extensive vocal training while they were in high school. You might thus reason *inductively* that high school students who wish to join their college chorus might increase their chances of selection by taking vocal lessons. On the other hand, if you knew that many or a majority of chorus members had special vocal training before they reached campus and were introduced to a member of the chorus, you might reason *deductively* that this person had this special training.

Deductive and inductive reasoning are quite crucial to our everyday thinking processes, and the two kinds of reasoning complement each other in the writing process. We apply them directly in organizing and developing persuasive texts when we move from specific details to generalizations (inductive) and from generalizations to specific instances (deductive). Inductive reasoning is thus used to generalize from observation and is essential to cause/effect analysis. It is the foundation of scientific inquiry. Deductive reasoning helps you arrive at sound principles by validating some assertions while arriving at others.

Examples of effective argumentation are harder to excerpt than other modes since an effective argument depends so heavily on a chain of reasons directed to a specific audience, but here is an argumentative paragraph that illustrates some of the four principles stated above:

> Ignorance of books and the lack of a critical consciousness of language were safe enough in primitive societies with coherent oral traditions. In our society, which exists in an atmosphere of prepared, public language—language that is either written or being read—illiteracy is both a personal and a public danger. Think how constantly "the average American" is surrounded by premeditated language, in newspapers and magazines, on signs and billboards, on TV and radio. He is forever being asked to buy or believe somebody else's line of goods. The line of goods is being sold, moreover, by men who are trained to make him buy it or believe it, whether or not he needs it or understands it or knows its value or wants it. This sort of selling is an honored profession among us. Parents who grow hysterical at the thought that their son might not cut his hair are *glad* to have him taught, and later employed, to lie about the quality of an automobile and the ability of a candidate.[6]

This paragraph is excerpted from a Wendell Berry essay that defends literacy as an essential possession in modern culture. In this paragraph he attempts to convince his audience that while an earlier culture, less "literate-bound," may have escaped the need for universal literacy, "the average American" needs these skills as a defense against the manipulating advertiser. Note that early in the paragraph he moves inductively, from specific details ("average American . . . surrounded by . . . newspapers . . . billboards . . .") to a generalization ("This sort of selling is an honored profession among us."). In addition, Berry defines his terms well ("prepared, public language" is annotated as "language that is either written or being read") and addresses his intended audience with a delicate balance of hard facts and personal appeal ("Parents are hysterical . . . glad to have him taught . . .") while making a clear presentation of his proposition (". . . illiteracy is both a personal and public danger.").

---

[6] Wendell Berry, "In Defense of Literacy," in *A Writer's Reader,* Eds. Donald Hall and D. L. Emblen (Boston: Little, Brown, Co., 1985), 45.

EXERCISES

1. Examine the following argumentative paragraph written to an audience of PTA members by a young woman concerned about her three year old son. How effective is it in (a) articulating a clear claim or proposition; (b) defining key terms clearly and adequately; (c) effectively employing deductive and inductive reasoning; and (d) appealing to its intended audience?

TV Is Ruining Our Kids

TV is ruining this generation of children. Every day brings news of declining SAT scores and increasing juvenile delinquency. Most of our kids watch TV for 75-100 hours a week and you know that they are not watching Mr. Rogers and Capt. Kangaroo. With the advent of video music, cable porn channels and more sexual and violent network TV, we can rest assured that our children will know more about ''life'' than ever before when they hit high school. My own children hardly read anything, even though we have a two-hour a day limit on TV watching. They simply go over to their friends' houses to watch. I propose that Congress pass a law which prohibits children from watching TV unless there is an adult in the room to monitor them. Something must be done.

2. Choose one of the following statements and craft a plausible argumentative paragraph which either defends or opposes the stance taken, keeping in mind the four principles suggested above and the indicated audience.

    a. Faculty should not be allowed to use student recreational facilities for free. (audience: readers of a campus newsletter for faculty)

    b. Treatment for drug abusers should be offered without charge to those unable to pay for it. (audience: citizens committee for drug control)

    c. Boxing is a sport that should be banned. (audience: readers of *Sports Illustrated*)

    d. The U.S. invasion of Grenada in 1983 was warranted. (audience: readers of a conservative political magazine)

    e. Most students would prefer to live in co-ed dorms. (audience: campus newspaper)

CHAPTER 6

Revising

on a Microcomputer:

An Overview

THE BASICS OF REVISION

After spending some time in prewriting and creating a first draft of a text, the writer naturally moves on to the most important and essential element of the composing process: *revision.* Revision can, of course, take place at any time during the composing process as ideas, shape and form come together in the writer's mind and on paper or VDT. But many apprentice writers make the mistake of thinking of revision as merely ''tinkering'' with a text—here and there correcting a spelling mistake, adding a comma, making a paper ''neater,'' and so on. These activities, important as they may be, are better understood as part of *editing*—the process of bringing a paper into its final manuscript form for a reader. Revision is a much broader activity, governing not only word and sentence editing, but also global changes in organization and content that successful writers make as they gain more and more control over the evolution of their texts. It is here where composing with a microcomputer is most advantageous over paper and pen.

Most writers do not revise extensively because revising represents a daunting task of erasing, whiting out, retyping, and sometimes literal cutting and pasting—an unpleasant task no matter how compelling the end result is. The advantage of revising on a microcomputer is that all of the time-consuming activities that formerly discouraged the writer because of their difficulty can be accomplished with a few keystrokes—and the microcomputer will painlessly do all the ''retyping'' in a matter of minutes. If writers ever had any excuse for failing to revise their texts appropriately—or for hating revision altogether—the microcomputer or word processor has taken it away.

Learning to revise involves, among other things, learning how to criticize your own draft as another reader would and learning how to do what needs to be done to make it reader-ready. That *you* understand the thesis and intention of your text does not necessarily mean that your reader will. You are so intimately involved with the process of drafting your text that you tend to see what should be there even if it isn't! Revision, or, "re-seeing" your text, is a crucial component of the successful writer's composing process. Putting distance between yourself as a writer and yourself as a reader is thus one of the goals you will work toward as you practice the revision strategies presented throughout the next four chapters.

Practically speaking, however, revision is primarily a matter of addition to, deletion from, substitution for, and rearrangement of existing elements of your text. Revision becomes meaningful, then, only when you have a draft of a text to work with, and not before. Let me illustrate these operations by referring again to Selena Campbell's text about John Lennon. After Selena wrote her discovery draft, she took a break and did not work with her draft until the next day. When she took up her text again, she wrote an intermediate draft, adding, deleting, substituting, and rearranging elements of her text appropriately to move toward a final draft. We can look at just one paragraph of her text and see how these operations assisted her in revising her first draft.

Early Version:

(1) Lennon's death now haunts me like President Kennedy's assassination haunted my parents. (2) Many dreams died that day in Dallas; so too did a generation's dreams die at the Dakota that fateful night that the assassin's bullet took John Lennon's life. (3) What I didn't understand then was that Lennon's death was not just the death of one man, albeit a famous man, but the death of a whole generation whose dreams of peace and contentment were shattered. (4) Lennon's music captured the essence of the late 1960s hope of a better world. (5) In the 1970s, those dreams were destroyed, just as Lennon was entering a new phase in his life.

When Selena examined this paragraph, she found it covered the ground she wanted to cover, but it had some problems. It was, she thought, quite repetitious in places; for instance, "dreams" were mentioned four different times without any concrete elaboration of what these "dreams" were. Sentences 4 and 5 seemed to introduce a line of thought and then drop it; she knew this had to be spelled out for the reader better. She also noticed that the first sentence left ambiguous the relationships between Kennedy and Lennon, one more thing that needed clarification. Here is her revised version of the paragraph:

Final Version:

(1) Just as President Kennedy's assassination haunted my parents' generation and represented not only his death but that of a culture's dreams of peace and prosperity, so too does the death of John Lennon haunt me and my generation. (2) What happened at the Dakota that fateful night was not just the shocking murder of a famous pop star, but the end of a post-60s dream of peace and respect for everyone in the world. (3) Lennon had entered a new phase in his life; he had settled down with a wife and child and was beginning to show us we could enter the 1980s with hope *and* responsibility. (4) He was one of the first rock-and-rollers to "settle down," to make a real home life for his family. (5) Instead of the dream, the assassin's bullet simply reminded us that nightmares—violence and insanity—were still a part of our culture. (6)

Lennon's legacy to us was nothing more than a callous memory, stained in blood, that one man's senseless act can destroy the aspirations and dreams of many.

In rewriting her paragraph, Selena used all four revising operations successfully. For instance, she *substituted* a new sentence (1) for the previous one, clarifying the relationships between the Kennedy reference and her own experience. She *deleted* the earlier sentence (5) and *replaced* it with one which helped sum up the topic of the paragraph and offered a more extended interpretation of what Lennon's death meant. In sentence 3 she *added* information that helped clarify what she meant by "entering a new phase in life." Finally, she *rearranged* some of the information in some of the middle sentences to help "glue" her ideas together better for the reader.

Once you have decided what needs to be done to your draft, your task is to move systematically through the revision process, eliminating communication problems and progressing toward a final draft that is accessible to a reader. As you learn to read through and rewrite your drafts, spotting weaknesses and exploiting strengths, you will gain confidence in your ability to communicate your ideas to the audience you are addressing.

TIPS FOR REVISING ON A MICROCOMPUTER

• As you become comfortable with the revising operations of the microcomputer, you should be careful not to "over-revise," that is, become so obsessed with the tools and power at your disposal that you cannot stop tinkering with your text. Set your revision goals, meet them, then move on to final editing.

• Revising with a microcomputer is a very powerful activity. The ease with which you can make changes is undeniable. However, you may wish to work with a *copy* of your text file whenever you are making extensive revisions, just in case you inadvertently delete or recast your text in a way that later distresses you. (Some word processors have an automatic "back-up" function which makes a copy of the text you are working on while you are revising it. If so, this may lessen your need for working on a copy. Discuss this with your instructor.)

• Most word processor enthusiasts like to revise at the VDT with a hard copy of their text at hand. You will probably find it easier to examine your draft and choose revision strategies using a hard copy first. Although there are some reviewing functions that the VDT makes simpler, moving from the hard copy of your text to the screen will assist you in finding and remedying more problems than revising with either one exclusively of the other.

• If you have decided to remove a large portion of text, say a paragraph or two, instead of deleting it entirely, first move it to the end of your text. Later you may find it contains valuable ideas or phrasings you can use. If not, you can delete it later.

• Beyond the revision skills you can develop for yourself in isolation from other writers, you will find that collaborating with your fellow writers will be invaluable in becoming a more effective reviser. Exchange your draft with a partner and ask her or him to respond to its thesis, intention, overall development, organization, and style.

USING THE REVISING STRATEGIES
IN *PROCESSING WORDS*

The following template file will guide you in revising toward a final draft. Create a version of this file and use it to evaluate a text which you consider a final draft. Answer these questions about the draft as a check of your original intention for your text. Chapters 7 through 10 contain specific revision strategies for dealing with any problems you identify. If you answer any question ''No,'' scroll below it and explain what you plan to do in revision to remedy the problem.

Evaluation Template for Final Draft

1. Have I captured my reader's interest early in the text by avoiding false starts and beginning directly and interestingly? If not, what revision plans should be made?

2. Have I announced my thesis and revealed my intention clearly enough so that the reader knows what to expect and in what order? If not, what revision plans should be made?

3. Have I supported any statements or assertions that the reader might have reason to question or debate? If not, what revision plans should be made?

4. Have I avoided *telling* the reader my ideas and instead *vividly depicted* them, using concrete and specific word choice, and focusing sentences and paragraphs sharply? If not, what revision plans should be made?

5. Have I avoided confusing or awkward sentence structure? Have I carefully selected appropriate words to convey a precise meaning? If not, what revision plans should be made?

6. Have I concluded my text appropriately without being abrupt or excessively repetitive? If not, what revision plans should be made?

7. Have I avoided major sentence errors, misspellings, grammatical and mechanical errors that would distract or annoy my reader? If not, what revision plans should be made?

There are four main goals in revising: (1) clarity, or eliminating ambiguity in structure and content; (2) economy, or eliminating wordiness; (3) fullness, or telling the readers all they need to know; (4) grace, or communicating with personality and variety. Chapters 7 through 9 each deal with some aspect of achieving these goals while Chapter 10 summarizes the basic revision strategies of the previous chapters and presents a case study of John Bebb's revision process, demonstrating how he put these revising strategies into action.

After working through these discussions and exercises regarding clarity, economy, fullness, and grace, your real task should be to work with *your own texts in-process*.

One of the most important things you can do is to familiarize yourself with the global and local problems that you yourself are likely to face in your composing process. If you know, for instance, that you are likely to have a problem with focus in your paragraphs or jargon in your word choice or poor development, you should take special note of these categories when you begin a revision.

The Revising Tools at Your Disposal

You can familiarize yourself with basic revising operations by trying them out on the sample texts in the exercises. Then apply these operations to your own prose. The exercises in later chapters work best when you type a sample text *as is* on your VDT and then manipulate the text with the appropriate keystrokes.

As I have noted numerous times in this text, the word processor puts at your disposal enormous power to change and mold your text. No more retyping long into the night, hoping you haven't added a few more typos to an already flawed text. The keystrokes of your word processor make most of the revising you will do a simple—and pleasurable—matter. The activities I suggest here by no means exhaust the possibilities. You will undoubtedly discover other applications on your own as you work with your particular software and texts.

As explained earlier, the word processor can serve two different functions. First, it can serve as a tool to initiate changes in your text which you have *identified and worked out on a hard copy of your text.* That is, you can use the word processor as a window for retyping portions of text which you have revised with pen and paper. Secondly, the word processor can serve as an *on-line text editor* which allows you to analyze and alter portions of the text before or without making any changes on a hard copy. By "on-line" I mean that you are working with the text (or copy of a text) in memory, making changes on the screen itself. As you have composed thus far, you have undoubtedly been making changes as you drafted your text. Once you have completed an advanced draft of your text, however, you are formally shifting into a revising mode, interested in transforming your draft into a reader-oriented text.

Most experienced writers use the word processor in both ways: (1) making changes on a hard copy initially and entering these changes into the text later on-line; and (2) exploring their text with the various search mechanisms a word processor provides and making changes on-line whenever and wherever they find things to alter. After some experience with composing on a word processor you will determine which of these two methods are most productive for you.

For your review, here are a number of functions and keystrokes you'll be using while you revise your text.

1. ENTER/INSERT: You will be placing the cursor at various locations in your draft in order to add to or type over text already present.
2. DELETE: You will be placing the cursor at various locations in your draft in order to delete or cut out text already present.
3. MOVE: You will be making the appropriate keystrokes to select and move blocks of text from one place to another in your draft.

4. SEARCH AND REPLACE: You will be making the appropriate keystrokes to SEARCH FOR various whole and partial words, phrases, punctuation marks, and textual cues in order to locate problems in your draft. You will sometimes search for these elements in order to REPLACE them with something else or to omit them altogether. Other times you will be searching just to review and check these elements to see if they need alteration.

During your revision sessions on-line, remember to first save a copy of the text you are revising just in case you unintentionally alter or delete portions of the text which you want to preserve as they are. Most word processors have an ''undo'' or ''undelete'' function and if you mistakenly change a portion of text, you can usually yank it back in place if you know the appropriate keystrokes.

EXERCISE

Look carefully at the draft of your text with which you are currently working. What problems remain? How do you plan to address these deficiencies to make your draft more effective? As you read through the next three chapters you will discover strategies for dealing with these and other problems.

CHAPTER 7

Revising Paragraphs for Clarity and Coherence

The main subunits of any text are its paragraphs. A writer starting to draft a text naturally begins to weave ideas and sentences into a cohesive package. But a writer's attempts to create effective paragraphs are not always successful. This chapter thus contains information that will help you better understand how paragraphs should work and how you can use the word processor to examine and revise them.

After a general discussion of how paragraphs work, we will explore two other aspects of these important units of text: (1) unity, coherence, and completeness; and (2) special paragraph functions—introductions, transitions, and conclusions.

There really should be no mystery about paragraphs, despite the sometimes long-winded discussions about them. Paragraphs really serve two kinds of functions in a text: (1) as *text-level "punctuation marks"* which make your text more readable; and (2) as *content containers* for your text which serve to organize and shape the development of your thesis.

THE PARAGRAPH AS PUNCTUATION MARK

Readers of newspapers know that journalistic prose typically employs short paragraphs. Such paragraphing eases the processing of the information presented in the newspaper, breaking up the text into smaller chunks for the reader. The column format of most newspapers demands such "punctuation," for otherwise the eyes of the reader would soon glaze over from an overload of text. Thus this paragraphing is not so much for organizational purposes as it is for readability. Similarly, you may have found in crafting your text that you chose to "paragraph" a section of your text simply to help your readers avoid eyestrain or to help them find their way in a forest of ideas which is becoming too thick.

It is tempting to set an arbitrary length to paragraphs, such as, "paragraphs should contain at least two sentences, but no more than six." However, the decision to paragraph a text cannot be dictated by such arbitrary rules. Paragraphing depends a great deal on the intention of the writer, how much information needs to be presented in certain sections of a text, and the surrounding context of the paragraph in question, that is, whether or not the reader has been asked to read a large chunk of text before and after it. In the discussion of the paragraph in later sections of this chapter you will get more specific guidance in deciding *when* to paragraph within your text.

THE PARAGRAPH AS CONTAINER

Most apprentice writers have come to know the paragraph as a kind of "mini-text" within a larger text, containing its own thesis or **topic sentence,** and bearing the qualities of unity, coherence, and completeness. But besides the fact that paragraphs may make a text easier to read, why do writers express their ideas in paragraphs? The following example will illustrate the logic of segmenting one's text into paragraphs.

Imagine a text which simply contained the following sentences, listed one after the other:

1. It may be we are issued a hunting license but offered no game.
2. The right to pursue happiness is issued to Americans with their birth certificates, but no one seems quite sure which way it ran.
3. Jonathan Swift seemed to think so when he attacked the idea of happiness as "the possession of being well-deceived," the felicity of being a "fool among knaves."
4. It is, of course, un-American to think in terms of fools and knaves.
5. For Swift saw society as Vanity Fair, the land of false goals.
6. We shall all have made it to heaven when we possess enough.
7. We do, however, seem to be dedicated to the idea of buying our way to happiness.

Presented with these sentences, how do you make sense of them? What relationship exists between these seven sentences? Do the sentences seem to have any intrinsic logic to their placement? How are they connected to each other? What ordering principle, if any, do you detect? Even though individual sentences may be meaningful, is it possible to determine the specific purpose the author may have had in mind in listing these seven sentences? In the absence of text-level cues supplied by the writer, the reader is left to guess at the organizing principle at work.

Here is the original paragraph format of these sentences, divided into two separate paragraphs by their author, John Ciardi:

> The right to pursue happiness is issued to Americans with their birth certificates, but no one seems quite sure which way it ran. It may be we are issued a hunting license but offered no game. Jonathan Swift seemed to think so when he attacked the idea of

happiness as "the possession of being well-deceived," the felicity of being a "fool among knaves." For Swift saw society as Vanity Fair, the land of false goals.

It is, of course, un-American to think in terms of fools and knaves. We do, however, seem to be dedicated to the idea of buying our way to happiness. We shall all have made it to heaven when we possess enough.[1]

Notice how the paragraphing of these sentences provides readers with the cues they need to follow the organization of the text. By properly *ordering* these sentences in his "paragraph container," the author, John Ciardi, wants his reader to process the first four sentences as a "whole" to be read together. The first paragraph is an introduction to a thesis which will be developed in later paragraphs: "Happiness as an ideal is easier to pursue than produce." The second paragraph serves to focus the reader's attention on his now emerging thesis, "We . . . seem to be dedicated to the idea of buying happiness." The paragraph is thus a way to tell your reader *how to read your text:* what sentences belong together, what your key points are, what the relationship of this group of sentences has to the text as a whole.

But paragraphs not only *organize* sentences and *indicate* structure, they also *contain a structure of their own.* If you recall our discussion of intention from Chapter 4, you know that different intentions yield different kinds of texts. Likewise, intentions govern the kind of paragraph development a writer may employ when drafting a text. The intention to explain implies that many of a writer's paragraphs will have an expository structure; the intention to tell a story implies that a writer will use narration and description; the intention to persuade implies that a writer will use an argumentative structure, and so on.

In summary, paragraphs are used to: (1) segment the text for readability; (2) cue the reader to those ideas, expressed in sentences, which should be read together as a unit; (3) signal the reader that the writer is moving from one point to another or is further elaborating on a previously stated point; and (4) make clear the intentions of a writer, since a paragraph's mode (narrative, descriptive, expository, or argumentative) often indicates the purpose of the text itself.

GENERAL STRATEGIES FOR EVALUATING AND REVISING PARAGRAPHS

Analyzing and revising paragraphs at the VDT is greatly simplified since you can rearrange sentences, delete words and sentences which are inappropriate, and add or substitute other material at any insertion point in the text. In any revision session, remember always to work with a *copy* of the file containing your text—just in case you inadvertently delete important elements or muddle your ideas such that you prefer returning to the

---

[1]John Ciardi, "What Is Happiness?," in *The Riverside Reader,* Eds. Joseph Trimmer and Maxine Hairston (New York: Houghton-Mifflin, 1981), 290–291.

original draft. The following general strategies will be useful to you as you begin to analyze and revise the larger units of your text.

1. THE BLOCK COPY/BLOCK MOVE FUNCTION. One word processing function particularly useful in revising paragraphs is BLOCK COPY/BLOCK MOVE. This function allows you to mark the beginning and ending of sections of text so that you can move, rearrange, or delete them to better suit your intentions in the paragraph. If you discovered, for instance, that your topic sentence worked better as the second or third sentence in the paragraph instead of the first, you could easily make the change.

2. CREATING A WORK SPACE. When you are revising a whole paragraph it is useful to insert enough carriage return spaces underneath it to create work space for crafting another draft of the paragraph. Make sure you can still read the original version and then tinker with the wording, arrangement, or information presented in the paragraph. If you prefer the revised version, you may simply delete the first version with a BLOCK DELETION. If you find a few elements in the revised version you want to incorporate into the original version, you can simply insert them into the text appropriately and then delete the revised version. (If your word processor permits you to use a split-screen to alter a copy of the text while looking at the original, you can perform these operations even more efficiently. Consult with your instructor about this.)

3. GAUGING PARAGRAPH LENGTH. In regard to length in a paragraph, remember that a standard VDT screen has twenty-five lines, and eighty characters per line, visible to the writer. You might use the ''screenful'' as a convenient measuring stick for judging the length of paragraphs; paragraphs which are consistently longer than a screenful of text may be too long for the reader to process easily or may be too ''full,'' requiring that you break the paragraph into two or more manageable units.

4. PARAGRAPH BUSTING. When analyzing a paragraph you may find it useful to separate it into individual sentences, examining their relationships. This gives you a quite effective overview of the unity, coherence, and completeness of the paragraph. What would be an arduous task if you were trying to manipulate the paragraph in longhand, or even on a typewriter, becomes an easy task performed with a few keystrokes at your VDT.

When the paragraph is disassembled, not only check for ''problems,'' look also for opportunities to expand and elaborate important terms and points and to provide useful background information for your readers.

First, place a carriage return space after each sentence so that each sentence may be displayed as a separate unit. (Depending upon your word processing software, you may be able to perform this "paragraph busting" semiautomatically, using the SEARCH/REPLACE function, searching for periods at the ends of sentences and replacing them with periods and two carriage return spaces. Consult with your instructor or the documentation for your word processing software to see how this may work.) Here is a sample paragraph from a student writer as it appears in his text and then after performing the above functions:

Cancelling the party was the worst thing the University could have done. It infuriated the fraternities and sororities. And it made them more determined to conduct the party secretly. Bill and the boys got really drunk. The next day the football game was less than a treat, too.

Cancelling the party was the worst thing the University could have done.
It infuriated the fraternities and sororities.
And it made them more determined to conduct the party secretly.
Bill and the boys got really drunk.
The next day the football game was less than a treat, too.

The first sentence, "Cancelling the party ... " is the topic sentence of the paragraph, and yet the relationship of the four subsequent sentences to it is rather fuzzy. Sentences 2 and 3 indicate consequences of the cancellation, but 4 and 5 seem to be off the point. After analyzing the paragraph, the writer decided to develop and move the last two sentences to another paragraph, combine sentences 2 and 3, and add other sentences better related to the topic sentence. Italics indicate the changes the writer made:

Cancelling the party was the worst thing the University could have done, since it infuriated the fraternities and sororities, making them more determined to conduct it secretly. The Delta Deltas and the Sigma Rhos rented the old warehouse on 5th Street and ordered two dozen kegs of beer. As word spread over campus, over 500 students gathered at the new, "secret" site, blocking traffic and generally disrupting the neighborhood. The end result was further erosion of community support for the students and an embarrassed Dean of Students.

As you examine each part of your paragraph you may discover that some sentences are too short or long, some have poorly conceived topic sentences, some contain sentences that do not support the topic sentence, and others that suggest ideas that need fuller elaboration, lack a subject or verb, and so on. After you have looked at each sentence and have performed an appropriate revision, you can remove the carriage returns with simple deletion and reform the paragraph with the appropriate keystrokes.

5. TABBING TO ANALYZE SUBORDINATE SENTENCES. Another helpful way to evaluate and revise paragraphs is to use tabbing to segment subordinating elements. On a normal typewriter, of course, tabbing is used to indent paragraphs or set up columns. At the VDT, tabbing can also be a tool for examining subordinate points in a sentence or paragraph. A subordinate element in a sentence or paragraph occupies a less important or less emphasized slot. In a *sentence,* it may be a parenthetical word or phrase, an appositive, or a transitional or modifying word, phrase, or clause. In a *paragraph,* the subordinate elements may involve elaboration, defense, or illustration of the points made in the primary sentences in the paragraph.

Some paragraphs are little more than indented *lists,* that is, ideas or points that have been strung together to support a topic sentence basically *in the order they occurred to* the writer. As a result such sentences may not be *subordinated* properly. That is, it may not be clear to the reader how to link these sentences with the topic sentence since the writer has not taken care to indicate their relationship with appropriate subordinating words and phrases. In the following sentences, the subordinate elements are italicized:

> UNSUBORDINATED: Walter is a good cook; he usually eats dinner at McDonald's.
>
> SUBORDINATED: *Although Walter is a good cook*, he usually eats dinner at McDonald's.
>
> UNSUBORDINATED: The team won the game. The coach resigned at halftime.
>
> SUBORDINATED: The team won the game *despite the fact that the coach resigned at halftime.*
>
> UNSUBORDINATED: Roxanne is energetic. She has rarely been to work on time.
>
> SUBORDINATED: *Energetic as she is,* Roxanne has rarely been to work on time.

In the following paragraph, the subordinate sentences have been tabbed:

> Like a clock on a home thermostat, brain clockwork turns down body temperature at night and turns it up at dawn.
>
> > Adrenal-cortical and other hormones, sodium and potassium salts, and many other substances are similarly regulated through a daily cycle.
>
> The clock appears to run a little slow, normally—about an hour later every day.
>
> > This tendency for the clock to run a little slow is corrected daily at sunrise, when the brain resets it for the correct time.[2]

The tabbed sentences represent subordinate points which illustrate, elaborate, or summarize the main point that was made in the primary sentence. Tabbing thus puts the writer in a better position (1) to examine the relationship of subordinate sentences to the primary sentences they follow; and (2) to determine whether the kind and number of subordinate sentences is appropriate.

Some paragraphs will significantly lack subordination while others will contain primary sentences that have too many or too few subordinate sentences. Tabbing the sentences you intend as subordinate in a paragraph may graphically reveal how successful or unsuccessful you have been.

If you determine that your paragraph lacks effective subordination or that your primary sentence requires more support, it is a simple matter to insert appropriate elements and then reform the paragraph. Similarly, if you determine that you had an imbalance of supporting sentences, too many in one segment, too few in another, you could easily add, delete, or move sentences as necessary.

6. PERSONA PARAPHRASE. It is sometimes instructive to use the structure of someone else's paragraph as a template for one's own content, a kind of "paint-by-numbers"

---

[2]Monte S. Buchsbaum, "The Chemistry of Brain Clocks," *Psychology Today* 12 (1979), 124.

kit for writers.[3] In using the persona paraphrase, you would appropriate the basic sentence patterns within a given paragraph and supply your own nouns, verbs, adjectives, and so forth. The end punctuation is left where it is, with basically the same number of words between commas, periods, colons, and so forth.

How does it work? First, select a paragraph whose shape and sound is appealing and enter it onto the VDT. (This paragraph is from Stephen Becker's *A Covenant With Death*.)[4]

Mrs. Talbot showed her amusement, and the women chatted as women chat, passing the time, Mrs. Donnelley taller, ample, ordinary, Mrs. Talbot placid yet restless, her brown eyes in motion, her hands roving to her hair, her throat, her skirt. When Bruce Donnelley appeared, far down the road, Mrs. Donnelley waved, and Mrs. Talbot seized that moment to primp briefly.

Below it, make another copy of the text—since you are going to delete certain words and replace them with your own. And now the fun begins: as you can see in the following example, the writer has substituted *her own* content, whimsical as it is, while preserving the original structure, using the SEARCH/REPLACE function:

[3]I am indebted to Professor John Trimble, University of Texas at Austin, for introducing me to the idea of the persona paraphrase.

[4]Stephen Becker, *A Covenant with Death* (New York: Atheneum, 1964), 7.

Corporal Punishment stroked his mustache, and the *officers muttered* as officers mutter, cursing their privates, *Major Disaster* older, gruff, self-important, Corporal Punishment *attentive but bored,* his toe tapping, *his eyes stealing glances* at his watch, his carelessly trimmed thumbnail, his empty beer bottle. When Private Parts again belched, still louder than before, *Major Disaster erupted, and Corporal Punishment pronounced it capital."*

If you look closely at the italicized words, and at other elements in the paragraph, you can see that this student playfully substituted the characters Corporal Punishment and Major Disaster for Mrs. Talbot and Mrs. Donnelley, "officers muttered" for "women chatted," "his eyes stealing glances ... " for "her hands roving ... " and so on.

What's the purpose of the persona paraphrase? For one thing, it will increase your repertoire of sentence and paragraphing strategies: You are compelled to experiment with different structures that you may never have invented on your own. It is not the *content* of someone's paragraphs you are borrowing, only the structure. Secondly, you will find that, rather than curtailing your imagination, it will actually stimulate it, and increase your own creativity and sense of appropriate sentence variety and order within paragraphs.

If you need to describe something vividly, choose an effective descriptive paragraph and do a persona paraphrase of it. Similarly, it you need to construct a narrative, expository, or argumentative paragraph, sample an essay or two that you find effective and do a persona paraphrase. The worst that can happen is that you discover a new way to express yourself.

Try it yourself with one of the following paragraphs.

Descriptive:

The porch is about thirty feet long, almost the width of the house, and six feet, eight inches wide. The porch is enclosed with ten-foot-tall screens and we sit in old brown wicker chairs, rocker, couch, except me. I lie on the floor, feet to the house, and measure myself against that wonderful height. A six-eight person can pretty much write his own ticket.[5]

Narrative:

They moved hastily along and found a place where the wall seemed to stoop abruptly, almost as if it had been half-sunk into the earth; and a garden tree, flamboyant with the gayest garden blossom, straggled out of the dark enclosure and was gilded by the gleam of a solitary street-lamp. Bagshaw caught the crooked branch and threw one leg over the low wall; and the next moment they stood knee-deep amid the snapping plants of a garden border.[6]

[5]Garrison Keillor, *Lake Wobegon Days.* (New York: Viking Press, 1985), 130.

[6]G. K. Chesterton, *The Penguin Complete Father Brown* (New York: Penguin Books, 1981), 468.

Expository:

The few histories of invention that we have available seem to suggest that the art of invention declined and subsequently disappeared in the late nineteenth century, except for the purposes of formal debate. Several reasons have been given for the demise of classical invention: the influence of Coleridge and the Romantic emphasis on intuition; the rise of science with its stress on empirical research; and the advent of a large middle class whose main concern was with literacy and practical discourse.[7]

Argumentative:

The rules of this society are cruel to women. Brought up to be never fully adult, women are deemed obsolete earlier than men. In fact, most women don't become relatively free and expressive sexually until their thirties. (Women mature sexually this late, certainly much later than men, not for innate biological reasons but because this culture retards women. Denied most outlets for sexual energy permitted to men, it takes many women *that* long to wear out some of their inhibitions.) The time at which they start being disqualified as sexually attractive persons is just when they have grown up sexually. The double standard about aging cheats women of those years, between thirty-five and fifty, likely to be the best of their sexual life.[8]

[7]Frank J. D'Angelo, "Paradigms as Structural Counterparts of Topoi," in *Rhetoric and Composition*, ed. Richard Graves (Montclair, NJ: Boynton/Cook, 1984), 202.

[8]Susan Sontag, "The Double Standard of Aging," in *On the Contrary*, eds., Martha Rainbalt and Janet Fleetwood (Albany, New York: SUNY Press, 1984), 103.

MAKING PARAGRAPHS WORK:
UNITY, COHERENCE, AND COMPLETENESS

For the paragraph to work in your text as an effective *container* of ideas, it must bear each of the following qualities: unity, coherence, and completeness.

Unity

Every sentence grouped into your paragraph must be related to a central idea. In almost all paragraphs there is a *topic sentence* which serves as the center of that unit of your text. (Some paragraphs with special functions may not contain a topic sentence per se; these are discussed later in the next section.)

The topic sentence tells your reader what the main point of that unit of text is, and it usually, though not always, is found near the beginning of the paragraph. A paragraph without a clearly delineated topic or one whose supporting sentences stray from the topic is called *unfocused*.

The following paragraph contains a clearly delineated topic sentence (indicated by the italics) which is supported by the other sentences within the paragraph unit.

As many people have pointed out, *the only way to learn how to swim is literally to jump in and get wet*. No one can learn to swim by reading a book about it, just as no one can become a husband or wife merely by reading marriage manuals. Reading might make you a *better* swimmer—or spouse—providing you already are one, but it will do nothing for the timid being who is content to sit on the edge of the pool. So if you want to learn how to swim, take the plunge. It's the only way to go.

Coherence

Remember that the main reason to combine sentences effectively in a paragraph is to show your reader how to *read* your text. When you order sentences into a paragraph you are indicating to your reader how each sentence in it is related. However, although every sentence in your paragraph may be "about" the central idea announced in your topic sentence, that is no guarantee that the paragraph is well formed. If your reader has to guess at your reasons for moving from sentence to sentence in your paragraph, your paragraph is *incoherent*.

In the two sample paragraphs below, notice how the writers have used such devices (indicated by italics) as pronouns, synonyms, repeated structure, and transitional word cues such as "on the contrary" to tie sentences together and provide the reader with cohesive units.

(1) Caesar was right. Thin people need watching. I've been watching *them* for most of my adult life, and I don't like what I see. When *these narrow fellows* spring at me, I quiver to my toes. *Thin people* come in all personalities, most of them men-

acing. You've got your "together" *thin person*, your condescending *thin person*, your tsk-tsk *thin person*, your efficiency-expert *thin person*. All of *them* are dangerous.[9]

(2) In the Christian sense, love is not primarily an emotion but an act of the will. When Jesus tells us to *love* our neighbors, he is not telling us to *love them* in the sense of responding to them with a cozy emotional feeling. You can as well produce a *cozy emotional feeling* on demand as you can a yawn or a sneeze. *On the contrary*, he is telling us to *love our neighbors* in the sense of being willing to work for their well-being *even if it means sometimes* sacrificing our own well-being, *even if it means sometimes* just leaving them alone. Thus in Jesus' terms we can *love our neighbors* without necessarily liking them. In fact *liking them* may stand in the way of *loving them* by making us overprotective sentimentalists instead of reasonably honest friends.[10]

Completeness

Paragraphs must not only be unified and coherent, they must also leave the readers with the sense that they have been told all they need to accept your assertions. That is to say, each paragraph should evoke a sense of *completeness*. Your topic sentence is a promise to your readers that everything that needs to be in the paragraph to support it will be there: assertions are backed up by illustrations; arguments are documented with evidence; narratives are concluded appropriately; descriptions are developed and sustained with detail.

The following paragraph is rich in development, leaving the reader with a sense of completeness.

Friendship arises out of mere Companionship when two or more of the companions discover that they have in common some insight or interest or even taste which the others do not share and which, till that moment, each believed to be his own unique treasure (or burden). The typical expression of opening Friendship would be something like, "What? You too? I thought I was the only one." We can imagine that among those early hunters and warriors single individuals—one in a century—one in a thousand years?—saw what others did not; saw that the deer was beautiful as well as edible, that hunting was fun as well as necessary, dreamed that his gods might be not only powerful but holy. But as long as each of these percipient persons dies without finding a kindred soul, nothing (I suspect) will come of it; art or sport or spiritual religion will not be born. It is when two such persons discover one another, when, whether with immense difficulties and semi-articulate fumblings or with what would seem to us amazing and elliptical speed, they share their vision—it is then Friendship is born. And instantly they stand together in an immense solitude.[11]

In Chapter 9, *Revising for Fullness and Grace*, you will find more revising strategies for developing paragraphs that are complete and well supported. In summary, then:

[9]Suzanne Britt Jordan, "That Lean and Hungry Look," *Newsweek* 92 (October 9, 1978), 32.

[10]Frederick Buechner, *Wishful Thinking* (San Francisco: Harper and Row, 1973) 54.

[11]C. S. Lewis, *The Four Loves* (New York: Harcourt Brace Jovanovich, 1960), 96–97.

1. Paragraphs are the basic units of a text. They contain information, they manifest certain modes and reveal certain intentions, and, overall, indicate to the reader how best to read a text.

2. To be effective, paragraphs need to be (a) unified, that is, all the sentences in a paragraph should be related to one central idea; (b) coherent, that is, the arrangement of the sentences within a paragraph should reflect a logical order, apparent to a reader without guesswork; and (c) complete, that is, your paragraph should contain any and all information necessary to support the topic sentence which forms the center of the paragraph.

3. Each paragraph should itself bear a clear relationship to the paragraph immediately preceding it and the one following it in order to maintain coherence at the textual level, that is, each paragraph should make clear a progression toward the writer's goal or intentions in the completed text.

DEALING WITH AMBIGUITY AND INCOHERENCE

Consider the following opening paragraph written in response to an assignment to "analyze" a poem for a group of the writer's peers. Read it carefully and try to determine what the writer's real point and intention are:

> (1) History is indeed an interesting subject. (2) And when I was asked to read Shelley's poem, "Ozymandias," I was very excited since it is a very historical poem. (3) History study helps you understand not only the past, but also the present, and sometimes the future. (4) "He who forgets the past is doomed to repeat," as the saying goes. (5) When reading "Ozymandias," it is clearly a poem about history and about a great king whose only legacy to the present is the record of his death. (6) It is an ironic poem indeed.

The problem with this version of the writer's opening paragraph is that it is obviously written as an expression of the writer's discovery process and not as a communication to a reader. Note these features:

a. Sentence 1 gives mixed signals to the would-be reader: is this paper going to be about history? Or will it be about a particular poem (announced in sentence 2)?

b. Sentence 2 indicates something interesting about the writer (she evidently likes history), but this contributes nothing to the writer's ostensible intention to analyze a poem. In this case, her interest in history is beside the point—unless this is an essay about herself.

c. Sentences 3 and 4 are equally off target, given that the writer's real task is to explore the poem "Ozymandias" and not to offer cliches about history and the purposes of studying history.

d. Sentence 5 is the first sentence really to identify the possible thesis of the essay the writer is creating, but it is poorly constructed and still leaves the reader wondering about what the succeeding paragraphs might contain.

e. Sentence 6 offers a comment on the poem but fails to provide a frame of reference for it and thus leaves the reader again wondering what the point of the writer's text may turn out to be.

One can almost reconstruct the thinking processes of the writer from reading this paragraph—and that's the problem. First, she thought of history and how much see liked to study it—so she began with a reference to its "interestingness." Then she reflected on the actual assignment the instructor had given her—and again she placed that in her text. We discover that what we have here is a record of the prewriting notes of a student whose purpose is still not clear to her—or at least has not been expressed clearly in text.

Writers should always remind themselves that their task is to communicate to their readers—and not merely to express themselves in a way that satisfies them. Personal satisfaction may be an appropriate criterion for judging journal entries, but it is not appropriate for assessing writing done for other readers. Here are some of the typical sources of global ambiguity in texts:

1. *The use of vague words*, terms which are used inconsistently, loosely, or in a sense meaningful only to the writer. In the second sentence, the writer calls "Ozymandias" a "historical" poem; *historical* here is ambiguous and is used in a somewhat private sense.

2. *The presentation of information that is not germane to the ostensible purpose of the text* but serves only to pace the writer's own discovery process. In the case above, all the information the writer provides about her interest in history is irrelevant and can only confuse or alienate the reader.

3. *Unclear organization.* Some writers mistakenly write every writing assignment as if it were a story—that is, their organizational pattern is to relate events, ideas, situations in the order in which the ideas occurred to them. This is obviously the case with the "Ozymandias" paragraph as the writer orders her sentences for the reader according to the sequence in which she thought of them.

4. *Convoluted sentence structure*, that is, structure in which the true subject and verb are lost somewhere in a mish mash of ideas. In convoluted structure, the action of the sentence is often hidden in passive verbs (is, are, was, were), and the reader finds it difficult to understand what is "happening" in the sentence. This is the case with sentence 5 above. There is no true agent (doer of the action) in the sentence: *who* is doing the reading of "When reading"?

5. *Overall lack of clarity.* A text that moves from point to point without adequate transition or proceeds randomly is probably just a record of the writer's discovery process. It is in a shape to be "harvested" for ideas, but is not ready to be read by a reader other than the writer herself. The narrative structure of the "Ozymandias" paragraph contributes to this sense of general disorganization.

Consider this revision of the "Ozymandias" paragraph in which the writer attempts to structure its content with a better focus:

Shelley's "Ozymandias" is an ironic poem which chronicles in first person the achievements of an ancient Egyptian king who foolishly believed that he would outlive his own legend. The following analysis will explore the poem's irony and the effective way in which the poet has juxtaposed the usual platitudes about history with the reality of one man's confrontation with mortality.

In this revised paragraph, note that the writer has provided a context for understanding the direction of her text and has greatly improved the focus of her opening paragraph by eliminating the distracting personal information about her interest in history. She has riveted the reader's attention to the poem itself (as is appropriate for an analysis text) by a direct statement of the paper's thesis and plan of attack, and this gives her the impetus for completing a revision of the rest of the text. The writer has reduced the number of sentences and this more compact structure helps underscore the text's direction.

USING THE MICROCOMPUTER ON-LINE

These pointers will assist you in making paragraphs clearer and more coherent using your word processor.

Search Procedures

Searching for problems of ambiguity and coherence is a matter of *scrolling* through the text sentence by sentence and paragraph by paragraph, to determine if each unit (sentence; group of sentences; paragraph; group of paragraphs) is consistent with the intention of the writer. One effective way to do this on-line is to use the "WAITS" system:

a. *Scroll* through your text *paragraph by paragraph.*

b. After each paragraph *space* a few lines and nutshell the main thrust of that paragraph by answering "WAITS": *What Am I Trying to Say?"*

c. Use this nutshell of the paragraph to help you decide if you have expressed yourself clearly in individual sentences and in groups of sentences, and among the paragraphs where this paragraph is located.

d. After you have made the appropriate changes, delete your WAITS nutshell from the text.

Revising Strategies

Revising to make your paragraphs clear and coherent for your reader involves the operations of addition, deletion, substitution, and rearrangement. Use the keystrokes appropriate to your word processing software to: (a) add appropriate sentences and words; (b) delete inappropriate sentences and words; (c) substitute more appropriate sentences and words; or (d) rearrange sentences and words to facilitate the meaning and effect you want your text to have. Here is an example of how one student used WAITS to revise his text:

Although many computer buyers are aware of the advantages that their machines provide, most of them probably don't know how computers are manufactured. I do. I spent a summer internship in Silicon Valley last year. I got to see the whole process at work. I believe most of us would be surprised to find out how they are produced.

WAITS:

I begin ok, but I get too personally involved in the next four sentences. What I am trying to do is introduce what this paper is going to be about—and not how I got the information.

The chips are always the key element in the manufacturing of a new computer. Even though the engineers have designed the functions and cabinet of the computer, nothing gets done without the chips. They are either purchased from overseas or manufactured. If they are purchased, that makes the machine more expensive for the consumer.

WAITS:

What I am really trying to do is prove how important the microchip is to the computer industry. As is, this paragraph jumps right into my topic. I need a smoother transition from the broad topic of how computers are manufactured to a narrower vision of the importance of the computer chip.

In revising this portion of his draft, the student made these changes:

1. Rearranged sentence 1 so that the introductory sentence clearly focuses on how computers are manufactured and not the ignorance of computer users.

2. Deleted sentences 2 to 5 which introduced distracting, unfocused personal comments and added these new sentences:

(2), whose analogy effectively illustrates the point the writer is making;

(3), which emphasizes the point made in 2;

(4) and (5), which specify the source of the writer's information and interest.

3. Deleted sentences 6 to 9, while harvesting the most useful information contained in those sentences.

4. Substituted a new sentence 6, which provides a context for understanding subsequent sentences by focusing the reader's attention on "miniaturization," the key to the writer's thesis.

5. Added new sentences 7 to 9 which focus the reader's attention on the computer chip and its effect on the industry. Throughout these sentences, the writer has employed effective synonyms, pronouns, and signal words that help the reader discern the writer's focus.

Here is the revised version:

(1) Although many microcomputer users have enjoyed the advantages in word and information processing which their machines provide, few of them have probably inquired into how their computers are manufactured. (2) Like the automobile driver who doesn't know what's under the hood of the car, most of us are content that these marvels of technology do our bidding. (3) We are not that interested in discovering the process whereby they are made. (4) I felt the same way until I held a summer internship at the Bracewell Computer Company in Silicon Valley--the manufacturing and design capitol of the computer industry, located between Palo Alto and San Francisco. (5) There I was introduced to the fascinating world of computer design and production.

(6) What few of us would have guessed is that the most amazing aspect of microcomputer design and production is how much it depends on miniaturization for its development. (7) The tiny computer chip is the heart of the 1980s microcomputer. (8) Smaller than a postage stamp, the silicon-based chip is a miniature circuit board, a reservoir of information the microcomputer uses to understand and carry out the programs and commands of the user. (9) The computer chip is, in fact, responsible for bringing the cost of computers down to levels accessible to the average consumer.

SPECIAL PARAGRAPH FUNCTIONS

We have considered the paragraph as a unit within a text which may bear certain structures and reveal certain intentions of the writer. In addition to these, paragraphs may perform still other special functions. In this section, we will consider more closely the uses of the paragraph for *opening* a text, for *concluding* a text, and for *providing transition between* sections of a text.

Beginnings

Of course, you must begin a text somewhere; yet, you may wish to write the "opening paragraph" last—or, at least, choose to write only a tentative opener until it appears what direction the text is going to take. Having decided to craft an opening paragraph, you should keep in mind that the first paragraph is especially crucial in getting the attention of your readers and "hooking" them for the rest of the text. Consequently, the opening paragraph should quickly reveal to the reader something of the text's thesis, direction, and tone.

Each of these text openers is effective, though each begins differently:

> (1) There are 4,000,000 starving people in the United States. You read it correctly: 4,000,000. The question is, what are we going to do to help these poor and forgotten fellow citizens? We need more than bombastic rhetoric and grand promises; we need action. In this essay, I want to show you how we can help the 4,000,000 today, this hour, this moment. When you have finished reading it you may not have the courage to act on its exhortations but you will no longer have the excuse, "But what can anyone do?"

In this opening, the writer startles the reader with a blunt fact, and focuses the reader's attention on the text's thesis with a rhetorical question. This is followed by an explanation of exactly what the writer intends to do in the context of the essay.

> (2) Our age has produced a new kind of eminence. This is as characteristic of our culture and our century as was the divinity of Greek gods in the sixth century B.C. or the chivalry of knights and courtly lovers in the middle ages. It has not yet driven heroism, sainthood, or martyrdom completely out of our consciousness. But with every decade it overshadows them more. All other forms of greatness now survive only in the shadow of this new form. This new kind of eminence is "celebrity."[12]

This opener tantalizes the reader with an opening topic sentence which declares the thesis of the text ("our age has produced a new kind of eminence") but which withholds explicit mention of what the "new kind of eminence" is until the last sentence of the paragraph. In between, the writer builds the suspense by alluding to earlier historical epochs and the kind of "eminence" which they honored.

> (3) The first thing that strikes the careless observer is that women are unlike men. They are the "opposite sex"—(though why "opposite" I do not know; what is the "neighboring sex"?). But the fundamental thing is that women are more like men than anything else in the world. They are human beings. *Vir* is male and *Femina* is female: but *Homo* is male and female.[13]

This opener begins directly enough, focusing the reader's attention on what appears to be a conventional thesis ("women are unlike men"). However, the reader quickly realizes that the writer has used the opening sentences as intentional misdirection to unsettle the reader with the antithesis of what at first appeared to be the text's thesis ("women are more like men than anything else in the world").

---

[12]Daniel Boorstin, "From Hero to Celebrity," in *On the Contrary*, 268.
[13]Dorothy L. Sayers, "The Human-Not-Quite-Human," in *On the Contrary*, 10.

An opening paragraph need not be long-winded, overly general, or filled with self-conscious attempts to shock or startle the reader. These three ''approaches'' are singled out here because sometimes well-intentioned textbook admonitions are translated by apprentice writers into some very counterproductive responses. For instance, ''reveal your thesis'' may be construed as an invitation to capsule the whole essay in one paragraph, or, worse, to create an unnecessarily vague and general ''background'' against which the thesis may be placed. Likewise, ''get the reader's attention'' may lead some writers to go out of their way to be novel or peculiar, thus alienating their readers.

The most important consideration in crafting an opener is *consistency*. The writer's initial approach to the reader should fairly indicate the thesis, scope, direction, and tone of the text which follows. If the opening is ''funny'' but the rest of the text is sober, if the opening is filled with statistics and hard evidence but the rest of the text abounds with ill-founded assertion and speculation, if the opening promises a broad discussion but is then followed by a text which considers only a narrow portion of the announced territory, the writer has misled the reader and will suffer the consequences of a hostile audience and an unread manuscript.

EXERCISE

Examine the following text openers. How effective are they in terms of: (1) their specification of thesis and scope of coverage; (2) their attempt to interest a reader; and (3) their revelation of tone and direction? At your VDT, compose a note to the writer suggesting what might be done to revise the opener to improve it. Print a copy for class discussion.

a. (opening for a biographical essay on Sigmund Freud)
Freud hated women. That sobering fact colors everything one might say about this controversial but incontrovertibly great man. To speak, then, of Freud the psychologist is to speak of Freud the misogynist. I will attempt to prove in this essay that my thesis about Freud hating women is accurate and that other psychologists, like Carl Jung, can't escape that charge either.

b. (opening for an article in *American Film* on violence in film)
''Go ahead, make my day.'' The magnum explodes on the screen and another full house revels in the bloodbath of another Dirty Harry movie. Studies show that, while some filmgoers find a release for their pent-up frustrations, a significant majority actually vent their violent emotions after viewing such a flick. What has happened to American values? How are these distorted values reflected in the kinds of movies Hollywood makes and the public clamors for? The time is coming when all of this violence will backfire on us and we will see an armed camp in every city in America.

Endings

If openers should be written only as the text emerges and provides the writer with a good grasp of where it is headed, should ''endings'' be written first? Not necessarily, although there is some advantage in being able to visualize what your concluding paragraph should look like. A writer who has a strong sense of how the text should end will be able to craft the beginning and middle of it that much more resourcefully.

Apprentice writers tend to acquire as much well-intended folklore about conclusions as they do about beginnings. Many writers believe they have been instructed to write the stereotypical "conclusion" which reiterates the "argument" of the preceding text—thus taking the risk not only of boring the readers (who have, after all, just experienced the writer's argument for themselves), but of insulting their intelligence as well by implying that they couldn't make heads or tails of what they have read.

Ultimately, you should try to avoid three extremes: (1) the text which simply *stops*—abruptly and perfunctorily—leaving your readers wondering if they're missing part of the text; (2) the conclusion which *merely* repeats the text's introductory premises; and (3) the conclusion which inadvertently introduces a *new line of inquiry* which is not pursued.

The following concluding paragraphs can serve as models for ending a text effectively.

The first is the conclusion to a text which reflects on the death of Marilyn Monroe, asking if she were, like Charles Lindbergh, a victim of fame.

> This doesn't mean that I don't think she was a "victim." But she was not primarily a victim of Hollywood commercialism, or exploitation, or of the inhumanity of the press. She was not even primarily a victim of the narcissistic inflation that so regularly attends the grim business of being a great screen personality. Primarily she was a victim of her gift, a biological victim, a victim of life itself. It is one of the tragedies that are inherent in human existence—at least, inherent in human existence in civilization. I think Marilyn Monroe was a tragedy of civilization, but this is something quite else again from, and even more poignant than, being a specifically American tragedy.[14]

In her conclusion, Diana Trilling takes the occasion to reemphasize her thesis by distinguishing her views of Monroe and of "victimhood" from more typically believed notions. The last sentence is particularly effective in tying together all of Trilling's views without repeating all that she has said before.

The following paragraph is the conclusion to a famous letter written by Dr. Martin Luther King from a Birmingham, Alabama jail. The letter explained to his fellow clergymen, skeptical of his motives in the civil rights movement, why he was imprisoned.

> I hope this letter finds you strong in the faith. I also hope that circumstances will soon make it possible for me to meet each of you, not as an integrationist or a civil-rights leader but as a fellow clergyman and Christian brother. Let us all hope that the dark clouds of racial prejudice will soon pass away and the deep fog of misunderstanding will be lifted from our fear-drenched communities, and in some not too distant

---

[14]Diana Trilling, "The Death of Marilyn Monroe," in *On the Contrary*, 286.

tomorrow the radiant stars of love and brotherhood will shine over our great nation with all their scintillating beauty.

> Yours for the cause of Peace and Brotherhood,
>
> Dr. Martin Luther King[15]

There is a decided undercurrent of irony in Dr. King's conclusion—a testimony to his keen sense of audience. Embattled as he was—fighting for the rights of minorities while trying to maintain his credentials as a clergyman—his conclusion necessitated a careful balance between explaining his stance and rebuking his fellow Christians for their ignorance and slowness in dealing with the important issue of civil rights. His conclusion accomplishes both goals.

The final example is a conclusion written for a text which has explained how to deal with creditors who harrass their clients.

> In conclusion, remember that no matter how much you may owe and no matter to whom you owe it, as long as you are making a reasonable effort to repay the balance (even if it is only $1.00 a month!) no creditor can garnish your wages or repossess any of your belongings. You have just as many rights as your creditors do, and if they continue to harrass you by phone at home or at work you may gain a court order to stop them. Take the initiative. The debt you save may be your own.

This text ends fairly conventionally, but competently. The writer announces that he is concluding, and then closes with a reminder and an exhortation. The last two sentences are intentionally short to drive the writer's point home with as much impact as possible.

EXERCISE

Examine these concluding paragraphs. How effective are they in (1) avoiding an abrupt ending; (2) satisfying the readers' need for closure without insulting them; and (3) avoiding an introduction of new lines of inquiry? At the VDT, compose a note to each writer, explaining how the conclusion might be improved. Print a copy for class discussion.

a. (conclusion to a text which argues for the legalizing of marijuana)

So, in summary, the case for the legalization of marijuana is unassailable: (1) Marijuana is safe; (2) young adults can get it if they want it anyway; (3) a society which is allowed to drink hard liquor ought to have access to marijuana as well; and (4) more revenue for the government would result.

b. (conclusion to a movie review)

I don't want to spoil the ending for you, but suffice it to say that in the end, the kids won't be disappointed by the intergalactic combat. Science-fiction cinema has come a long way since the days of the old Buck Rogers films.

---

[15]Martin Luther King, *Why We Can't Wait* (New York: Harper and Row, 1963), 100.

c. (conclusion to a text which explains how to start a home typing service)

Finally, be sure to keep track of all your start-up expenses. Every one of them—from the purchase of the computer/printer to the paper clips which you attach to invoices—is deductible. And here's to a successful first year!

d. (conclusion to a composition textbook)

Writing is not pretty.

In-betweens

As we have seen, paragraphs serve as idea-bearers in the development of texts, and they are used both to begin and to end texts. In between, they also (1) provide transitions between various sections of a text, serving as "pointers" to indicate where a text has been and where it is headed next; and (2) serve as "containers" for the further exploration of a thesis presented in a previous paragraph.

Paragraphs used to provide transition typically are shorter than usual paragraphs and explicitly indicate a change in the direction or focus of the text, as in these two examples:

(1) Having surveyed the major sources of food poisoning in mammals, we will now turn our attention to an equally important division of veterinary pathology: the classification of diseases of the alimentary canal. In doing so, we will discuss, first, the more typical occurrences of alimentary dysfunction, and then move on to the rarer forms.

(2) These, then, are the reasons I support the Equal Rights Amendment. But one must also be aware of the opposing view as well, and I will now address the common objections to the ERA, one by one.

A paragraph employed to elaborate points already made in a preceding paragraph "shares" the topic sentence of that preceding paragraph without explicitly duplicating it. Notice this symbiotic relationship between these two paragraphs in this excerpt from Frederick Buechner's memoir, *The Sacred Journey:*

As my father moved from job to job during the Great Depression of the thirties, we moved from place to place and house to house. In the section of Washington, D.C., called Georgetown, we had a brick-walled garden where I sat with a nurse named Mrs. Taylor, who said one day, "Now I am going to show you something that you have never seen before." Then she opened her mouth wide and sang out a single loud, clear note, and as she held it, her teeth dropped a full half inch before my marveling eyes. She was right. I had never seen such a thing before.

This was the same Mrs. Taylor who, another time in that same garden, showed me a cut of raw beefsteak and, pointing to a small knot of white gristle somewhere toward the center, said, "That is the soul. Now you know what a soul looks like . . . ."[16]

[16]Frederick Buechner, *The Sacred Journey* (San Francisco: Harper and Row, 1982), 13.

The second paragraph in this sequence serves to elaborate the eccentric character of Mrs. Taylor, who was introduced in the preceding paragraph. Strictly speaking, the topic sentence is found in the first paragraph, ". . . we had a brick-walled garden where I sat with a nurse named Mrs. Taylor . . ."

Each of these paragraph functions are useful, even crucial to a writer. Learning how to fashion effective beginnings, middles, and conclusions is nearly as important as coming up with the original ideas for the text itself. As you work through drafts of each text that you write you will develop your own strategies for evaluating and revising them in addition to the ones that are suggested in this text.

EXERCISES

1. At your VDT, scroll through the text you are currently working with, examining each of its paragraphs. Use the general on-line strategies introduced in this chapter to evaluate each paragraph according to the criteria of unity, coherence, and completeness.

2. Examine each of the following passages for problems of ambiguity and incoherence. Write a note to the writer, suggesting how the problematic paragraphs might be rewritten using the revision techniques discussed in this section.

   a. (Task: To prove that *Splash* is a better movie than *Cocoon*)
   When I went to see *Cocoon* I was disappointed. Having seen Ron Howard's other smash hit, *Splash*, I expected a light-hearted sense of humor. Instead there was something else. A lot of moralizing. This is something I can't stand in a movie. Those people shouldn't have gotten on the space ship. At least when Tom Hanks swam out to become a merman in *Splash* it was logical.

   b. (Task: To convince a reader to buy a VCR instead of paying for subscription cable service)
   Though cable TV has become big business over the last few years, there has been an even bigger story: the VCR explosion. Too many people have rushed out to subscribe to cable to get first-run movies and the like. Instead, they could have bought a VCR and rented whatever movies they wanted. That is a better deal.

   c. (Task: To explain conflicting American positions on the topic of abortion)
   Abortion is not an easy problem to discuss. There are many positions on the issue. There are those who say that a woman should have complete control over her own body. Then there are those who believe that there are no good reasons for an abortion. Finally, there are those who say there is a compromise position. The issue will not go away just by ignoring it.

   d. (Task: To relate a personal experience to teach a lesson)
   The storm that night on Lake Erie would have scared off even experienced boaters. But here we were, my mom, my dad, and little sister, Theresa, adrift on a small inflated raft, waiting to be picked up. The radio had quit working two hours ago. We were afraid no one would ever come. Then they did. My mom had tears in her eyes when the Coast Guard vessel pulled alongside us and lifted Theresa into the safety of its deck.

3. Read each of the following paragraphs carefully. Write a brief analysis of each paragraph, identifying the features that help make the paragraph effective.

a. (Task: To argue that welfare entitlements hurt, not help, those who receive them)

(1) The intention of welfare entitlements is to supply only the "truly needy," as if they were somehow a sharply distinguishable class. (2) The idea is that they will know who they are, and will step forward to collect benefits, while others (with a few exceptions, of course) will abstain from making false claims. (3) Obviously it doesn't work that way. (4) Welfare is less a temporary expedient for many people than an addictive way of life.[17]

b. (Task: To explain why the writer began to raise chickens)

(1) When I was five, I had an experience that marked me for life. (2) Pathe News sent a photographer from New York to Savannah to take a picture of a chicken of mine. (3) This chicken, a buff Cochin Bantam, had the distinction of being able to walk either forward or backward. (4) Her fame had spread through the press, and by the time she reached the attention of Pathe News, I suppose there was nowhere left for her to go— forward or backward. (5) Shortly after that she died, as now seems fitting . . . .

(6) From that day with the Pathe man I began to collect chickens. (7) What had been only a mild interest became a passion, a quest. (8) I had to have more and more chickens.[18]

[17]Joseph Sobran, *Single Issues* (New York: The Human Life Press, 1983), 6.

[18]Flannery O'Connor, *Mystery and Manners* (New York: Farrar, Straus, Giroux, 1962), 3–4.

CHAPTER 8

Revising
for Economy

Wordiness, using more words than necessary to convey one's meaning, is the bane of every reader, who expects and delights in information and ideas expressed crisply, economically, and forcefully. Wordiness bores readers, makes them work too hard, and ultimately compels them to stop reading altogether.

Wordiness is typically present in situations like this: a writer lazily uses four words when one will do; writers opt for a sentence structure that compels them to use extra words; or writers settle for a weak verb that forces them to pack the action of the sentence into nominalizations and modifiers. Before examining three common sources of wordiness, here are three general principles to guide your sentence construction. These will help you avoid wordiness in your prose:

1. The basic English sentence pattern is Subject-Verb-Object. Readers expect and are comfortable with this pattern; consequently, make sure you place the real subject and the real action of your sentence in these slots and avoid hiding or omitting them, as this sentence does:

> There is considerable evidence to the effect that nobody should be allowed to swim on this beach.

2. Whenever you can, use specific verbs, adverbs and adjectives rather than abstractions and nominalizations (typically -tion/-sion/-ness words) to express the action of your sentences.

> **PROBLEM:** The *intention* of this organization is the *inculcation* of *improvement* in office morale.
>
> **BETTER:** This organization *intends* to *improve* office morale.

3. For all practical purposes, avoid negative constructions, which ultimately force the reader to translate the sentence into a positive in order to understand it. The negative states something indirectly (usually so the writer can hedge a bit), while the positive states something forthrightly:

NEGATIVE: *In order not to misunderstand me*, pay attention.

POSITIVE: Pay attention so you can understand me.

At the end of this chapter are some exercises which will give you practice in recognizing and eliminating wordiness. While the sources of wordiness are many, there are three main ones that this section will explore and show you how to transform into economical prose. I am greatly indebted in this chapter to the pioneering work of Joseph Williams and Richard Lanham in identifying the sources of wordiness in prose.

THE PASSIVE PREDICATE

The passive voice is typically the enemy of economical prose. Why? Because it usually compels the writer to use extra verbs, nouns and prepositions to convey the action of a sentence that might have been expressed in one strong verb. Here is an example:

ACTIVE PREDICATE: The team *broke* the record for wins.

PASSIVE PREDICATE: The record for wins *was broken by the team.*

In the passive version of the sentence, the writer must add "was" and "by" to convey the same idea. Of course, in isolated, short sentences like this one, the passivity of this sentence is no major problem. In fact, there may be a very good reason for the writer to choose the passive voice in this sentence, for instance, to emphasize the record itself, rather than the team who broke it. No, the problem with passive predicates occurs when the writer strings together a number of them and cripples the energy of the sentence—as in this example:

It *was found* that information concerning microcomputer prices allocated to local dealers *was not obtained.* This action *is needed* so that a determination of redirection is permitted on a timely basis when economic conditions change. A system *must be established* so that information on economic conditions and consumer buying patterns *may be collected* on a regular basis.

The italicized constructs represent passive predicates that obscure the meaning and slow down considerably the reader's processing of the information. A revision would replace the passive predicates with active ones:

We *found* that the business office *did not obtain* the proper information about microcomputer prices that local dealers *need.* The dealers *require* this information so they can determine how to *redirect* their sales campaign. The business office *must create* a system for gathering information about consumer buying patterns on a regular basis.

In each case, the true agent (i.e., the person(s) or object performing the action) is inserted into the sentence's subject slot so that the reader immediately knows *who is doing what and to whom.* Since in passive sentences, the subject expresses the goal of an action, the more direct order of agent-action-result is reversed. When the passive pattern becomes the rule rather than the exception in a writer's sentence patterns, his prose is inevitably long-winded, opaque and generally unreadable.

TIPS FOR REVISING PASSIVE PREDICATES

• Locate passive constructions by searching for "be" verbs (is, are, was, were) and typical prepositions which accompany them: by, of, for, to.

• Identify the true agent and action of the sentence. The agent may be tucked away in a prepositional phrase or absent altogether, needing to be supplied; the true action may be hiding in a modifier or nominalization. Ask *"Who's doing what to whom?"*, and reconstruct the sentence so that the recovered agent and action are placed appropriately in the subject and verb slots.

EXAMPLE: The registrants received information that they would be reimbursed for their travel expenses, but a *decision has been made* that such a gesture *cannot be extended* at this time.

REVISED: The council decided not to reimburse the registrants for their travel expenses even though they had earlier promised them that they would.

• Don't feel compelled to revise the passive predicate in these three specific instances:

a. Don't revise the passive into active when the agent of an action is irrelevant:

"When a garage *is adequately ventilated,* the children will find it a convenient place to play." (*Who* ventilated the garage is unimportant here.)

b. Don't revise the passive into active when the purpose is to emphasize a particular action or state of affairs:

"When *teachers* are required to take proficiency exams, *they* sometimes feel as if *they* are being treated like incompetents. And if *they* are emotionally distressed by these exams, *they* can be expected to perform poorly.

c. Don't revise the passive into active when the identity of the agent is intentionally vague:

"The museum was broken into last night by an unknown vandal."

REDUNDANCY

Even when writers have the subject-verb-object pattern stable in their sentence construction and use true agents and actions consistently, they can still fall into a pattern of wordiness. Writing economically involves not only mastering basic patterns, but also learning how to compress one's meaning for easier processing and learning how to avoid stating the obvious. Prose can be inflated in so many ways, it is perhaps foolish to try to list all the ways that we can be wordy. The following example, however, illustrates many problems of redundancy:

> My personal belief is that we should really just consider and think about in a very meticulous manner each and every suggested plan of attack that is offered to us.

First, beliefs are always personal, so *personal* can be cut. And since the whole sentence is basically the person's belief, even *my belief* can be cut. *Consider* and *think about* are virtual synonyms here. *Really* and *just* are empty intensifiers and *in a very meticulous manner* means *meticulously,* which means no more than *carefully. Each and every* is a redundant pair that drifts over from speech; *each* works well. *Suggested* and *that is offered to us* say the same thing and one or both of them might be eliminated. What's left is leaner and more direct:

We should consider each plan of attack carefully.

What we are considering here is simple *redundancy:* stating the obvious, repeating what has already been said, carrying over popular formulae from speech. What may be useful as cueing devices for speech-makers or conversationalists becomes turgid and off-putting in written prose. Revising redundancy in prose is usually a simple operation: cutting, pruning, condensing, deleting. Little actual "rewriting" is usually necessary.

Redundancy also occurs when writers add modifiers to words which simply repeat or emphasize an identical meaning, or include the general category of an item along with the item itself. *Future plans* is an example of a redundant modifier; plans are always "in the future." And in this example, the categories "period," "area," and "level" are unnecessary:

PROBLEM: Within a short *period of time,* the *student union area* improved to a *decent level of quality.*

REVISED: Within a short time, the student union improved in quality.

Prepositional phrases often signal redundancy and can be collapsed into single adverbs or pruned phrases, as in these examples:

in a frivolous manner/frivolously
used *for accounting purposes*/used for accounting
owing *to the fact that*/since (because)

In fact, the *fact that* construction itself adds a great deal of extra verbage to prose and probably can be deleted from most sentences and replaced by expressions like these:

> the fact that he had not arrived/his delay
> in spite of the fact that/though
> call your attention to the fact that/remind you

One other source of redundancy is the use of false modifiers and intensifiers such as *really, basically, definitely, different, interesting,* and *generally*—modifiers that are often meaningless within a sentence, and serve only to clutter the sentence and convey insincerity. In this example, note how many empty words and phrases are used:

> *For all intents and purposes,* the recent baseball strike *generally* represents an *interesting* episode in labor-management relations that may *really* set a precedent for *the modern world of today.*
> **REVISED:** The recent baseball strike may set a precedent in labor-management relations.

Such modifiers can be deleted with no harm to the meaningfulness of the sentences they inhabit.

JARGON

Jargon is characteristic of prose which is carelessly excessive in employing cliches, pretentious qualification or caution, or euphemisms.

Cliches:

> it takes all kinds of people to make a world
> high hopes
> never expected it in a million years
> the bottom line
> ball park figure
> modern world of today
> from the beginning of recorded time.

Cliches are overused or well-worn phrases that rob a text of its vitality and freshness; they are the province of the writer who lazily reaches for the nearest and most familiar expression to convey an idea. They contribute to wordiness usually by their length.

Pretentious Qualification or Caution:

> it is by no means completely apparent that
> due to the fact that
> to a great extent

rather/somewhat

in this respect.

Pretentious qualification or caution is used by a writer to affect distance and considered scrutiny. Its effect on readers, however, is to convince them of the writer's insincerity or unreliability, and certainly to add to a text's wordiness.

Euphemism:

relieved of his position

terminated with extreme prejudice

under the influence of intoxicants

less than productive.

Euphemisms are expressions used by a writer to hedge or blunt the impact that a more direct statement would have upon the reader. Hence, an employee is not "fired" but "let go"; a close friend is not "dead," but "has passed away." If you find jargon in your prose, follow these revision suggestions:[1]

1. Where possible replace abstract subjects with definite, concrete ones.
2. Where possible replace passive, weak predicates with active, strong ones.
3. Replace cliches with fresh expressions or images.
4. Replace needless qualifiers with direct statements; if a qualifier is necessary, use a specific one.
5. Replace euphemisms with direct statements; writing with tact need not exclude forthrightness.

USING THE MICROCOMPUTER ON-LINE

Search Procedures

1. The search function of your word processing software can be put to good use in looking for wordiness in your prose, especially if it has a PARTIAL WORD SEARCH function. Here are some specific searches you can make to eliminate wordiness in your prose:

   a. Place typical passive or prepositional constructions in the SEARCH slot (usually the *to be* verbs: *is/are, was/were;* and prepositions such as: *by, of, for* and *to)* to locate areas in your text which are inappropriately passive. Examine each instance of a passive verb or prepositional phrase to determine whether the sentence should be revised. If so, use the revising strategies discussed in this section to alter your text appropriately.

   b. Place typical nominalizations or nominalized endings in the SEARCH slot to locate stifling word choice which buries the action of your sentences. These include most words ending in *-tion, -sion, -ness, -ence, -ance,* and *-ity.* Examine each instance of a nominalization to determine if you have used an ineffective nominalization or a com-

---

[1] I am specifically indebted to Joseph Williams and the work of E. B. White and William Strunk for these strategies.

pound noun structure. If so, use the revising strategies discussed in this section to alter your text appropriately.

c. Place prepositions (*by, of, to, in*) and the conjunction *and* in the SEARCH slot to locate redundant modifiers. Since prepositions are often used redundantly to indicate location, manner, or quality (for example, ''in the union area,'' ''in a rough manner, ''blue in color'') and the conjunction *and* frequently couples redundant terms (''first and foremost''), a search with these terms can help you spot troublesome wordiness. Revision in these cases involves simple deletion.

d. Place meaningless modifiers and intensifiers (for example ''interesting'' or ''really'') or jargon (''due to the fact that,'' ''modern world of today'')—those elements which *you know you frequently use*—in the SEARCH slot to determine if you have employed them in your draft. If so, revise them by substituting more appropriate words and phrases that condense your meaning and make it more direct to the reader.

Revision Strategies

Revising to eliminate wordiness in your draft involves primarily the operations of deletion and substitution. Use the keystrokes appropriate to your word processing software to: (1) delete inappropriate words or phrases: and (2) substitute more sentences, words, or phrases to facilitate the meaning and effect you want your text to have.

EXERCISES

You should check the first draft of your text for evidence of any of the problems surveyed in this section. If you determine that longer passages, individual sentences, or words cause wordiness, revise them using the techniques discussed in this section. The following exercises will give you practice in locating and remedying these problems.

1. Examine the following passages for problems with passive predicates. Rewrite each passage, using the techniques surveyed in this chapter.

a. When an indoor baseball stadium is adequately air-conditioned there will not be a problem with balls hit by batters. Comfort will be felt by the fans and the game itself will be enjoyed.

b. The message was to be received by the doctor before the end of the meeting. Because it was delayed by the slow delivery by the mail room, the decision had to be postponed until a meeting was rescheduled by the board of directors.

c. It was discovered that the report detailing the events of the past few weeks was scheduled to be released by the provost's office no later than Monday afternoon. A determination has been made that an action is needed to speed the process of publishing the report so that those concerned by the report can receive it as soon as possible.

d. The supermarket was burglarized last night. An investigation by the police is not expected to turn up a likely suspect. This is something which many have gotten used to.

2. Examine the following passages for problems with nominalizations. Rewrite each passage, using the techniques surveyed in this chapter.

    a. The analysis of the decisions which was to have provided a determination of the proper course of events has disappointed a number of the president advisory council committee members.

    b. The confrontation between the students and the press was an unlikely ramification of the recent selection of a new press liaison official, in consideration of the carefulness with which the original decision was made.

    c. The preparation of the case against the senior vice-president reveals the intelligence and the cooperation that can be expected from the education implementation board.

    d. Presentation of the final grading report by the graduate assistant English instructor occurred during the profiling of her students at the annual department discussion of teaching techniques.

3. Examine the following passages for problems with redundancy and jargon. Rewrite each passage, using the techniques surveyed in this chapter.

    a. It is, and has been for a long time, the personal position of this august and revered body that unless we consider each and every case with optimum carefulness and scrutiny, we will be unable to render a just and righteous decision.

    b. The team should try to win the game or the final result will be, all in all, failure to achieve victory.

    c. Nearly in an unconscious state, the firefighters rescued a total of seven persons at Grand Central Station.

    d. The victims lost their right arms due to injuries received during the explosion that completely destroyed the old warehouse. Insurance investigators had warned the owners a hundred times that the building was less than safe.

    e. Presently, there are six federal laws that prohibit the distribution of obscene literature in the states.

    f. The experience I had there was not disimiliar to one I had a few years ago at the ranch not too far down the road from it.

    g. Putting it on the line, the department chair made it quite clear that she fully intends, once and for all, to request salary increases for all the faculty members within her department.

    h. All things taken into account, it would not seem too far out of line to expect that less than fully mature students would seek their eventual degree from an educational institution where they can pursue with vigor and energy a study of a field with which they feel comfortable.

CHAPTER 9

Revising for Fullness and Grace

The purpose of this chapter is to teach you strategies that will help revise your text for two important qualities: fullness—telling your readers all they need to know; and grace—communicating your ideas with effective sentence structure. Fullness is a measure of a text's completeness and comprehensiveness. Readers should finish your text with a sense that they have been told everything they need to understand your ideas, follow your directions, act on a particular circumstance, and so on. There are two extremes which can plague writers seeking fullness in their texts: overdeveloped prose and underdeveloped prose. Overdeveloped prose is inflated, dense, and opaque to a reader; instead of telling readers what they need to know, the writer tells them more—filling the text with unnecessary or irrelevant detail. Underdeveloped prose is thin, skeletal writing which leaves the reader wanting to know more; instead of providing readers with essential background or developing key ideas, the writer leaves too much that is implicit and unexplored.

Graceful prose communicates ideas not only clearly and accurately, but also with a sense of flair and skill appropriate to the subject matter and intention of the writer. Although writing with grace entails many of the factors we have already examined in preceding chapters—effective paragraphing, setting a context, sharpening the focus, eliminating wordiness, and so on—in this chapter I want to examine effective ways to combine sentences and improve readability.

REVISING FOR FULLNESS: TELLING YOUR READERS ALL THEY NEED TO KNOW

One of the challenges of learning to write is knowing when to present information and evidence to support one's main points, and how much. As writers we tend to assume too much knowledge on the part of our audience, and so what seems perfectly clear and justified to us may come off as shallow and rather perfunctory to our readers.

The goal of the writer, nevertheless, is to tell readers all they need to know, no more and no less. That is to say, we want neither to bore the reader with unnecessary or obvious information nor to leave out anything essential. A successful text leaves the reader with a sense of *fullness;* that is, it contains prose that is neither inflated nor barebones. Here is a negative example that illustrates overinflated writing.

> Basketball, one of the older and most energetic indoor
> sports in terms of weight loss during actual playing time,
> has the kind of breathtaking action pattern to it on the
> court that excites both the casual fan who attends only a
> few games during a basketball season and the intense fan
> who holds season tickets to all the games.

In this paragraph we find a brand of redundancy that can't be traced to the use of a few extra words or to poor word choice itself. Such excessive or obvious detail is sometimes employed by apprentice writers in order to fill up their text, giving the impression of fullness. Perhaps a writer has been told to "supply more detail" or "elaborate" a point. Unsure about what to do, the writer simply adds—literally—more "stuff," whether or not it is relevant or meaningful to the context.

To the student who wrote it, the paragraph above appears to be filled with helpful information, well placed and relevant to the reader. Because it looks "full"—packed with facts, ideas, and detail—the writer ignores the fact that the readers are told things they either don't want to know or know already. When we "unpack" the paragraph we see that it is riddled with unnecessary and obvious detail:

> Basketball, (1) one of the older (2) and most energetic
> indoor sports (3) in terms of weight loss during actual
> playing time, has the kind of breathtaking action (4)
> pattern to it (5) on the court that excites both the casual
> spectator (6) who attends only a few games during a
> basketball season and the intense fan (7) who holds season
> tickets to all the games.

Each of the numbered units above represents a questionable chunk of information. Are units 1 and 2 meaningful comments about basketball within the context of the sentence? Is unit 3 a useful clarification on the excitement of the sport? Are units 4 and 5 anything more than excessive detail that bogs the sentence down? Can units 6 and 7 be construed as anything but unnecessary explanation? Of course not. In the name of "fullness" this writer has merely added verbiage. The basic sentence can stand as:

> Basketball's breathtaking action excites both the casual spectator and the intense fan.

Fullness, then, is not mere clutter and data-dumping.

Another example can illustrate the reverse of this problem—lack of detail.

```
Poltergeist was the scariest movie I have ever seen.
Everyone else thought so too. I'll never go to a movie like
that again. From now on, I'll just see nice, adventure
movies.
```

In the above passage, the writer obviously wants to convey to her reader that (1) the movie she saw was scary, (2) others thought so too, (3) she'll avoid movies like *Poltergeist,* and (4) it has affected her future choice of movies. But the writer is not conveying this information; it is only mentioned in passing to the reader as if everything were perfectly obvious. In a *conversation* between two friends who know each other well, perhaps this writer's description would "say it all." For a *reader,* however, it comes off as sparse, naive, and uninteresting.

Consider the following revision. It emphasizes *showing* the reader the evidence or information that undergirds the writer's *telling* of the conclusions.

```
I've never seen a movie scarier than Poltergeist. Its
gruesome ghosts and incredible gore sent several of us to
the bathroom to ward off our nausea. I've resolved never to
see another horror movie again; I'll stick to adventure
yarns like Raiders of the Lost Ark or Romancing the Stone
to spare my stomach such tension.
```

Here is another example of a sparsely developed paragraph:

```
During the early days of the Soviet invasion of
Afghanistan, few Western reporters were aware of what was
happening. Soon, the reports leaked out through rebel
radio communiques. By then it had really become old news
even to the networks.
```

Like the *Poltergeist* example, this passage calls for elaboration and examples at several points. Now read the revised version below. It creates a sense of fullness for the reader through the use of meaningful detail and illustration. In other words, more "showing," less "telling."

> During the early days of the Soviet invasion of
> Afghanistan, the only Western reporters within the borders
> and in a position to issue stories were Associated Press
> correspondents. Other news agencies depended upon
> interception of rebel radio broadcasts for the information
> they provided. By the time camera crews from the major
> networks could sneak their way into the country, the
> Associated Press reporters had easily scooped the
> electronic media.

How does a writer avoid the two extremes of excessive, obvious detail and sparse, underdeveloped prose? What we tell our readers depends on what they need to know, what they already know, and our overall intention in saying something in the first place. We can never be fully explicit in our writing, and we can never fully anticipate everything that a reader must know to process the information we are providing. But we can look for the key features which help us analyze our prose to determine if we are falling into either extreme.

Strategies for Locating
Excessive or Obvious Detail

Revising excessive or obvious detail means deleting extraneous information. Locate such details by using the following strategies:

1. Consider carefully your intention in each unit of your text (paragraph, sentence, word). What are you trying to explain, elaborate, or illustrate? Review each section of your text to determine whether you are consistent with your intentions. In the basketball paragraph above, the writer's ostensible purpose was to discuss the excitement of basketball, not to define basketball in terms of its age ("one of the older . . .") or its relationship to the health of its participants (". . . in terms of weight loss during actual playing time").

2. Note repetition of specific words or related ideas and concepts in consecutive clauses or sentences. Ask yourself, Does this word or idea add new, relevant information, or does it merely clutter up the text? In the basketball example, such phrases as "the casual spectator who attends only a few games during a basketball season" and "intense fan who holds season tickets to all the games" do not really amplify the writer's meaning; instead they distract the reader from it. ("Casual" and "intense" are concrete adjectives that can work well without elaboration in this context.)

3. Note the use of the useless "particles," appositive phrases or prepositional phrases that convey little new or relevant information. Certain particles—for example, "in terms of" or "kind of"—often introduce extraneous or obvious detail. Likewise, in the basketball paragraph the appositive phrases modifying "spectator" and "fan" introduce unnecessary identification.

Prepositional phrases that indicate relationship and location can also mask irrelevant verbiage. The reader doesn't need to be told that basketball is played "on the court"; technically, that's the location (whether a driveway or arena) on which any basketball game is played.

Strategies for Locating Underdeveloped Prose

To revise underdeveloped prose a writer usually needs to do some more prewriting and then weave the additional information into his or her prose, using one of the modes of development discussed in Chapter 5. Here are some strategies for locating underdeveloped prose:

1. Note weak verb choices (linking verbs: *is/was, was/were;* flat verbs: *thought, see*) that force the writer to convey information in adjectives, ones which describe the writer more than the object or idea. In the *Poltergeist* example, the writer calls the movie "scary," but this adjective describes the emotion of the writer more than it does any quality of the movie itself.

2. Note paragraphs whose sentences merely form a *list* of propositions, qualities, or characteristics which are not illustrated or elaborated upon in the text. The Afghanistan paragraph reveals this problem.

3. Note places where conclusions are announced unaccompanied by examples or evidence. For instance, we knew that one writer felt *Poltergeist* was "scary," but not why. She had not shown readers what made it scary, but merely forced them to accept her word without corroboration.

4. Note inexplicit or ambiguous relationships between propositions. In the Afghanistan example, the writer suggested that "few Western reporters were aware of what was happening," implying that his point was that news was difficult to obtain. In actuality, his point was that print reporters were in a better position to issue stories than TV reporters.

5. Note weak or meaningless intensifiers used to modify equally weak adjectives. In several examples above the writers have used inexpressive or weak modifiers to cover the absence of concrete descriptive detail ("*nice* adventure movies"; "By then it had *really* become old news").

USING THE MICROCOMPUTER ON-LINE

Search Procedures

As you *scroll* through your draft paragraph by paragraph, you can use the WAITS nutshelling strategy discussed in Chapter 7 to help you decide if you have told your reader too much or too little. If you have overdeveloped or underdeveloped your draft, you can use the SEARCH function of your word processing software to look for such problems in your prose:

Place in the SEARCH slot any *sentence particles* you rely on to carry the meaning of your text (for example, "in terms of," "kind of"). If you find that you have been using such particles to relate trivia, delete any information which is extraneous to your main topic in that section of the text.

Place in the SEARCH slot any *weak verbs* (for example, *is/are, was/were*) that force the writer to store key information in single adjectives and thus tend to encourage poor detail. If your search indicates that these verbs do mask an underdeveloped section of your text, revise these sections using the strategies discussed in this section.

Place in the SEARCH slot any *weak adjectives* or *meaningless intensifiers* that you commonly use (for example, "interesting," "different," "really," "very"). Revise any underdeveloped sections of your text using the strategies discussed in this section.

Revision Strategies

Revising to provide fullness for your reader involves the operations of addition, deletion, substitution, and rearrangement. Use the commands appropriate to your word processing software to: (1) add appropriate information and illustration; and (2) delete irrelevant or trivial content to facilitate the meaning and effect you want your text to have.

EXERCISES

You should check any draft of your text for overdevelopment or underdevelopment of detail. The following exercises will give you practice in locating and remedying these problems.

1. Examine each of these short passages and determine if the writers have used unnecessary or obvious detail. Write a note to the writer explaining any changes you think necessary to avoid these problems.

    a. In our time today, that past event in history known as World War II looms large in our memory. Hundreds of movies have been photographed and edited by some of Hollywood's most illustrious directors, actors, and actresses which depict the events which happened during this period of time. Hardly any one of us as citizens can avoid knowledge of the incidences which took place during World War II.

    b. What a healthy phenomenon it is in terms of morale for this business, which has been in existence for more than 75 years in two different and various locations, that we recently received and accepted the city's nicest and most interesting award. This award, which is the only one the city gives to the best business of the year, is unique in that we are the only ones who won it this year.

    c. As a result of what has happened in the past few days, weeks, and months, the President of the student body has had no choice but to decide to eliminate the annual spring festival dance. Since he has decided that, barring a miracle, a set of unusual events which make the seemingly impossible occur, there will not be enough funds available to rent the hall, which has been reserved for the college each year, consecutively, since 1957. The only alternative to this state of affairs seems to be an alternate site for the dance which would not cost the student body anything in terms of its own treasury.

2. Examine each of these short passages to determine if the writers have "shown" more than they have "told." For each passage, write a brief explanation to the writer detailing what should be clarified to make the passage more effective.

   a. That game last Saturday was really something else. There was no chance the Celtics could win but somehow they did. The only explanation is the fantastic play of their marvelous center. He must have scored forty points. What a game!

   b. The problem with the American auto industry is simple. We lost the pride we used to have in creating quality products. When our Japanese counterparts go to work in the morning their sole purpose is to make the very best vehicle that can be made. In contrast, our workers are preoccupied only with making money. Until and unless we regain the craftsmanship which allowed us once to lead the world in production and quality, our auto industry will lag behind the Japanese.

   c. The local election was very close. The vote was split between three candidates almost equally and for a time two of them were actually deadlocked. As the night wore on, the atmosphere at the Harris Hotel suite was tense since few of her supporters felt an incumbent could be defeated. Many of her supporters got pretty emotional when the results were announced and knew that she had lost for the first time. Ms. Harris was really perturbed by the slowness of the count.

   d. The only way the problem could have been handled worse is if the parties involved had had a duel. The negotiators for both sides seemed disinterested in compromise. No one gave ground.

   e. The cable contract was ratified by the city council after a prolonged and spiteful debate. Mr. Jacobs, an advocate for the consumer action group, disliked clause H, which limited the number of channels available. His arguments were easily countered, however, by Ms. Garabaldi.

REVISING FOR GRACE

Creating Effective Sentences

The style of a text includes, among other things, the appropriate choice of words and the effective construction, combination, and placement of sentences for emphasis. In the remainder of this chapter you will find helpful advice for creating effective sentences.

A sentence consists of a *subject* (what the topic or theme of the sentence is) and a *predicate* (what is said about the topic—a statement of action or state of being which affects or explains something about the subject):

Subject	Predicate
The Farnsworths	built their own log cabin.
Their choice of carpet	reflected their good taste.
President Carter	was formerly Governor of Georgia.

To be punctuated as a sentence, a group of words must contain a subject and predicate and be able to "stand alone," that is, contain all the information the reader needs to make sense of it.

Basic sentence order—including the placement of modifiers, dependent clauses, punctuation, and so on—therefore depends upon the intention of the writer and the effective choice of subject and predicate. (See Chapter 11 for a variety of common sentence errors such as fragments, comma splices, and dangling modifiers.) Revising for grace at the sentence level means analyzing each sentence and asking, "What do I want this sentence to *do*?" The writer's particular revising goals, then, generally include these: (1) to expand sentences with effective modification, (2) to balance each sentence containing parallel elements, (3) to combine sentences with effective coordination and subordination, and (4) generally to achieve pleasing variety in sentence patterns. In the following section, I will describe these four strategies for achieving grace in sentence structure. At the end, you will find strategies for examining and revising convoluted sentences on-line with your microcomputer.

Adding Modifers

One way to improve sentence style is to locate subjects and predicates and enrich them by adding modifiers, such as adjectives, adverbs, and other clausal structures, that bring to life the writer's world for the reader. Adding modifiers can, of course, be abused; wringing the last possible drop of "description" out of every sentence can muddy the readers' perception of your topic and cause them to dismiss your text as immature.

Still, bare-bones sentences that provide only an obscure statement of the writer's point leave the reader with unanswered questions, as in these terse sentences:

1. In high school, we had a pretty good band.
2. My best friend, Karla, is probably the best chess player in the city.
3. The dog chased the salesman.

The reader of such statements may want to know:

1. Where was your high school? What made your band good? Did it win any awards? Who was the director? Did you compete against other bands?
2. When did Karla start playing chess? Does she play in tournaments? How good is she? How did you meet Karla? Who taught her how to play?
3. What kind of dog was it? Was the salesman at someone's house, in his car, or at his own business? Was the dog being playful or angry?

Of course, it may not be the writer's intention to answer all or any of the questions, but the thinness of these sentences leaves too much for the reader to guess about. In the following revised versions, the italicized elements represent modifiers which have been expanded to amplify the original subjects and predicates:

During my high school days in northwest Kentucky, our marching band *placed first in statewide competition twice.*

My best friend *and next door neighbor,* Karla, has been *playing chess since she was five years old, and has won the city championship four of the last five years in her age group.*

The Andersons' german shepherd chased the *uninvited* salesman *out of their yard and down to the grocery.*

Achieving Parallel Construction

Effective parallel construction within a sentence means repeating a pattern or grammatical form to emphasize the equality of two or more parts of a sentence. Parallel construction thus keeps coordinate relationships within sentences (items joined by a conjunction like *and*) clear, as in these examples:

Not Parallel:

Football players must be fast and coaches think they are quick.

He opened the broiler, inserted the steaks, and the temperature control was turned to broil.

The Senator's office is difficult to find and at noon few people find it open.

Parallel:

Football players must be *fast* and *quick.* (Parallel adjectives)

He *opened the broiler, inserted the steaks,* and *turned the temperature control to "broil."* (Parallel predicates, consisting of verbs and direct objects)

The Senator's office is difficult to find, and it usually closes at noon. (Parallel independent clauses)

Parallel construction may also be extended over a *series* of sentences, increasing the coherence of your text by knitting together equal and related ideas with parallel structure.

Less Parallel:

Children seem to improvise. A teacher may give a child a writing task during a class session. In this session, the child could begin with her own version of the teacher's instructions. Some children decide to launch off on the assignment, doodling, stopping later to begin serious writing. The child might be very scrupulous to understand each detail of the assignment in the classroom. At home, she may forget the teacher's instructions entirely and make up her own assignment.

More Parallel:

>   Children seem to improvise. *When given a particular writing task* during a class session, *a child may begin* writing down her own version of the teacher's instructions. Or *she may* proceed directly to the assignment, doodling to illustrate her ideas, only to stop and begin serious writing. *In the classroom,* she might be very scrupulous to understand each detail of the assignment. *At home,* she may forget the teacher's instructions entirely and make up her own assignment.

In the revised example, parallel construction helps both to provide connecting links between sentences and to bind information within the sentences. The subject-verb parallelism (". . . a child may begin . . .", ". . . she may launch . . .") and the parallel prepositional phrases ("In the classroom . . .", "At home . . .") help achieve better cohesion than first version.

Combining Sentences[1]

Another way of creating effective sentences is to use the technique of *sentence combining*, a task that the microcomputer makes very easy. In sentence combining, the writer puts the elements of several sentences into one in order to achieve coherence, to reduce wordiness, and to create better variety in overall structure. To combine sentences with word processing, the writer uses such functions as deletion, insertion, block copy/block move, and search/replace.

Separate Sentences:

The education department is being hurt by inflation.
It is being hurt by the increased cost of photocopying.
It is being hurt by the increased cost of student assistant wages.
It is being hurt by the drop in revenue from state taxes.

Combined Version 1:

>   Considering the increased cost of photocopying and student assistant wages and the drop in revenue from state taxes, the education department is beginning to face the pinch of inflation.

Combined Version 2:

>   The education department is being hurt by inflation as photocopying costs and student assistant wages increase and state tax revenues begin to drop.

There is, of course, no one right way to combine these sentences. The two examples here, however, reflect the basic philosophy of sentence combining: the writer should strive to produce tighter, smoother, and more economical sentences by combining elements from a series of sentences that are related to one another.

---

[1] I am indebted throughout the next two sections to Maxine Hairston's discussion of sentence combining and sentence variety in her *A Contemporary Rhetoric* (Boston: Houghton-Mifflin, 1982), 113–123.

There are two main strategies that writers use to combine sentences: *embedding* and *transforming*. In embedding, the writer incorporates information from one sentence or clause into another by inserting appropriate modifiers (adjectives), grammatical forms (for example, appositives), or modifying phrases. Here is an example of embedding:

Original:

Richard Nixon once served as vice-president to Dwight Eisenhower. He himself ran for the presidency three times. Once he lost to John Kennedy. The other two times, in 1968 and 1972, he won.

Revision 1:

Richard Nixon, one-time vice-president to Dwight Eisenhower, ran for the presidency three times, losing to John Kennedy in his first try, and winning his second attempts in 1968 and 1972.

Revision 2:

At one time vice-president to Dwight Eisenhower, Richard Nixon unsuccessfully ran for president against John Kennedy, later winning his second and third attempts in 1968 and 1972.

What you choose to "embed" depends upon your intention, that is, what you wish to emphasize in the sentence or series of sentences. Embedding is not a difficult task, but it is possible to pack too many sentences into one, causing confusion for the reader. If, in reading your sentence aloud, you find yourself having to gasp for breath or lose track of the subject, perhaps you have tried to embed too much!

The other sentence-combining strategy you will find useful is *transforming*. While embedding selects elements from one or more sentences and incorporates them using modifiers or appositives, transforming involves a more extensive rewriting of sentences by joining several elements and rearranging them for efficiency, clarity, and emphasis. Choppiness and repetition plague many apprentice writers simply because they do not have a large repertoire of strategies to use in constructing sentences.

Original:

Garbage collectors in New Orleans make more than $20,000 a year with little or no formal education. Many college graduates apply for these jobs in New Orleans.

Revision:

Many college graduates apply for the $20,000 garbage collecting jobs in New Orleans, positions that require little or no formal education.

Original:

The Japanese are baseball lovers like Americans. However, their reason for loving baseball is different from ours. The Japanese love baseball because it is a graceful, gentle sport. Americans love baseball as a power, "homerun" sport. In contrast, the Japanese emphasize the qualities of inner strength and endurance in the sport.

Revision:

The Japanese, like Americans, love baseball; however, they have their own reasons for this devotion. While Americans view baseball as a power sport and love the home-run, the Japanese see it as a graceful, gentle sport which emphasizes inner strength and endurance.

As you can see, the revised versions not only reduce the wordiness of the originals, they are also clearer and reflect the relationships between the sentences better.

Achieving Sentence Variety

Revising for sentence variety helps the writer achieve emphasis, prevents reader monotony and, generally, makes a text more readable and interesting. While no rules can be established to regulate how *long* each sentence should be in a text, a healthy balance of long and short sentences—again, dependent on the writer's intention—will make a text less predictable or "sing-song." Likewise, tinkering with the subject/verb/object slots in sentence patterns—for instance, moving the subject to the end of one sentence to give it greater emphasis—can add to the particular effects the writer is trying to achieve. Here are three strategies you can use to achieve sentence variety:

MATCH SHORT, SIMPLE SENTENCES WITH LONGER, MORE COMPLEX SENTENCES. Short sentences are punchy, to-the-point, and can be used to introduce or emphasize the topic or the summing up of a point. Longer sentences are useful for elaboration, detailed explanation, or qualification of the main topic. Notice how the balance of long and short sentences is effective in this example:

> The bone in my ankle was cracked. I knew the football season was over for me. But, refusing to accept my fate, I foolishly attempted to run the ball one more time— "for the team," I thought to myself. Little did I know that one extra play would make the difference. Unable to cut sharply on the next handoff, I was an easy prey for the onrushing free safety, who promptly dislodged the ball and returned it seventy yards downfield. It was a winning touchdown for our dreaded rivals. I could only wince.

INVERT WORD ORDER. Varying the placement of subject, predicate, and modifiers in a sentence can help the writer achieve variety of structure. Any shift in the basic subject-verb-object pattern focuses special emphasis on the word groups that are moved. Of course, modifiers should always be placed close to the words they modify to avoid ambiguity, and the writer should take care not to alter word order in such a way that confusion instead of variety invades the text. Nevertheless, the inversions of word order in the following two examples effectively spotlight the writer's intention:

Throughout his life, Dietrich Fonzer's one ambition was to become a famous violinist. *Such ambition* he constantly dreamed of; and *such ambition* he squandered a lifetime to achieve. (Intention: to focus on the subject's desire for fame)

No longer could I count on the extra income my receptionist's job had provided. *No longer could I* continue to support my elderly aunt. *What I had to do now* was go back to school and start over. (Intention: to highlight the change a loss of a job brought)

USE FREE MODIFIERS EFFECTIVELY. Certain modifiers—adverbs, adverbial phrases and clauses, absolute phrases, and many prepositional phrases—can be placed at different positions in a sentence without causing ambiguity. Moving such *free* modifiers around can also help the writer achieve variety and create emphasis in sentence slots appropriate to his or her intention. Note the effect which the placement of the modifier has on the following three examples.

Adverb Phrase:

The senator's husband kept dodging reporter's questions *to cover his own embarrassment.*

To cover his own embarrassment, the senator's husband kept dodging the reporter's questions.

The senator's husband, *to cover his own embarrassment,* kept dodging the reporter's questions.

Participial Phrase:

Flinching at the sound of the referee's whistle, the coach reluctantly called a time out.

The coach, *flinching at the sound of the referee's whistle,* reluctantly called a time out.

The coach reluctantly called a time out, *flinching at the sound of the referee's whistle.*

Absolute Phrase:

Mr. Buechner ducked into the sheriff's office, *his head down, his eyes glazed over, his suit wrinkled and damp.*

His head down, his eyes glazed over, his suit wrinkled and damp, Mr. Buechner ducked into the sheriff's office.

Mr. Buechner, *his head down, his eyes glazed over, his suit wrinkled and damp,* ducked into the sheriff's office.

Participial phrases must be located carefully because, quite often, they can modify more than one item in the sentence, causing ambiguity or unintentional humor. On the other hand, adverbial and absolute modifiers can usually be placed anywhere in the sentence since they generally modify the whole sentence.

USING THE MICROCOMPUTER ON-LINE

Search Procedures

Again, the SEARCH function of your word processing software can be put to good use in looking carefully at the style of your sentence structure. Here are some searches you can make to locate awkward sentence patterns:

a. In the *search for slot*, place a period and a space (or two spaces, if you space twice after final punctuation), then select the global SEARCH option to move through your text sentence by sentence. The cursor will stop at the beginning of each sentence.

b. Examine each sentence and series of sentences carefully, looking for:

- thin, underdeveloped sentences that could use more modification to expand or make more concrete the information you are providing the reader.
- nonparallel structures within sentences that make your meaning ambiguous or difficult to follow.
- sentences that basically concern the same topic and could be economically embedded into one sentence or transformed into one or two new sentences with rearranged or rewritten elements.
- a series of sentences that are consistently the same length (long or short) or consistently feature the same word order.

Revision Strategies

Revising sentence structure involves primarily the operations of deletion, addition, block copy/block move, and substitution. Use the keystrokes appropriate to your word processing software to: (1) delete inappropriate words or phrases; and (2) substitute, add, or move more appropriate words or phrases into place to facilitate the meaning and effect of your text.

Rewriting Convoluted Sentences

Some sentences must be rewritten because they have a convoluted structure, that is, the true subject or verb is hidden or absent from the sentence and the reader is forced to guess at the writer's meaning. Examine the italicized sentences in this first paragraph from a discovery draft about business in Akron, Ohio:

(1) Akron, Ohio, is one of the most industrialized cities in the midwest. (2) Its rubber tire industry is world-famous. *(3) Because of its industrial climate, a relocation would be smart for any company. (4) Offering all sorts of tax breaks, it would be an advantage especially for some start-up business. (5) Especially locating in the already-established industrial park, this would be a great advantage.*

Sentences 3 through 5 do not communicate clearly what the writer wants to say and serve only as place markers for the writer to return to later to clarify the meaning. The writer intends these sentences to be about the advantages of a new business in Akron, focusing on the considerable tax breaks and attractive industrial park. Note that, instead, the writer confuses the reader by filling the subject slot of the sentence with false or dummy subjects like "a relocation," "it", and "this":

(3) Because of its industrial climate, a relocation would be smart for any company.

The grammatical subject of this sentence is "relocation." However, is this sentence about a *relocation,* or is it about Akron's *industrial climate* or is it about the *writer,* who would like to persuade someone to visit Akron? Likewise, sentences 4 and 5 offer a problem with their true subjects:

(4) Offering all sorts of tax breaks, it would especially be an advantage for some start-up business. (5) Especially locating in the already-established industrial park, this would be a great advantage.

In sentence 4, "it" takes the place of a true subject which, in this case, appears to be "Akron." In sentence 5, "this" masks the absence of a real subject. A revision of this paragraph to eliminate this ambiguity would employ true subjects in the grammatical subject slot and delete extraneous demonstratives and pronouns:

(1) Akron, Ohio, is one of the most industrialized cities in the midwest. (2) Its rubber tire industry is world-famous. *(3) Relocating to Akron would be smart for any company, given the already-favorable industrial climate present there. (4) Offering all sorts of tax breaks, Akron would be an especially attractive city for some start-up business. (5) Likewise, locating in an already-established industrial park would be a great advantage.*

TIPS FOR REVISING CONVOLUTED SENTENCES

Here are some common sources of convolution in sentences and techniques for revising them:[2]

Source of Convolution	Revising Technique
1. Sentences whose grammatical subject is "it" or "there" and whose real subject is hidden in a *sentence modifier.*	*Locate the true subject and place it in the subject slot.*

EXAMPLE: Speaking of *revising first drafts*, it should be of value to every student.

REVISED: Revising one's first drafts should be valuable for every student.

[2]I am indebted to my colleague Alice Heim Calderonello for these strategies.

Source of Convolution	Revising Technique

EXAMPLE: With respect to *speed and agility*, there is a need for such persons on our rugby team.

REVISED: Speed and agility are prerequisites for our rugby athletes.

2. Sentences whose modifiers really do not modify anything in the sentence itself or are misplaced. | *Supply the real subject of the sentence or move the modifier next to the item it modifies.*

EXAMPLE: Playing the match skillfully, the fourth set lasted more than two hours. (Who was "playing skillfully"?)

REVISED: Playing the match skillfully, the *two opponents* prolonged the fourth set more than two hours.

EXAMPLE: Traveling to Europe, the committee might reach her at the Rome office.

REVISED: *Since she is travelling* in Europe, the committee might be able to reach her at the Rome office.

3. Sentences which lack a grammatical subject altogether. | *Supply a subject for the sentence.*

EXAMPLE: By cooperating with the Latin American consolate can bring an end to the crisis.

REVISED: *Cooperating with the Latin American consolate* can bring an end to the crisis.

4. Sentences which shift focus within the subject slot. | *Clarify the relationship between the competing subjects, by selecting one over the other.*

EXAMPLE: The place to which we have come, I feel good about it.

REVISED: *I* feel good about the place to which we have come.

USING THE MICROCOMPUTER ON-LINE

Search Procedures

Pay careful attention to the subject and predicate of your sentences. Does your sentence contain a true subject? Is the action of the sentence focused in the predicate or is it hidden in a modifier or nominalization? Is there a gerund (participle used as a noun) heading your sentence or clause? Many sentences are convoluted because a participial modifier is misplaced—note these places especially when you examine your text.

As you *scroll* through your text, line by line, note each subject and predicate. *Who is doing what to whom?* If the agent and action in your sentence is not readily apparent, revise that sentence using the four principles discussed in this section. In addition to the careful analysis of each subject and predicate, you may use the SEARCH/REPLACE function to look for these specific indications of convoluted structure:

a. Place "it" and "there" in the *search for slot* and select the SEARCH ALL option. For each "it" or "there" that the search procedure uncovers, determine whether the word is appropriate as the grammatical subject. If you find that "it" and "there" are inappropriate, *locate the true subject and place it in the sentence's subject slot.*

b. If your word processing software permits PARTIAL WORD search (some allow you to use a wildcard indicator like "*"), *look at each "-ing" word in your text* to see if misplaced modifiers are causing ambiguity in your text by masking the true subject and predicate of your sentences. If you determine that you have used one of these modifiers inappropriately, you may use the revision strategies discussed in this section.

Revision Strategies

Revising to eliminate sentence ambiguity for your reader involves the operations of addition, deletion, substitution, and rearrangement. Use the keystrokes appropriate to your word processing software to:

a. Delete an inappropriate subject or predicate

b. Substitute an appropriate subject or predicate

c. Rearrange sentences and words to facilitate the meaning and effect you want your text to have.

One student used the search function of the word processor and uncovered a number of sentences that seemed to have a number of misplaced modifiers and problematic subjects:

(1) The events to which I refer, *it* seems impossible now. (2) *By coming from behind in the bottom of the ninth* more than once in a season can seem unlikely. (3) But, *leading in the final inning*, the screws just come unloosed. (4) The Wildcats, nevertheless, did *it* three times that season, and thereby cost them the championship.

In revising, the writer made these changes:

a. Deleted "it" from sentence 1 and rewrote it as: "The events to which I refer seem impossible now."

b. Deleted "by" from sentence 2, supplied a subject, and rewrote it as: "Coming from behind in the bottom of the ninth more than once in a season can seem unlikely, but the Wildcats' opponents did just that this year."

c. Rearranged the modifier and clarified the true grammatical subject of sentence 3: "When the Wildcats are leading in the final frame, the screws just come unloosed."

d. Clarified the predicate in sentence 4: "Incredibly, the Wildcats lost a ninth-inning lead three times this season, thereby costing them the championship."

EXERCISES

1. Make the appropriate changes in each of the following sentences or groups of sentences to achieve parallel construction.

a. Ryan's children took his dog for a walk, fed him his supper, and they rested at the park.

b. The concert was completely sold out, the entertainers began the show on time, and he laughed at the scalpers who thought they would make a killing.

c. I thought the ordeal would never end, but I decided to study and my friends came over later.

2. Revise the following sentences by adding modifiers that expand or amplify the subject and predicate in the sentence.

a. The mayor opposed the legislation.

b. Wall Street was really active today.

c. Chemical dependency is a bad thing.

3. Combine the following groups of sentences using the strategies of embedding and transforming.

a. The senior class president has had a severe cough.
It has lasted three weeks.
He has been to the doctor twice.
He has purchased prescription drugs.
He may have to check into the hospital.

b. Joe Namath had a short movie career.
He was in *Norwood* with Glen Campbell.
He was in another movie with Ann-Margret.
I saw him in *Chattanooga Choo Choo* on TV last night.
He is now a football announcer for ABC.

c. The universe is a wondrous place.
The stars are beautiful.
The constellations are intriguing.
The moon is a mystery.
The earth is a marvel of creation.

4. Combine the following series of sentences into one coherent *paragraph,* using the strategies of embedding and transforming.

a. The Cleveland Indians are the worst team in baseball.
They don't have any pitching.

They don't have any hitting.
Their defense is terrible.
Their coaching staff is the worst.

b. The fans don't get their money's worth.
The ballpark is cold.
The weather is rainy.
The playing surface is ragged and unkempt.
The price of a ticket is high.

c. There are no changes in sight.
There is not enough operating capital.
The front office is strapped by the mistakes of the past.
The future of the Indians is only more failure on the field.
The best hope is that they will leave the city.
The city might get a better expansion team.

5. Revise the following paragraphs using the strategies of inverting word order and employing free modifiers to bring variety to the sentence structure.

a. The children's home had to be closed. It was getting too crowded. The neighborhood was beginning to complain about the noise level. No more orphaned children could be housed there. To house more children would have been criminal. They could not even take care of the ones there. It is a good thing that the city has elected to shut it down.

b. No one in her right mind would have had the slightest inclination to have boarded such an untested vessel as the *Titanic,* but still thousands tried to book passage. The tale is an old and sad one to be sure, since so many famous and not-so-famous passengers died on that star-crossed journey. And yet there is a fascination with that trip, marked by the fact that there have been three movies made and thirty-four books written about that fateful and heart-rending voyage. Who can say that the next generation's attempt to fly in the space shuttle crafts will not end the same way: in death, in despair, in ignominy.

6. Examine each of the following passages and sentences for problems of *convolution.* Where possible, rewrite problematic sentences using the revision techniques discussed in this sentence.

a. While working toward an advanced degree, it is good to consider the job prospects available. Especially in the arts, this would be a wise move.

b. To be the first woman astronaut in space, Sally Ride, she had to train harder than her male counterparts.

c. Speaking of shrewd judges of character, it would not be unusual for an unqualified candidate to be selected.

d. Setting aside the court's decision, this really put the convicted thief in jeopardy.

e. By completing the mission started there can effect the changes desired.

f. The battle site to which he referred, I've been there.

g. Traveling in the Orient, it would be great if she would consent to the offer.

CHAPTER 10

A Case Study in Revision

In Chapter 3 you glimpsed at the discovery draft of an explanatory essay by John Bebb about buying a computer printer. In this chapter we return to John's essay and explore his work on it in two parts: (1) a consideration of John's revision strategies for making his next draft more effective; and (2) a presentation of John's final draft. The purpose of this chapter is to tie together all that *Processing Words* has been saying about composing and revising, by applying to John's essay the rewriting strategies presented in Chapters 6 through 9.

Here, as elsewhere in *Processing Words,* it is important to keep in mind that it is the writer's intention which governs the revising process. Each revising decision should evolve out of a sense of the writer's overall design; each component of the essay should contribute to the writer's goal of communicating content clearly and meaningfully to its intended readers.

As you recall, John determined that this draft of his essay contained a meaningful thesis and intention, as well as the beginnings of a useful organization. Thus revision of his text would involve adding, deleting, substituting, and rearranging material in the text.

In the following sections, transcripts of John's own notes appear, as he "talks himself through" his analysis of the essay draft. In them, John discusses what he thinks needs to be revised and describes what revision strategies he will decide to use. You will also see a sampling of his actual work while rewriting his draft. At the end of the chapter you will find John's edited, final draft. In reading through John's work on his essay, from rough to final draft, you should examine your own essay drafts and begin plotting the appropriate strategies for making your draft more suited to your intended readers.

JOHN'S DISCOVERY DRAFT

To make it easier to analyze individual features of John's text, I have numbered each paragraph and each of the sentences in his discovery draft.

How to Buy a Computer Printer
by John Bebb

(1)   (1) The computer revolution has affected every corner of our society today. (2) Especially in education, computers are more and more prominent. (3) If one doesn't know how to use them, then he is just about out of luck. (4) Therefore, it is important for each and evbery individual student to become cognizant of the features of computers and printers.

(2)   (5) The purpose of this essay is to help the reader understand how computer printers assist in the accumulation and disseminationg of data for business, school, and home. (6) A computer without a printer is like a car without gasoline. (7) Unless there is a way to store and transmit the information that a computer assists the user in accumulating, there is no way for it to become as resourceful a tool as it should be.

(3)   (8) If you are in the market for a printer, then the information I am about to present will be of interest to you. (9) But there is good news and bad news. (10) First, the good news: printers have more and more features these days, are compatible with almost any computer, and users can count on a greater speed than before. (11) But the buyer should beware: there is also some bad news too. (12) There are a bewildering array of models and choices. (13) And the retail stores are usually full of high-pressure salespeople who want to sell you whatever they can, whether it is what you need or not. (14) Finally, if you decide to order through the mail, there are the hassles of dealing with companies in which you don't know anyone and far away.

(4)   (15) The first thing to decide when you are ready to buy a printer is what kind of print quality you will need. (16) There are three general descriptions of computer printer quality: letter quality, which is the best, near-letter-quality, which is faster but not as good, and draft-quality, which is for the writer's eyes only. (17) The second thing to decide is how fast you need your data printed. (18) If you are going to write only a few letters or reports a day or a week, then a letter-quality printer will suffice. (19) On the other hand, if you will be producing hundreds of

letters and reports you may want a dot-matrix one. (20) Finally, cost is a big factor. (21) How much do you want to spend? (22) The letter-quality ones are slow and expensive; the dot-matrix ones are fast and cheap. (23) Only you can determine this.

(5)   (24) The following chart will help you decide what features, speed, and price you need: [<u>note</u> <u>to</u> <u>me</u>: <u>insert</u> <u>chart</u>]

(6)   (25) I myself recently bought a computer and printer and I can say that I am glad that I read a lot about them before entering the store. (26) Since I was well-informed I was not bamboozled by a high-pressure salesperson. (27) I knew the right questions to ask and knew what models would be suitable, (28) The only catch was coming up with the money to pay for it!

EXAMINING JOHN'S PARAGRAPHS

To examine your work globally means to look closely at the coherence and clarity of its larger structures, using your intention and intended audience as your guide. In this task you analyze individual paragraphs and groups of paragraphs to determine if a clear thesis is sustained throughout, and adequate transition exists between paragraphs. In addition, the text's fullness is examined, focusing on how well the writer has elaborated and illustrated the text's main points. Finally, global evaluation also involves a careful examination of the writer's stylistic choices to determine if they are consistent and appropriate for the text's subject matter and intended audience.

John had set aside twenty-four hours between the completion of his discovery draft and his evaluation, which gave him a fresh perspective when he took a second look at his text before he began to revise. John began his initial evaluation with a hard copy of the draft and a sharpened pencil. John read through his draft several times, writing comments in the margins and circling specific features he wanted to be sure to examine carefully.

John then took this marked-up copy to the computer lab with him to begin work on-line. He decided to create a separate file just to record his analysis of each portion of his text. He named the file REVISION 1, and in it he registered his reactions to the global and local features of his text. Here are John's on-line comments about text-level features, paragraph by paragraph.

PARAGRAPH 1: I'm not sure this sets up the context for the reader that I really want. The opening sentence is overgeneralized and, really, too filled with jargon, like "computer revolution."

Part of the problem is my audience. I think I should narrow it, maybe to recent computer buyers and not the complete novice I seem to be writing to now. It needs to be more concrete and specific. I don't think I should move so quickly from "the computer revolution" to "therefore, you better know about computers and printers." This seems very thin now.

PARAGRAPH 2: There's not much buffer between the first and second paragraph—no easy transition, just BOOM! Here's the purpose of my essay. The first sentence just doesn't communicate my real intention: to help a buyer buy. Needs a new focus, more in line with my true intention. What I really need is a paragraph that explains the value of the printer to a computer user.

PARAGRAPH 3: "In the market for a printer?" I sort of drop the reader in the middle of something again. It's audience again. I know what I mean, but the reader doesn't. No transition. The pieces are here but not the glue. It all goes back to the opening paragraph. I'll have to clear that up before fixing the rest of these paragraphs. There is a lot of background info I need to supply—that's clear. Too many vague words. I'm not sure the stuff about the high-pressure salespeople works. It's exaggerated.

PARAGRAPH 4: This one works OK if I have set up the previous two paragraphs successfully. Focus is fuzzy though. The organization is just too listlike. No subordination. The reader has to guess about my purpose. Skeletal. I need more flesh and blood! All of this feature stuff needs extensive elaboration.

PARAGRAPH 5: What about the chart. Do I need it? There are so many options and printers and so on. Maybe a modified version—no prices or model names, but a few of the features presented so the reader can see the kind of decisions he has to make. It can't be a name-brand buying guide. That's too much trouble. I'm not *Consumer Reports*.

PARAGRAPH 6: This doesn't work at all—too personal, all out of whack. The stance and tone change too abruptly. Does the reader want to know, suddenly, about me and my printer? Probably not. At least not after I have been so distant and "objective" throughout the text previous to this. It may be useful for the reader to know I have recently bought a printer to give me some authority in this.

Summary

In examining his essay globally, John determined that his failure to establish an opening context in his essay had made the rest of his draft unclear. It had encouraged a listlike structure in later paragraphs and, overall, made his essay seem more thin and superficial than it was. Further, as he examined the opening sections, he realized that his original audience analysis had yielded too broad a spectrum; he needed to limit his audience further. As he revised he would need to do some more prewriting, considering his audience again in order to clarify and elaborate many of the points only hinted at in his discovery draft.

EXERCISES

1. John suggests that his first two paragraphs are the most crucial in deciding how the rest of his text will be revised. Do you agree? How has John's sense that his audience is too broad helped him to make some important revising decisions? What, specifically, is the problem with these two paragraphs?

2. What other global features of John's draft need attention? Do you think his evaluation of each paragraph rings true? How much elaboration do you think is required for expanding his various points about printers and their features?

3. How would you go about revising the text features he identifies as problematic?

EXAMINING JOHN'S SENTENCES

To examine your work locally means to look closely at the structure of individual *sentences,* noting convoluted, excessively passive, or generally ambiguous structure. It also involves monitoring clusters of sentences for wordiness, variety, and balance. After John had looked at his essay globally, he zeroed in on individual sentences. Here are his hard copy comments about sentence structure. I have added sentence numbers to identify the sentences to which John refers.

```
Sentence        John's Comment

1        Limp; vague; starts the essay off too generalized.
2        Passive; prominent for whom? Blah!
3        What does "out of luck" mean? Passive again.
4        Whoops, a typo--evbery. Where's the focus?
5        Sentence OK; but that's not my purpose! Another
         typo.
6        Good analogy? Check later.
7        Sentence OK; but does it fit? Where's the
         transition?
```

```
8        Needs to be a transitional sentence; flat.
9-11     This cluster needs development and varied
         structure; need to combine some of these and
         indicate how they fit together.
12-13    Focus problems. What are these sentences doing?
14       Convoluted; "far away" isn't attached to anything;
         "finally" is a false transition.
15       The beginning of a listlike series of sentences;
         need to find a better way to set up these "steps."
16-20    Focus again; transition problems; relationship of
         "factors" needs better set-up and context.
21-23    Very awkward to suddenly ask the reader a question
         or address him directly.
24       To chart or not to chart???
25       What is this sentence doing? Change of stance.
26-28    Bamboozled? I've exaggerated the sales pressure
         stuff. The last sentence is just plain
         inappropriate.
```

Summary

John's analysis of sentence structure both cheered and distressed him. On the one hand, he found few structural problems per se, that is, convoluted or excessively passive sentences. On the other hand, there were other problems at the sentence level. While he felt confident that the right ''pieces'' were present, he knew nevertheless that he needed to clarify a number of sentences and expand key portions of the essay to make it accessible to the reader.

EXERCISES

1. What are the main kinds of sentence problems John found in his analysis? What other problems do you find?

2. John suggests that sentences 16–20 reflect transition problems. How are these problems revealed at the sentence level?

3. How would you go about revising the sentence features he identifies as problematic?

EXAMINING JOHN'S WORD CHOICE

To examine your work locally also means to look closely at individual words, noting obscure expressions, needless repetition, and vague, inaccurate, or imprecise word choice. John had already uncovered a number of vague and imprecise words as he examined the essay globally. On his hard copy he jotted the symbols ''vw'' (for vague word), ''ww'' (wrong or imprecise word), and ''wdy'' (wordiness) near any word or expression which he thought might be problematic to a reader. He decided to compile a list of questionable expressions he found, paragraph by paragraph. His list of words (underlined) and commentary follow.

PARAGRAPH 1:

each and every (redundant pair; has to go!)
computer revolution (too vague--it's not much of a
   revolution if I can't pin down its impact in concrete
   terms)
our society today (a cliché I can do without)
prominent (imprecise; prominent to whom? in what way?)
cognizant (where'd I get this big word; maybe "aware of"?)

PARAGRAPH 2:

accumulation and dissemination of data (wordy! unpack it--
   remember the audience)
store/transmit (audience--will they know the term?)
resourceful as a tool (be precise)

PARAGRAPH 3:

high-pressure (I'm sure I want to keep this anyway)
more and more features these days (audience again; will
   they know any of the "features," let alone what
   constitutes more?
hassles (slipped in my own jargon)

PARAGRAPH 4:

print quality (I sort of explain this, but I can do it
   better)
big factor (pure code; what does "big" mean, compared with
   the other factors?)
slow and expensive (reader doesn't have a context yet to
   judge this)

PARAGRAPH 5:
[none]

PARAGRAPH 6:

bamboozled (out of left field; probably won't keep it
   anyway)
high-pressure (same thing as above; do I need it?)

Summary

John's analysis convinced him that these instances of vague expressions, verbose diction, and imprecisions were directly related to the global problems he had earlier identified. His main task in revising these word-choice problems would be to clarify his intention in the text itself and thus orient his word choice more specifically to his intended readers.

EXERCISES

1. At what places in the text did John seem to have trouble choosing clear and concrete words? Are there other problems you think he missed?

2. How would you go about revising the local word-choice problems he identified?

JOHN'S REVISING STRATEGIES: AN OVERVIEW

We cannot, of course, give you a detailed transcript of all that John thought about as he considered possible revision strategies for his text; few writers can articulate, with any precision, exactly what they do when they revise a text. But we can give you a sense of John's thinking process, to demonstrate the kind of decisions and choices that a writer who takes revision seriously must make.

After John completed his global and local analyses, he opened up the file containing his discovery draft and began to plot, on-line, strategies for revising it. John knew that he needed to do some more prewriting about his audience and about the various features he needed to explain to his readers. This extra prewriting would also assist him in discovering the best organization for his intended readers.

To prepare for a new prewriting session, John read through his own printer manual and a few articles in computer magazines that focused on tips for buying a printer. After spending a half-hour brainstorming, he determined that he would direct his second draft to a more limited audience: recent personal computer buyers who are considering buying a printer to complement their purchase. This, he felt, would make his other revision chores more manageable since most of his global problems seemed to emanate from this lack of audience awareness. He then took a break and scheduled another session for later in the day.

Returning to the lab, John decided to begin revising his text by scrolling to each paragraph, inserting some carriage returns beneath it, and then typing in some specific strategies that he would carry out after he had worked through the entire draft. After John completed this task, he printed a hard copy and took a break before proceeding with his revision. Here are excerpts from John's hard copy containing his revision strategies.

How to Buy a Computer Printer
by John Bebb

(1)   (1) The computer revolution has affected
          every corner of our society today. (2) Especially
          in education, computers are more and more
          prominent. (3) If one doesn't know how to use
          them, then he is just about out of luck. (4)
          Therefore, it is important for each and evbery
          individual student to become cognizant of the
          features of computers and printers.

STRATEGIES:

1. Create a new opening context for the essay which
explains clearly and directly the intention of the essay
to my newly defined audience.
2. Explain why printers are useful to the computer owner.
3. Provide the necessary background information to avoid
obscure phrasings and generalizations.
4. Add appropriate sentences to clarify intention;
delete sentence 3; and refocus each of the remaining
sentences to serve the overall context.
5. Choose real subjects and strong predicates for each of
the opening sentences.
6. The title seems pretty dull now. Change to ''Ifs,
Ands, and Bytes''?

(2)   (5) The purpose of this essay is to help the
          reader understand how computer printers assist
          in the accumulation and disseminationg of data
          for business, school, and home. (6) A computer
          without a printer is like a car without gasoline.
          (7) Unless there is a way to store and transmit
          the information that a computer assists the user
          in accumulating, there is no way for it to become
          as resourceful a tool as it should be.

STRATEGIES:

1. Delete the first sentence, since it isn't really part
of my intention. Again, link the new audience analysis to
the development of the information.
2. Devise a new analogy between computer and printer;
explain the basic focus of the essay in more reader-
oriented terms.

3. Add an additional paragraph after this one to present a better transition between the discussion of computers and printers and the advice to be offered about how to buy a printer.

(3)   (8) If you are in the market for a printer, then the information I am about to present will be of interest to you. (9) But there is good news and bad news. (10) First, the good news: printers have more and more features these days, are compatible with almost any computer, and users can count on a greater speed than before. (11) But the buyer should beware: there is also some bad news too. (12) There are a bewildering array of models and choices. (13) And the retail stores are usually full of high-pressure salespeople who want to sell you whatever they can, whether it is what you need or not. (14) Finally, if you decide to order through the mail, there are the hassles of dealing with companies in which you don't know anyone and far away.

STRATEGIES:
1. Clarify the purpose of this paragraph, explaining key terms and features of printers more comprehensively.
2. Create one paragraph or section for each of the kinds of features that printers have so the relationship between speed, quality, and cost will be clear later. A lot more needs to be said.
3. Try adding "headers" to distinguish different sections and introduce each "feature" for the reader.
4. Delete the reference to "high-pressure salespeople," since it doesn't really fit my own experience or the tone of the rest of the essay. Fit the sale people stuff in a different way: contrast buying from a discount store and a store that specializes in computers.
5. Keep terminology as simple and clear as possible or the reader will get lost.

(4)   (15) The first thing to decide when you are ready to buy a printer is what kind of print quality you will need. (16) There are three general descriptions of computer printer quality: letter quality, which is the best, near-

letter-quality, which is faster but not as good, and draft-quality, which is for the writer's eyes only. (17) The second thing to decide is how fast you need your data printed. (18) If you are going to write only a few letters or reports a day or a week, then a letter-quality printer will suffice. (19) On the other hand, if you will be producing hundreds of letters and reports you may want a dot-matrix one. (20) Finally, cost is a big factor. (21) How much do you want to spend? (22) The letter-quality ones are slow and expensive; the dot-matrix ones are fast and cheap. (23) Only you can determine this.

STRATEGIES:

1. This is a long section that should be broken into several paragraphs, each one exploring one particular aspect of buying a printer in order to keep my intention clear.
2. The listlike organization is evident; find a more appropriate organizing principle to avoid the list.
3. Combine sentences appropriate to sidestep the choppiness and sameness now present.
4. The potential for ambiguity is large here; watch it.

(5)   (24) The following chart will help you decide what features, speed and price you need: [note to me: insert chart]

STRATEGIES:

1. Create the chart that compares various features, but without specifying particular brands. There are too many and it is not a buyer's guide, but a discussion of how to buy, period.
2. Make sure the terminology is direct and simple.

(6)   (25) I myself recently bought a computer and printer and I can say that I am glad that I read a lot about them before entering the store. (26) Since I was well-informed I was not bamboozled by a high-pressure salesperson. (27) I knew the right questions to ask and knew what models would be suitable. (28) The only catch was coming up with the money to pay for it!

STRATEGIES:

1. It was important for me to write this, but now it should be deleted.

2. Create a concluding paragraph which briefly summarizes the key points, but which ends without excessive repetition.

3. Avoid the editorializing.

EXERCISES

1. Given his earlier evaluation of the essay, how well do you think his plans for revision address the problems he identified?

2. How has John's new sense of audience assisted him in revising globally? What difference do you think the "headers" will make in cueing the reader to important information?

3. What other strategies would you suggest to John to help him make his draft more effective, that is, more suited to his intended audience?

SAMPLING JOHN'S REVISION STRATEGIES

Before going back to the microcomputer to begin work on his next draft, John poured over the hard copy of his text one more time, looking at the revision suggestions he had inserted and reflecting once more on his overall intention. He hoped that after this revising session the resulting draft would be ready to be edited as his final draft, but he still had some questions about what needed to be done.

John planned a two-hour session, but as soon as he began he realized that he would need at least four hours to complete the expansion and elaboration needed to fulfill his revision plans. He spent a great deal of time crafting paragraphs and moving them around in his text as he searched for the best order. John ended up organizing his text into ten sections: an overall introduction to the essay, a section on basic printer information, an introductory section on how printers work, one section each on various printer features, the chart, and a concluding section.

In the following you will find excerpts of revisions from three different sections of John's text. These revisions illustrate the kinds of decisions John made and how he used the microcomputer to his advantage in adding, deleting, substituting, and rearranging material in his draft. To show you every change John made would be tiresome and probably unproductive. The important thing is that you recognize the strategies John used to evaluate and revise his text. All told, John spent six hours evaluating and revising his first draft.

Revision of Opening Paragraph

John worked through most of his second draft before returning to the beginning to rewrite the introductory paragraph. He needed to see where he was going before he could tell the reader. After a few false starts, John wrote three different versions of the opening paragraph:

FIRST VERSION

If you are one of the thousands who have recently purchased a personal computer but have yet to take the plunge in buying a printer, you don't know what you're missing. Linking your computer to a printer gives you access to many different options.

COMMENT: John rejected this way of opening the essay because it started off too generally and did not begin with the clarity he needed both to hook his reader and make sense of what followed.

SECOND VERSION

Most of us are aware of how quickly computer technology has infiltrated and revolutionized the business world. Executives who once dictated their memoes to secretaries are now creating their own on sophisticated word processors. Secretaries who once spent hours retyping the same letter to fifteen different customers now type it once and have their high-speed printers print out a hundred custom-tailored versions for individual customers. From a distance this revolution seems miraculous.

COMMENT: This looked and sounded good to John at first, but he quickly realized that it took him too far afield of the real topic and intention of his text: buying printers wisely.

FINAL VERSION

As helpful as a personal computer is for recording and storing data, a printer will make it even more versatile and useful to you. The addition of a printer and the appropriate software can turn your computer into a word processing work station, making all your writing chores--from important reports to everyday correspondence--easy and professional. In addition, a printer gives you the option of backing up important files with paper copies. Despite all the safeguards built into today's computers, a disk can always become defective; paper copies ("hard copy") of essential information will help you sleep better

at night. As one who recently took the plunge, purchasing a
computer and printer myself, I can offer you some guidance
in choosing the right machine for your needs.

COMMENT: John finally settled on this version because it adequately introduced his subject matter and clearly stated his intention. It provided the necessary overview to help the reader find a way through the rest of John's text.

Revision of Middle Paragraphs

Once John reached the thick forest of ideas in the middle portion of his text, he was anxiously trying to find an organizing principle. He ended up giving each printer feature its own section. In the following versions of the same paragraph, John attempted to put printer speed in context and explain its relationship to print quality.

FIRST VERSION

How fast you want your printer to work will depend on
how much work you will be doing, how often you will need to
reprint materials, and your overall budget. Most dot-
matrix and ink-jet printers, for instance, can print at
speeds above 100 cps. That's about one double-spaced page
per every 30 seconds.

COMMENT: John decided there was vague word choice in this version (for instance, "overall budget") and that its sentences were rather convoluted.

FINAL VERSION

How much work you will be doing and how often you will
need to print and reprint materials will determine how
fast a printer you should select. Most dot-matrix and ink-
jet printers, for instance, can print at speeds above 100
cps (that's about two double-spaced pages per minute) and
are usually $200-$300 cheaper than LQ printers. If you
will be printing only a few pages a day and want the
highest quality of print, the LQ printer will serve you
well. If, however, you will be printing lots of pages daily
or will be making multiple drafts of various writing
tasks, you will want something that prints at a faster
speed. A difference of 100 cps can affect your
productivity--and patience--greatly.

COMMENT: This version greatly extends and elaborates the differences between letter quality and faster printers, giving the reader a much clearer approach to the information than the first.

Revision of Closing Paragraph

John wanted his conclusion to reinforce certain principles he was trying to instill in the reader without rehashing everything. In his first attempt, John goes overboard in avoiding the "rehash" and ends too abruptly. The second version more suitably ends the essay with a gentle exhortation to the reader and a personal concluding sentence which brings the essay full circle.

FIRST VERSION

```
    In conclusion, then, a printer buyer should remember
what features he or she needs and enter the store with the
confidence that an intelligent, wise choice can be made.
```

COMMENT: John knew he was groping for a suitable ending, but he so feared repetition that this version became so terse it almost restated the obvious anyway.

FINAL VERSION

```
    Heading unprepared to a computer store to a buy a
printer can be like going to a grocery store when you are
hungry: you could end up buying anything, including
something you don't really need or want. Smart buyers
survey their needs, determine which printer model
satisfies those needs at the price that fits their budget,
and then select a store which offers the most
knowledgeable salesmen and helpful service. In my own
case, my prior preparation made all the difference in
getting the machine that fit my needs and at a price I
could afford. Here's hoping the information presented here
will do the same for you.
```

COMMENT: This version more satisfactorily reminds the reader of John's original point in the first version: that being prepared helped him buy a printer successfully, meaning he can now pass along that wisdom to others.

EXERCISES

1. Examine each of the paragraphs John wrote for his opening paragraphs. What are the strengths and weaknesses of each? Do you agree that the "final" version is better than the others?

2. Examine the two versions of John's middle paragraph about printer speed. What makes the second version more effective? How has John changed this paragraph from the original one in his first draft?

3. Examine the two versions of John's conclusion. What makes the second version effective? How else might John have ended his essay on buying a printer?

JOHN'S FINAL DRAFT

Using the revising strategies he had plotted, John wrote a second draft. Overall, he had succeeded in expanding his original draft a great deal. John's second analysis of his audience had helped him immensely in creating a more coherent draft. After completing it, he again left it alone for twenty-four hours. He wanted to gain some perspective before deciding whether or not it was a final draft.

When he picked it up again a day later, he performed many of the same reading strategies that he had used in examining his first draft. First, he read through his draft paragraph by paragraph, examining individual sentences. He then carefully analyzed the diction in the text, looking for evidence of such problems as wordiness, ambiguity, and imprecision. He decided that he had been successful in eliminating all or most of the problems which had plagued his first draft.

Before John could consider this version a final draft, however, he had one more component of the writing process to perform: editing. John's task was to locate and correct any structure, diction, or punctuation problems which would interfere with understanding of the text or which would unnecessarily alienate the reader. (In the next chapter, you will learn strategies for effective proofreading of your text, and how to go about locating and correcting common problems at the microcomputer.)

John did his proofreading in two ways. First, he did a proofreading on-line, using the SEARCH function of his word processing software to locate the specific kinds of editing problems—especially those he usually fought with and expected to find. Then he examined his hard copy carefully, marking the errors he found for correction at the VDT. Here are some of the editing changes John made:

> Changed "salesmen" to "sales personnel"
> Added words he had unintentionally omitted
> Corrected a comma splice
> Rephrased several sentences in middle paragraphs to reduce wordiness
> Deleted one redundant phrase in the final paragraph
> Moved one sentence from the end of the paragraph to the beginning of the next paragraph for better transition
> Inserted a footer which included his page number
> Changed "his" to "his or her" in two places
> Corrected the spelling of "complement"
> Made two paragraphs out of one for better readability.

After this editing process was complete, John was ready to print a final copy of his text for submission to his instructor. John selected the appropriate option from the menu, electing to print two copies, one for himself and one for his instructor. Here is John's final draft:

John Bebb
Introductory Composition
September 5, 1987

Buying a Printer for Your Computer: Ifs, Ands, and Bytes

(1)   As helpful as a personal computer is for
recording and storing data, a printer will make it
even more versatile and useful to you. The addition
of a printer and the appropriate software can turn
your computer into a word processing work station,
making all your writing chores--from important
reports to everyday correspondence--easy and
professional. In addition, a printer gives you the
option of backing up important files with paper
copies. Despite all the safeguards built into today's
computers, a disk can always become defective; paper
copies ("hard copy") of essential information will
help you sleep better at night. As one who recently
took the plunge, purchasing a computer and printer
myself, I can offer you some guidance in choosing the
right machine for your needs.

(2)   Whether you will be using your computer for
charting the stock market, extensive word
processing, or just managing your checkbook, you will
quickly find the printer an essential complement to
your computing. Using a computer without a printer is
somewhat like owning a large collection of 45 RPM
records and a phonograph that only plays at 33 1/3
RPM. Such a collection may be impressive, but unless
you can play the records once in a while or share them
with others, the phonograph is marginally useful.
Likewise, if you store and access your information
exclusively on diskettes, you will always be
handcuffed to your computer and can never share this
information in hard copy with anyone else. A printer
thus becomes an important access tool for understanding and disseminating your work.

1

Basic Information

(3)   Before you walk into a store, there are some basics about buying a printer that you'll want to be familiar with. This information includes a grasp of basic terminology and typical printer features, and a sense of which options you will need. Printer technology has progressed about as fast as computer technology, providing the consumer with a wide variety of choices of features, models, and prices. It's presently a buyer's market, but that doesn't mean you can't make a mistake and be disappointed.

(4)   I recommend that you buy your printer at a store which specializes in computers, rather than at a discount house. Questions about how your printer operates and later repairs won't be handled as well by a clerk with no special computer competence; better to spend a few extra dollars and have the security of a specially trained sales and service staff backing your purchase.

(5)   What follows is not a name-brand buying guide, but an overview of what to look for when choosing a printer. I will begin with an overview of how printers work, and then narrow my focus to the specific kinds of features you will choose from in selecting a printer. Toward the end of the text I will supply a helpful chart which summarizes the basic options and choices you will face when you decide to buy a printer.

How Printers Work

(6)   There are three basic ways printers print characters on a page, and these three methodologies represent three different kinds of machines from which to choose.[1] Letter-quality (LQ) printers are "impact" printers which form characters by hitting a "daisy-wheel" or other print head against a ribbon and platen much like a typewriter. (Most LQ printers

---

[1] I am ignoring in this discussion the new technology of laser printing since laser printers are out of the price range of most individual buyers.

use interchangeable "daisy-wheels," circular print
wheels with alphabetic and numeric character type on
them.) Their print quality is excellent; each page
looks like it was freshly typed by a talented typist.
But the user usually gains this quality at the
expense of speed, since LQ printers print between
only 12-20 characters per second (cps)--not as fast
as most good typists can type. Though some LQ
printers can print as fast as 40 cps, they are usually
more expensive.

(7)   The main alternatives to LQ printers are dot-
matrix printers and ink-jet printers. Dot-matrix
printers are impact printers that produce characters
by "firing" rows of pins against a ribbon and platen.
Ink-jet printers are nonimpact printers whose
characters are formed by spraying streams of ink
through "portholes" at a sheet of paper. Both are
much faster than LQ printers, printing anywhere from
80 to 200 cps. Dot-matrix printers are fast
approaching LQ printers in print quality, while the
quality of ink-jet printers often meets or exceeds
the quality of the more expensive LQ printers.

Printer Speed and Special Printing Modes

(8)   How much work you will be doing and how often you
will need to print and reprint materials will
determine how fast a printer you should select. Most
dot-matrix and ink-jet printers, for instance, can
print at speeds above 100 cps (that's about two
double-spaced pages per minute) and are usually $200-
$300 cheaper than LQ printers. If you will be
printing only a few pages a day and want the highest
quality of print, the LQ printer will serve you well.
If, however, you will be printing lots of pages daily
or will be making multiple drafts of various writing
tasks, you will want something that prints at a
faster speed. A difference of 100 cps can affect your
productivity--and patience--greatly.

(9)   As I said, LQ printers are much slower, but they
do produce text that looks like original typewritten

3

print. If the typewritten appearance is important to you and those who will read your text, the LQ printer is the one for you. On the other hand, the newer dot-matrix and ink-jet printers are capable of printing with different "modes," or qualities of print. One mode, sometimes called "near-letter quality" or correspondence mode, overprints characters several times, making the print darker and closer to typewritten print. Readers have to look very closely to note that the characters have not actually been typewritten. There are, clearly, advantages and disadvantages to both kinds of printers.

Pitch, Font, and Paper Feeding Features

(10)   Most printers, whether LQ, dot-matrix, or ink-jet, allow you to select the size of type or pitch in which you want to print your text. Almost all dot-matrix and ink-jet printers feature pica (10 characters per inch); elite (12 characters per inch); condensed (17 characters per inch); and enlarged (6 characters per inch). Pitch changes on LQ printers depend upon your choice of daisy-wheel, and the selection switches available on your machine.

(11)   In addition to pitch options, all three kinds of printers allow the user to select font and format options like italics, underlining, boldface, double-strike, superscript, and subscript. (Selecting a different font in a LQ printer means changing the daisy-wheel.) In selecting a printer you will need to determine how important some of these features are to you. If, for instance, your writing tasks demand a lot of scientific or mathematical notation, you would want to be sure your printer could print superscripts and subscripts. If not, you may be able to select a less expensive model.

(12)   Two other important features concern the size of paper you can use in your printer and how the paper may be fed to your printer. Most printers feature either 10-inch or 15-inch carriages. The 10-inch carriages allow the user to use paper 8 1/2 inches wide; the 15-inch carriages, 13 1/2 inches wide. The 10-inch carriage suffices for most word processing

functions, but if you were going to use the printer to
record financial "spreadsheets" requiring a wider
page size, the 15-inch carriage is a better option.

(13)   How paper is fed to the printer is also an
important consideration. All printers permit
"friction feeding," that is, loading single sheets of
paper which are advanced in the printer like a
typewriter: pressure is applied to the paper between
a platen and roller as it moves up through the printer
mechanism. Friction feeding is adequate if you are
only going to print one page at a time. For most
applications, however, a continuous feeding process
is more convenient, and either tractor feeding or
cut-sheet feeding options serve this function. The
tractor feed, a separate or built-in mechanism,
advances specially perforated paper through pinholes
during the printing process. The cut-sheet feeder
literally sits on top of the printer and
automatically feeds paper into the printer as each
preceding sheet is ejected. The tractor feeder and
cut-sheet feeder are rarely included in the purchase
price of a printer, but are crucial extras the buyer
should consider seriously.

Interface and Cable

(14)   Selecting the printer you want doesn't end the
decision-making process for the buyer. One
especially crucial factor to determine is the
interface you will need to link your computer to the
printer. An interface is the "translation" device you
need to send data to your printer from the disk drive
or internal memory of your computer.

(15)   Some personal computers have this interface
built in; others require that you purchase a special
piece of hardware to enable your computer to access a
printer. You should check on this when choosing a
printer. In addition to the interface itself, you
will also need to purchase the appropriate connecting
cables to link the two machines. These are almost
always extra costs and are not included in the price
of either the computer or the printer.

5

(16)   Printer interfaces basically come in two kinds: serial and parallel. The parallel interface is becoming more and more standard and is easy to use. The user simply plugs in the connecting cables to the computer and printer and begins printing. The serial interface can be trickier since sometimes a special cable must be created to allow the two machines to be linked. You will want to ask the salesperson which kind of interface the printer (and computer) requires and make sure you take home the right kind of cable.

Price

(17)   As you might guess, the price of a printer is determined by the number and kinds of features the printer contains. There are economy models, ranging from $200-$300; mid-range models, ranging from $300-$500; and upper-range models, over $500. Generally, one should expect the higher priced models to bear more and better features, but this is not always the case. Most LQ printers will be in the upper-range bracket and, in fact, one could easily pay over $1000 for a multifeatured model. Most first-time computer and printer buyers will, however, find an economy model more than adequate to fulfill their printing needs.

Other Options to Consider

(18)   In addition to all of these features and options, there are some other questions you might like to mull over. Put these questions to the salesperson if you don't find them answered in the brochure for the printer you're considering. How easy to use are the printer's controls? How does the feeding mechanism work? How much noise does it make? How easy is it to replace the ribbon and load the paper? How expensive are the ribbons for the printer? These questions involve the convenience of the user and do not represent important printer functions--but they could make the difference in your choice.

A Summary Chart

(19)   The following chart identifies the various features and options which you should consider when

purchasing a printer for your computer. Place a check
in the appropriate slot--Essential, Important, or
Optional--depending upon how you rate the particular
feature in importance.

	Essential	Important	Optional
Speed			
Print quality			
Letter quality			
Near LQ			
Print features			
Italics			
Underlining			
Boldface			
Double-strike			
Super/subscripts			
Emphasized			
Price			
Economy			
Mid-range			
Upper-range			
Interface			
Parallel			
Serial			
Pitch			
6			
10			
12			
17			
Paper feed			
Friction			
Tractor			
Cut-sheet			

Conclusion

(20)   Heading unprepared to a computer store to buy a printer can be like going to a grocery store when you are hungry: you could end up buying anything, including something you don't really need or want. Smart buyers survey their needs, determine which printer model satisfies those needs at the price that fits their budget, and then select a store which offers the most knowledgeable sales personnel and helpful service. In my own case, my prior preparation made all the difference in getting the machine that fit my needs and at a price I could afford. Here's hoping the information presented here will do the same for you.

EXERCISES

1. Examine John's final draft globally. How has he addressed the organizational problems that he identified in his earlier analysis? How did his narrowing of the audience for this essay contribute to his success in revising?

2. The final version of John's text is more than quadruple the original length. Is this expansion justified?

3. What effect do the ''headers'' which introduce each section have on the coherence of his essay? Do you think he has adequately dealt with the transition problems that plagued his first draft?

4. John chose to drop one line of argument—''high-pressure salespeople''—when it didn't seem to work. Why did he do this? What did he replace it with in his final version?

5. Has John refined his stance toward his audience in this new draft? If so, in what way? Is it an improvement over the original?

6. What does the title mean? Why did John choose the phrase ''Ifs, Ands, and Bytes'' to come after the colon?

7. How has John pushed his own experience, which was once the key ingredient in his prewriting and in the first draft, to the background? Is this a useful tactic?

8. Examine the sentences in John's final draft. How has John addressed the problems of convolution, ambiguity, and lack of variety he identified in his earlier evaluation? Can you identify specific sentences or clusters of sentences which he has revised particularly well? Do you think he has adequately dealt with the sentence problems that plagued the first draft?

9. Examine individual words in John's final draft. Can you identify specific instances of word changes that have increased the effectiveness of his text? How has John addressed the problems of vagueness and imprecision that he identified in his earlier evaluation? Do you think he has adequately dealt with these problems?

10. Do you agree with John that he has produced a *final* draft? Are there editing changes (grammar? usage? mechanics?) you would make before submitting it to an instructor? If so, what changes?

CHAPTER 11

Editing:
Polishing
the Final Draft

Editing is the final component in a writer's composing process. In *Processing Words* I have been exhorting you to distinguish *revision,* a set of dynamic, comprehensive strategies for creating a coherent, well-developed text suited for its intended audience, from *editing,* a set of strategies for *polishing* the final copy of a text so that it reflects appropriate conventions of grammar and mechanics.

When writers reach the editing stage of their writing process most of the larger, major revising decisions will have been made. Unfortunately, editing has often been confused with revising, and both processes have suffered because of this confusion. If one attends to smaller, isolated errors too early in the composing process—especially at the expense of text-wide, global revision—the writer may miss the forest for the trees, ending up with a grammatically correct, mechanically perfect text that communicates little of importance to the reader.

Some very good writers feel that serious editing is an admission of poor writing or grammatical ignorance. But writers should be neither defensive nor timid about editing. *All* writers make mistakes of transcription and judgment; even a composition instructor must turn to the reference book—a dictionary, thesaurus, or handbook—to settle questions or affirm a particular stylistic choice. Even the most famous and best-selling writers need a proofreader specifically to monitor grammatical, usage, and mechanical problems in their texts.

This chapter will help you become a better proofreader of the hard copies of your text and show you how to use the microcomputer to search for and identify typical errors as well. If your instructor gives you access to commercial software that checks spelling, grammar, or style, you will certainly want to use it. The chief value of these programs is that they are already designed to look for specific kinds of errors, omissions, and spelling problems; your task is simply to select an option from a menu and start the program running. You can, however, duplicate most of these functions manually, using the search/replace function of your word processing software.

152

Though it is focused on the editing process, this chapter is not intended as a replacement for a solid, comprehensive writing *handbook*. Instead it is intended to provide you with search strategies for locating selected errors that the microcomputer is best suited for uncovering. It is by no means exhaustive. For more specific instruction or extended information about any of the issues discussed in this chapter you should consult your handbook.

While editing at the VDT, the two greatest tools at your disposal are the scrolling and searching functions that almost every word processing program possesses. The scrolling function permits you to examine the text at your own pace, line by line or screenful by screenful. If you can set the speed of your scrolling function, you can slow it down or speed it up, depending upon what you are looking for. The search function permits you to locate every instance of a particular character, word, string of words, particular control characters, carriage returns, and even, as we noted earlier, each space. The search/replace function will enable you to make global changes in punctuation, spelling, even format, if you determine that they are necessary.

Computers treat information very "literally"; if you inadvertently use a lower-case "r" when you need an upper-case "R," it will not perform the desired function. While this literalness can be unnerving when you are trying to perform a certain function, it is a great advantage when searching for particular characters, words, or control codes. The word processing program's search function will stop at each instance of the item you are looking for, never skipping even one character or string. You could, for instance, look at every "space" in your text to see if you have forgotten to punctuate a sentence. This would not be the most economical way to perform this task—but you could do it if you needed or wanted to! Check Appendix I if you need more specific help in learning how to use the search/replace functions of your word processor.

The microcomputer is thus particularly well-suited for searching for certain kinds of "repeatable" errors and omissions, but no global search will locate every error or stylistic problem you may create. Thus, you should always follow up any "on-line" editing session with a careful look at the hard copy of the same text. Studies show that writers who only proofread on-line miss many of the errors they might catch on hard copy. You will want to make sure that any formatting instructions you have sent to your printer are working as you designed them; margins, special typefaces, underlining, and so on should appear just as you imagined them. You should especially be wary of "toggled" functions like underlining or centering which require you to enter a beginning and ending control code to work; you could end up underlining large portions of text or centering every line of your text without intending to.

Helpful as the microcomputer is in the composing process, it can also multiply certain kinds of errors. For instance, if your keyboard repeats all or some keys, it is possible for you to unintentionally enter characters doubly or triply without realizing it. When typing characters faster than the VDT can register them, you may omit words or transpose letters in words, particularly words you use frequently. (I often type "teh" or "hte" for "the.") Smaller diacritical marks like the apostrophe, and even the period, can sometimes be missed with an on-line reading. Therefore, you should not consider any draft "final" until you have examined and corrected it both on-line and on hard copy.

PROOFREADING HARD COPY

Generally, I recommend that you do all "final" polishing of your text on hard copy, transferring changes to the VDT in a final on-line session. It is too easy for eyes tired from staring at a VDT for several hours to skip even obvious mistakes. What makes one a good proofreader of hard copy? Someone who is willing to take the time to examine his or her text critically and carefully. "Once overs" are rarely helpful in spotting the kinds of nagging errors that can creep into a text. Having a friend read a text is usually a good idea, but, realistically, most of us have to rely on our own powers of perception to spot errors and problems. Even the most gracious outside reader will not have the same stake in your text as you do.

What can be done to increase your ability to locate and correct editing problems? Here are three strategies for improving your proofreading and editing efforts:

1. *Distance.* Put at least twenty-four hours between the completion of your final draft and your editing session. You need to be fresh, awake, and relaxed to be a good proofreader. If you are too familiar with the text you will "find" what you want to find, and thus miss some errors.

2. *Create a file for your typical errors.* Before you examine the hard copy of your text, you may find it useful to create separate files on a disk that catalogue specific problems, one for spelling words you frequently misspell, for instance, or one for dangling modifiers. When you are proofreading on-line, you can then call up these files as a reminder of the problems you typically face.

Off-line, you will want to use a hard copy of these files to examine your text. If you know you have trouble spelling words that contain a certain vowel combination ("receive," "deceive," etc.), spotlight those kinds of words when you proofread. If you are likely to leave the past tense marker off of certain verbs, you will want to make such predicates a priority in your proofreading. If you have problems with comma or semi-colon use, look for these in your text and check your usage against your handbook's instructions.

3. *Don't rely on silent reading.* When you begin proofreading, read your text aloud, *slowly,* looking and listening for possible errors of grammar, confusing sentence structure, agreement problems, and inconsistent punctuation. Reading aloud is not foolproof, but you will discover awkward phrasing, repetition, and other problems that you might miss in a purely silent reading.

The remainder of Chapter 11 is divided into four brief sections: (1) Monitoring Sentence-Level Problems; (2) Monitoring Word-Level Problems; (3) Monitoring Grammatical Problems; and (4) Monitoring Mechanical Problems. If you need to locate a section on a particular editing problem quickly, check the index at the end of the book.

MONITORING SENTENCE-LEVEL PROBLEMS

Sentence-level errors force the reader to guess at your meaning because they leave conceptual gaps in your text. The following search strategies will help you locate four particular kinds of sentence problems in your text. If you locate errors in your text, correct them with reference to your handbook.

FRAGMENTS

Each of your sentences should be complete with a clear subject and predicate. A sentence that contains a subject and predicate and can "stand alone," requiring no additional information from the writer to make sense, is sometimes called an independent clause. A group of words that contains a subject and predicate but does not make sense without additional information is called a dependent clause. Compare these two would-be sentences:

> **DEPENDENT CLAUSE:** Although she won the race. [The reader needs additional information to make sense of this group of words even though it contains both a subject (she) and a predicate (won).]
>
> **INDEPENDENT CLAUSE:** She won the race. (A complete sentence)
>
> **DEPENDENT CLAUSE COMBINED WITH AN INDEPENDENT CLAUSE:** Although she won the race, she was not happy.

The relationships between the clauses in your sentences should be unambiguous. Fragments are incomplete sentences, that is, sentences lacking either a subject or predicate, or dependent clauses masquerading as sentences:

> **FRAGMENT:** She running the race.
>
> **CORRECTED:** She is running the race.

> **FRAGMENT:** Although he fixed the engine.
>
> **CORRECTED:** Although he fixed the engine, he wasn't finished.

To use the microcomputer to help you search for fragments, in the *search for slot* place:

1. *End punctuation* (period; question mark; exclamation point). Search globally, looking at the end of each sentence, and the sentences which precede or follow it. Check for

> **a.** *Completeness.* Does each sentence have a clear subject and predicate? If not, supply them.
>
> **b.** *Unattached clauses.* Are any dependent clauses punctuated as sentences? If so, attach them to the independent clause or complete sentence to which they belong.

2. *That* or *which.* Search globally, looking for relative pronouns which may make a clause dependent and thus fragmentary. Check for completeness. Correct any fragment with the methods illustrated above.

COMMA SPLICES

A comma splice occurs when a writer uses a comma to join two independent clauses or sentences that should be punctuated separately or joined with a conjunction or semicolon.

> **COMMA SPLICE:** I went to the store, I forgot to get bread.
>
> **CORRECTED:** I went to the store. I forgot to get bread.
>
> **CORRECTED:** I went to the store, but I forgot to get bread.
>
> **CORRECTED:** I went to the store; I forgot to get bread.

To use the microcomputer to assist you in your search for comma splices, in the *search for slot* place:

> *A comma* (,). Search globally through your text and note each comma use. Determine whether you have used a comma improperly to join two or more independent clauses or sentences. Correct, if necessary, using one of the strategies discussed above.

DANGLING PARTICIPLES AND MISPLACED MODIFIERS

Participial phrases may be used as modifiers, but their placement in a sentence is crucial. A writer can inadvertently confuse (or amuse) a reader by dangling such a modifier in a sentence. Other kinds of modifiers, including single words, phrases, and clausal structures, can also be misplaced, confusing writers themselves and forcing them to create awkward sentences whose true subjects and predicates are obscured.

> DANGLING PARTICIPLE: Hanging by the roof, Walter removed the flag.
>
> CORRECTED: Walter removed the flag that was hanging by the roof.
>
> MISPLACED: Coming to Pittsburgh, the train ride was long. ("Train ride" is not the true subject here since the writer refers to someone "coming" to Pittsburgh who is not named.)
>
> CORRECTED: The train ride to Pittsburgh was long. (Ambiguity is resolved by deleting the modifier.)
>
> CORRECTED: Coming to Pittsburgh, I felt the train ride was long. (Ambiguity is resolved by supplying a true subject, "I.")
>
> MISPLACED: We couldn't conveniently tell her how to park the car. (As it stands, "conveniently" modifies *tell;* if the writer's intention is to modify *how to park,* the modifier is misplaced.)
>
> CORRECTED: We couldn't tell her how to park the car conveniently. (The ambiguity is resolved by moving the modifier closer to the word or phrase it modifies.)

To use the microcomputer to assist in your search for dangling participles or misplaced modifiers, in the *search for slot* place:

1. "-ing" verbs. Select the "partial word" option. Search globally, noting any constructions in which the real subject or object in the sentence is missing. This will help you locate participial phrases which may be dangling modifiers. Correct, if necessary, by recasting the sentence and supplying the missing item.

2. A comma (,). Search globally, noting any constructions that contain modifiers that (1) do not seem to modify a specific item in the sentence; or (2) seem misplaced in the sentence. Correct, if necessary, by (1) recasting the sentence and supplying the missing item; or (2) using a block copy/block move to relocate the modifier closer to the item it modifies.

3. *It* or *there*. Search globally, noting any constructions in which *it* or *there* takes the place of the real subject or object in the sentence which is being modified. Correct, if necessary, by recasting the sentence and supplying the missing item.

FAULTY PREDICATION AND EQUATION

Faulty predication occurs when a subject and predicate are illogically joined. Faulty equation occurs when linking verbs join items that are not logically equal.

> **FAULTY PREDICATION:** The selection of the candidate was chosen by the board. (The *candidate,* not the "selection," was chosen by the board.)
>
> **CORRECTED:** The candidate was selected by the board.

Faulty predication can be corrected by locating the real subject and verb and placing them in their proper slots in the sentence.

> **FAULTY EQUATION:** For eighty years my grandfather's job was a farmer. (The *job* wasn't a farmer, the grandfather was.)
>
> **CORRECTED:** For eighty years my grandfather was a farmer.

Faulty equation can be corrected by making the linked items parallel or by substituting a more specific verb, as in this example:

> **FAULTY EQUATION:** A touchdown is when a ball carrier moves into the opponents' end zone. (A touchdown is not a measure of *time,* hence the use of *when* is inappropriate.)
>
> **CORRECTED:** A touchdown occurs when a ball carrier moves into the opponents' end zone.

To use the microcomputer to help you locate instances of faulty predication or equation, in the *search for slot* place:

1. *When.* Search globally, noting each instance of *when* used with a linking verb. Examine the sentence for faulty equation. Correct, if necessary, using the strategies presented above.
2. *Linking verbs* (is, are, was, and were). Search globally, noting each instance of a linking verb and examining the sentence for faulty predication. Correct, if necessary, using the strategies presented above.

EXERCISES

Consult your handbook if you need extra help in correcting the specific sentence errors in these exercises.

1. Edit the following sentences for fragment errors.

   a. Diane wanted the most expensive minivan. Not knowing that it was beyond her budget.
   b. The family headed for Sacramento. That California capital city full of Western history.
   c. Intercepting hijackers is a dangerous activity. A mission only for the most brave and noble.
   d. Burying the last remains of her childhood pet. Cecilia wept bitterly.
   e. Gandalf is the true hero of *The Lord of the Rings.* Which is one of the reasons people are disappointed by Frodo in the end.

2. Edit the following sentences for comma splice errors.

   a. Today was my birthday, I am glad it is over.
   b. Frankly, Joan isn't ready to take on two jobs, I told her so today.
   c. When the Cardinals moved to St. Louis from Chicago, football became an important pastime for this city of 900,000 but that didn't mean that baseball was any less popular.
   d. Candace was reluctant to tell Barbara that she wasn't going to the same graduate school, they had been friends for so long, she didn't want to hurt her feelings.
   e. The only reason the merger fell through was Frank's inability to convince the chief executive that she could make more money, she just didn't believe the stocks would rise that much.

3. Edit the following sentences for problems with dangling or misplaced modifiers.

   a. Coming to the party, it seemed a long drive.
   b. Jogging in the park, the pigeons bothered the summertime runners.
   c. Although they won fairly, the losers were disappointed in the victors' pompous post-game celebration.
   d. The program was set on Tuesday, instead of waiting until the last minute on Friday.
   e. Upset by the election returns, it was an early bedtime for the losing candidate, Mr. Struthers.

4. Edit the following sentences for faulty predication and equation errors.

   a. Teaching is when a person tries to educate someone in a skill.
   b. For many years, my uncle's hobby was a ham radio operator.
   c. The construction of the Carrier Dome was built in part by the Syracuse Alumni donations.
   d. A fast pitch is when it goes more then 85 miles-per-hour.
   e. His completion of the book was written just two hours ago.

MONITORING WORD-LEVEL PROBLEMS

Word-level editing problems include vague words and inaccurate words, and potentially offensive language. Compile your most common word-level problems in a file. You may examine various drafts of your previous writing tasks to discover and record examples of these problems. Such a list might include: (1) vague words (such as ''nice,'' ''different,'' ''interesting'') you frequently rely on to convey your meaning; (2) words which you have trouble distinguishing, and thus are apt to use inaccurately (for instance, ''their/there/they're''; affect/effect); and (3) words like ''policeman'' or ''businessman,'' or the exclusive use of the masculine pronouns (he, him, his) that may be interpreted as sexist.

Search Strategies

1. *Vagueness.* Scroll through your text slowly, each time selecting a particular grammatical slot to examine for vagueness. For instance, the first time through your text, look at each subject to determine if it is appropriately clear and specific to the context and intention of the sentence. Next, look at the predicate, both the verb and the object (if there is one). Next, look at modifiers. If, while scrolling through your text, you spot one of the vague words you usually employ (''different''; ''nice'') or find others that are inappropriately general, substitute a more specific and meaningful word.

2. *Inaccuracy.* Scroll through your text slowly, each time selecting a particular grammatical slot to examine for inaccuracy. For instance, the first time through your text, look at each subject to determine if it is accurate and clear within the context and intention of the sentence. Next, look at the predicate, both the verb and the object (if there is one). Next, look at modifiers. If, while scrolling through your text, you find words that are inaccurately used, substitute a more appropriate and meaningful word. If you know that you tend to use certain words inaccurately (*affect* for *effect,* for instance), place that word or phrase in the *search for slot* and examine each instance of it in your text. Correct, if necessary, by substituting the appropriate word.

3. *Sexism.* Scroll through your text and examine words that end with the suffix -man or -men. You may use the ''partial-word'' option to perform a global search for such words. Examine each third-person pronoun use. Have you consistently used the traditional masculine pronouns? Consider your audience; it may be appropriate to alternate masculine and feminine pronouns or to make plural those subjects and objects that can be altered without awkwardness. Consult your handbook for further discussion of your stylistic options.

EXERCISES

Edit the following passages for vague, inaccurate, or potentially offensive word choice. Consult your handbook if you need extra help in correcting these word-level problems.

1. The trip we took to Long Island was really interesting. We had a great time there, and the scenery was very nice. If you can except certain social customs, you will find the Long Island people friendly and ready to advice you if you need directions. There manners were also very different.

The first sight you'll want to visit is the home of President Theodore Roosevelt. It is a place bound to illict ''wows'' and ''far outs'' from the people who see it. To know that a real president formally lived their is amazing when one has thorough about it. And you won't loose too much money because the place is really cheap.

2. The children were already to go when the news came that Michael had flunked his social studies coarse. He came though the door, sulking; his conscious was clearly bothering him.

''Why didn't I study those state capitals?'' he groaned.

''Aw, mom,'' Tammy shrieked, ''does this mean we can't eat at that fancy restaurant?'' She was eluding to her mom's plans to celebrate Michael's graduation from junior high.

''It's a matter of principal, Tammy,'' mom explained. ''He's going to have to bare his own burden tonight. If he had asked for my assistants, he would have faired better. It's a waist of time to go to school if you're not going to study. Weather or not he's learned his lessen remains to be seen.''

3. I am very happy today to introduce the Prez of this great college, Meredith Dixon. She's been around this joint about five years now and it's about time somebody laid a welcome on here that's justified. You folks know all that jazz about her degree from Harvard, she's a bonifide Ph.D., but what you might not know is that she put herself through school after both her parents croaked in a plane accident when she was a teeny-bopper. Well, there's no use shooting my mouth off any more. Here she is, the first lady of the green, green grass of this student hostel, Doc Dixon.

4. This report will detail the mastication habits of young adolescents as they progress through the annals of time from age twelve to eighteen. Medical research promulgates the notion that such adolescents normally masticate only two or three times during a typical meal. Adolescents in this age bracket normally consume nutritional units twice during a twenty-four time period: once during a morning, pre-school meal, and later, during a mid-evening supper arrangement at the habitat of said individuals. Modern dentistry suggests that minimum mastication rate for adolescents should be 5-6 replications per spoon-sized serving. In fact, this rate is much lower among socially disadvantaged youths in urban areas of metropolitan landscapes.

5. The local police chief has released a report that verifies that a majority of his police force of 26 men fail to take their required physicals each year. As a result, the mayor suggested that some of them may be released and more policemen hired. ''I cannot,'' Mayor Lungstrum argued, ''tolerate such crass incompetence. A man's health is too important in such duties and I am shocked that each officer didn't take it upon himself to certify that his body and mind are in condition.''

MONITORING GRAMMATICAL PROBLEMS

Grammatical editing problems include the proper form of plural and possessive nouns, subject-verb agreement, and pronoun case and reference. Compile your most common grammatical problems in a file. You may examine various drafts of your previous writing tasks to discern and record examples of these problems. Such a list might include: (1) possessive forms which give you trouble (for instance, 's [apostrophe ''s'']); (2) past tense markers which you frequently omit (for instance, forgetting to put the -ed on the end of certain verbs); or (3) a tendency to use pronouns with unclear reference. Refer to this list first when you begin to edit for grammatical problems.

The following search strategies highlight three main areas of grammatical problems that apprentice writers face: noun and pronoun forms; verb form; subject/verb and pronoun/antecedent agreement. These are by no means the only grammatical areas which deserve attention as you edit, but these are those that the microcomputer can be most helpful in locating. Consult your handbook for other problems or issues with which you need help.

Search Strategies

1. *Noun/Pronoun Forms.* Begin editing with your list of the problems you typically face in noun or pronoun forms. If you tend to misform noun plurals, examine those; if you often struggle with consistency of person in using pronouns, start there. Before doing any general search for noun or pronoun problems, look carefully at your common problems by scrolling through your text sentence by sentence.

a. For plural or possessive formations, in the *search for slot* place "s " ("'s" and a space) "s' " ("'s' " and a space) or " 's" (" 's" and a space), selecting the partial word option. (The space is needed to locate only those items which appear at the end of words, rather than in the middle of a word.) Search globally, noting any misformed plurals or possessives. If you have particular problems with certain formations (for instance, man → man's → men → men's) place these in the search slot as well. Correct any misformations by deleting the inappropriate form and substituting the proper one.

b. For checking consistency in pronoun use and for identifying reference problems, in the *search for slot* place the typical pronouns you use: he/she/it, I/we, they/them, etc. Search globally with each pronoun, carefully noting ambiguous reference, improper form, or shifts in point of view. Correct any faulty use with deletion and substitution of the appropriate form of the pronoun.

2. *Verb Form.* Begin editing with your list of the problems you typically face in verb forms. If you tend to leave off the -ed in the past tense, examine those first; if you often struggle with consistency of tense, start there. Before doing any general search for verb form problems, look carefully at your common problems by scrolling through your text sentence by sentence.

a. For past tense problems, in the *search for slot* place "ed " ("ed" and a space) or "d " ("d " and a space), selecting the partial word option. (The space is needed to locate only those items which appear at the end of words, rather than in the middle of a word.) Search globally, noting any misformed verbs. Correct any misformations by deleting the inappropriate form and substituting the proper one.

b. For checking consistency in tense, in the *search for slot* place auxiliary verbs like: is/are/was/were; had/have/has; would/could/might/may. Search globally with each verb form, carefully noting sudden shifts in tense or point of view. Correct any faulty use with deletion and substitution of the appropriate form of the verb.

3. *Verb and Pronoun Agreement.* Begin editing with your list of the problems you typically face in creating consistent agreement between subject and verb, pronoun and antecedent. If you tend to use plural verbs with collective nouns, examine those; if you often struggle with using plural pronouns with singular antecedents, start there. Before doing any general search for agreement problems, look carefully at your common problems by scrolling through your text sentence by sentence.

For editing agreement problems, in the *search for slot* place selected pronouns (everyone; anybody; who; which; etc.), verbs (to be verbs; has/have/had), or sentence openers (there; it) which may introduce or forecast agreement errors. Search globally, noting any agreement problems between subjects/verbs, pronouns/antecedents. Correct problems by deleting the inappropriate form and substituting the proper one.

EXERCISES

Consult your handbook if you need extra help in correcting errors in the following exercises.

NOUN AND PRONOUN FORMS. Edit the following passages for problems in noun and pronoun forms or pronoun reference ambiguity.

1. During the registration period, students forms will be examined by a committee which check how many times they have changed majors.

2. Burke will not run again for the mayors' office; he said he had had enough complication's in his first term.

3. Who did she give the potatoes to, himself or Mary?

4. Having two television's may seem extravagant, but Rachel and me consider ours indispensible.

5. Cedric is a person whom, it is safe to say, never will come close to reaching his potential.

6. Between you and I, the steaks tasted terrible.

7. The building plans for the conference center and Billie's ideas for duplicating them were unusual; everyone was fascinated by them.

8. Fans of the Michigan Wolverines can't help but get excited when they play Ohio State.

9. It is hard to be unhappy during the holidays, but sometimes it's unavoidable.

10. Riding a bike in busy traffic while wearing earphones can be dangerous for a person. If you really have to have music that person should carrying a transistor radio and turn up the volume. This is a compromise solution that will help him avoid injury.

VERB FORM AND AGREEMENT PROBLEMS. Edit the following sentences and passages for verb form problems and subject/verb, pronoun/antecedent agreement problems.

1. KMOZ, the local top 40 radio station, has finish its 1986 100 Hits Countdown.

2. In her unbias report, Jamie Collins refutes the evidence that Mayor Keck was suppose to get a raise every three years.

3. Many of the concert goers were disappointed that the band play only two encore songs.

4. Jill McTavish will go to the 1988 Olympics for sure. She has complete her training and will naturally be resting this summer. Her fans hoped that she can win it all this time; she come so close in 1986 at the Mid-American Olympic Trials.

5. Tomorrow I go to Slayton, Minnesota. Even before I leave, pack my bags so Joan could drive me to the train station by 6:00.

6. Their discussion will be devoted to an analysis of how much a student must pay for their summer classes.

7. I can't remember if it is Bill or Kathy that bake their own pizza in a large kiln in the backyard.

8. Taylor Gordon and Janis Philby, veterans of the Janitorial Staff, was honored at a retirement party last night.

9. Everyone was excited about their visit to the zoo.

10. New word processing software is available to English department faculty; interested parties should contact his or her Computer Services Representative.

11. The price of coal and other alternative energy sources have climbed this year.

12. A video of duets by Janis Ian and Carly Simon were shown on Public Television last night. A majority of their fans was first introduced to them while in high school.

13. Kate never could use her backhand smash or overhead lob in a match; it was too hard to practice.
14. Canned fruit were placed in the traveller's suitcases.
15. A person shouldn't judge another by their clothes.

MONITORING MECHANICS PROBLEMS

Mechanical errors, that is, errors in spelling, punctuation, abbreviations, and so on, almost more than any other textual problems can communicate an image of "illiteracy" to your readers. A text filled with even a few spelling errors or lapses in punctuation may cause an audience to regard you as an incompetent writer. Editing for mechanical errors becomes, then, an important part of preparing the final copy of a text for the reader.

Editing for mechanical errors can be a tedious and problematic process, especially on-line. As I suggested in the preceding sections, you should create a file which compiles your most common mechanical problems. You may examine various drafts of your previous writing tasks to discern and record examples of these problems. Such a list might include words you frequently misspell or must look up in a dictionary every time you use them, or specific punctuation problems: semicolons; quotation conventions; etc. Refer to this list first when you begin to edit for mechanical problems.

Manuscript form deserves your special attention. It is influenced by many factors, including your instructor's specifications, the particular writing task you are working on, and the discipline or field of study in which you are involved. Since your word processing program will allow you to make many of the formatting decisions at the very end of the writing process, you should pay particular attention to conventions your instructor wishes you to follow in preparing the final copy. *Any* text you prepare for an assignment will require you to make decisions about these features:

MATERIALS. The text should be printed on white, high quality $8\frac{1}{2} \times 11$ paper. (Most computer printer paper measures $9\frac{1}{2} \times 12$ inches *before* its perforations are removed.) The ribbon on the printer should be dark and you should make sure the paper is properly aligned in the printer to allow the margins you have set to be spaced properly on an individual sheet.

MARGINS. On most writing tasks, top and left margins of $1\frac{1}{2}$ inches and bottom and right margins of at least 1 inch are standard. Paragraphs are usually indented eight spaces from the left margins. Check such variables as page length (number of lines per page, usually 66) and number of printed lines per page (usually 55) to make sure that you will be able to accommodate the margins you have set. This is especially important if you are working on a monitor that permits only 40 characters per line.

TITLES. Your instructor may or may not wish you to have a separate title page. Normally, a writer will (1) place such information as name, course, and date on the first page in the upper right-hand corner; (2) triple space and center the title of her text; and (3) double space and begin the text itself.

PAGE NUMBERING. You will normally select the page numbering function from within your word processing program. Rather than typing a page number on each page of your text, you will usually select a "header" or "footer" command which automatically numbers each page of your text. Your instructor may wish you to place the page number at a particular location. The first page does not usually receive a page number. Check your word processing program to determine how to select location and spacing for page numbers. You may wish to add additional information on the same line as the page number, for instance, your last name or the title (or an abbreviated version of the title) of your text.

SPECIAL FORMATS. Your instructor may have a particular style sheet you should follow in preparing your text. He or she may, for instance, require you *not* to *justify* your text or use *italics* to indicate emphasis. You should make sure that decisions like these, as well as the font and type size, are appropriate for the particular writing task you are completing.

EMPHASIS WITH UNDERLINING/ITALICS/BOLDFACE. Your word processing program undoubtedly provides you with a number of options for indicating emphasis in your text. Traditionally, a character, word, phrase, or sentence to which a writer wanted to draw attention was *underlined*. These included such items as titles of books, names of ships, and foreign words and expressions. In printed magazines and books, these usually appear *italicized*. With the newer options in word processing, you can select italics or boldface to accomplish the same task. *Underlining*, however, is still the preferred mode of emphasis by most instructors. You should, then, check with your instructor to see what his or her preferences are before you select italics or boldface as the mode of emphasis.

Since selecting underlining, like italics and other special typefaces and fonts, is a *toggled* function in most word processing programs, that is, something that must be turned on and then off with control characters within the text, make sure that you have "pairs" of the appropriate starting and ending commands for these formating features. Check your word processing user's manual if you have any questions about these functions.

Search Strategies

1. *Spelling.* If you have access to a spelling checker program, you should examine your text, using it to check each word in your text. Even the most exhaustive spelling checker, however, will only tell you if a word you have used matches a word in its dictionary. *It will not tell you if you have correctly spelled the particular word you intended to use.* If, for instance, you have used the word "human" in your text, but you meant to use "humane," the spelling checker will ignore "human," since its dictionary will undoubtedly contain it. There is no substitute for your own word by word scan for spelling errors in your text.

To use your microcomputer helpfully without such software, use the search/replace features in your word processing program. In the *search for slot*, place words, vowel combinations, prefixes, or suffixes which give you particular trouble, selecting the partial word option. Examine each instance of the item to determine if it has been used correctly. If you find a spelling error, correct it using deletion and substitution.

2. *Punctuation*. Punctuation covers a wide range of diacritical marks and characters, including end punctuation (periods, question marks), punctuation within sentences (commas, semicolons, colons) and even within and between words (hyphens, apostrophes, ellipses). Consult your handbook for the specific conventions that govern their use. To use your microcomputer helpfully to identify errors in punctuation, follow these suggestions:

a. In the *search for slot* place each of the punctuation marks that you know you use incorrectly or inconsistently, selecting the partial word option. Search globally, looking carefully at each instance of the particular punctuation mark, determining if it is used properly.

b. Note especially those punctuation marks, such as parentheses, quotation marks, dashes, that require you to use them in pairs. Place this punctuation mark in the *search for slot* and search globally. Make sure that you have used two of each.

3. *Manuscript form*. Manuscript form includes all the conventions appropriate to preparing a text for a particular audience. These include such common conventions as capitalizing the first word of every new sentence to the sometimes subtle rules governing abbreviations and the use of numbers in a text. In editing your text for manuscript errors, you will need to be familiar with the specific kinds of conventions that govern your discipline and your subject matter.

You should be careful to note errors related to word processing features such as toggled functions (underlining, bold print, etc.) that require control characters in the text that turn them on and off. In addition, if your search/replace function allows you to use "wildcard" characters, like "\" (backwards slash) or "*" (asterisk), you may search for unintentionally doubled letters, selecting the partial word option. For instance, in the *search for slot*, you may enter "\ \" which will tell the program to look for any instance of doubled letters. In the sentence above, the program will stop at the "oo" in "look," as well as the "tt" in "letters." It will also uncover, however, characters which are simply typographical mistakes.

EXERCISES

Consult your handbook if you need extra help in correcting these errors in manuscript form.

SPELLING. Edit the following passages for errors in spelling.

1. Its not going to make any difference, but Ted really should have complemented them on the choice of a convention sight. I prefered Buffalo from the start, but Sidney had all ready excepted the advise of the comision.

2. Before the advint of the prenting press, few people could have copys of books. Books were the propertie of an elite group of clergymen and nobles. Learning to read was holy a matter of living in the home of one who's social status was above the middle class. To recieve a well-rounded educasion, one began at the age of sevin, learning Latin grammer and Greek rhetorik. Such training was not availible to young girls.

PUNCTUATION. Edit the following passages for errors in punctuation.

1. After they completed the first draft of the text (which took them forty minutes, the council decided to end the debate on the funding issues—something long hoped for: by the council itself, and by the citizens.

2. Well be leaving on March 14 1987 for Manhattan Kansas if that means anything to you,'' Michael yelled out the door.

3. I dont always agree with Mark he is, after all a stubborn fellow); but I cant help but applaud him for getting that position in the chemistry department.

4. Bring me: those pliers; the hammer—and the two-inch nails.

5. ''Can't you come over, she replied, ''by the end of the month—you promised''!

6. My dad, the city council chair just finished his PhD in agriculture at Louisiana State University.

7. Lucy could have just said, I don't have time for this; instead, she ruined the party, our friendship; and any chance we would take a summer trip again.

8. The train was late nevertheless; Joes parents we're still there to meet him—as they had always promised.

9. Frankly, John's remark that ''Letitia has a ''bad attitude'' toward me'' doesnt make sense (unless you remember his brother once dated her.

10. Be certain that, when you get to Des Moines you call Fred.

11. What we had expected, and what we actually got were two quite different things: even if you like your steaks cooked medium rare.

12. The fire marshalls who had just finished a refresher course in preventing injuries from smoke inhalation had no idea how the infants lungs became filled with smoke, especially since she was not in the room where the fire began.

13. Barth always spoke in clipped terms; I remember the time he told the student leaders: ''It makes no difference. . . . who you vote for, just vote''.

14. The campers were asked to bring; binoculars, sleeping bags, insect repellant; and canteens.

15. The crusade will last only two more nights; which is more than enough time to: clear your schedule; organize a car pool; and (it goes without saying. attend the precrusade volunteers meeting—held at the arena.

MANUSCRIPT FORM. Edit the following passages for errors in capitalization, abbreviations, hyphenation, numeric form, and emphasis.

1. My physician, doctor Morgan, told me that the latest copy of the new england medical journal has an article about german measles.

2. More than two hundred thousand four hundred and twenty-nine people attended the billy graham crusade in warsaw.

3. Mr. and mrs. Felix Duncan request *your presence* at their daughter's wedding. Sheila will marry Professor Galen maxwell.

4. Give me 36 hours and i can find any Missing Person.

5. The New York times reported today that the Union of Soviet Socialist Republics was hosting the 1986 goodwill games.

Edit the following passage for general mechanical errors.

Dear Dr. Gebhardt:

Approximately 2 weeks ago—we sent letters to each of the candidates for a book scholarship an application forms. We excepted them to respond formerly, with these items: three letetrs of recommendation; two copys of their resumes; and several samples of there writing. Well—we have yet to here from any of them, and dont anticipate being able to make a decision until at least February 20 1987.

Anything you can do to speed up this process will be appreciate. As one of our staff recently remarked, ''You would think that students who could get a book scholarship would be anxious to complete the proper form. We have decided to host a seminar about how to complete the form next week at the j. zabriskie concert information center on Forbes drive. Dr Williams and I will both be there to answer student questions however; if this seminar is poorly attended, its possible we will simply cancel the scholarship program itself.

I know that you have played a special part in past scholarship decisions, along with Ms Prentiss coordinator of the student funding program. We desparately need you're help now to see that students are aware of our book scholarship: and to help us locate worthy candidates.

Thanks for you help,

Kevin Xavier

CHAPTER 12

Writing
for Self-expression

This chapter and Chapter 13 each present three writing tasks that your instructor may assign during the term. Before I introduce these assignments, it might be useful here to elaborate briefly on the idea of *global intentions* first presented in Chapter 4.

In composing a draft for the writing assignment at the end of Chapter 2, you already have some experience in writing either a personal narrative or a persuasive essay. Both of these writing tasks represented a different kind of *intention*. In writing the personal narrative, you were expressing yourself—or writing a story about your experiences that would interest your reader. In writing the persuasive essay, you were attempting to convince readers that the position you were taking was valid and that they should adopt it. The global, or overall, intention to write expressively or persuasively guides the writer in making other, local choices in a text.

DEFINING GLOBAL INTENTIONS

After writers spend time in prewriting, they are in a position to compose an actual draft of the text. As I suggested in Chapter 4, writers have intentions, both global and local, in writing their texts. At the *local level,* the writer makes choices about which words to use to convey meaning, how to form individual sentences, whether to use underlining, and so on. At the *global level* the writer makes choices such as what thesis should be explored and what intention will guide that thesis.

Out of these global intentions come the kind of *text* the writer eventually creates. It is helpful for writers to *envision the whole text*—to see its primary nature and to clarify the strategies they should use—as they begin to draft. In *Processing Words* we focus on the two main global intentions in the writing process: expressive intentions and transactional intentions.

Expressive Writing

When you write basically to express yourself, that is, to declare your ideas to yourself or whomever will listen, you create expressive writing. **Expressive writing** proceeds from the writer's desire to "get something off his chest," to suggest opinions, or even to declare allegiance to certain principles. Expressive texts include the following kinds of texts:

> prayers and meditations
> sermons and declarations
> manifestoes
> letters to the editor
> editorials and opinion columns
> journal entries and diaries

In writing expressively, writers focus mainly on their personal stake in an issue, a situation, a relationship, or a circumstance. Of course, the writer wishes to be understood, to be clear, to be forthright, but the primary intention is to get said what the writer feels deeply inside. The intention to be expressive thus causes the writer to ignore some of the considerations one might have in writing a different kind of text, say, a transactional text designed to obtain a refund for a toaster that no longer works. In summary, expressive writing is much more personal, self-focused, and inner-revealing than other kinds of writing.

Some of the texts you will be asked to create will have their origins in personal experience and in personal writing from journals, notes to the self, and personal letters. Even if you have no interest in writing stories or poems ("creative writing"), there will come a time when you will feel provoked to respond—or to declare what is on your mind—to a friend, to an editor of a newspaper, to a group of associates. To express yourself, you will employ an expressive mode of writing.

Transactional Writing

A *transaction* is an exchange or set of activities that occurs between two or more people and which achieves a particular goal. I may agree to buy your car from you for a certain price. When we complete the deal, we have completed a transaction. **Transactional writing** is thus writing in which a writer intends to produce a specific response in an audience.

In transactional writing, self-expression takes a back seat to the clear presentation of information so that the reader may understand and respond appropriately. Transactional writing explains or informs, trains, provides analysis, and persuades a reader. Some examples of transactional texts are: (1) reviews of books and movies, (2) political speeches calculated to win votes, (3) cooking recipes, (4) manuals for repairing automobiles, (5) historical analyses of the causes of war. Most of the writing you will be asked to do in college, and in your future career, will be transactional in nature. Transactional writing is the main focus of Chapter 13.

To better understand how expressive and transactional writing may be distinguished, consider these five different versions of a text that John Bebb might have written about computer printers:

Expressive:

1. *Personal narrative:* How I got interested in computers and ended up knowing a great deal about the printers which may be purchased to facilitate data and information processing.
2. *Opinion text:* I think every college student should own a computer.

Transactional:

1. *Explanatory text:* How to buy a computer printer. (This is the kind of transactional writing John Bebb undertook in his actual essay.)
2. *Analytical text:* How computer printers have evolved to become an essential component in computing.
3. *Persuasive text:* Why every college student should own a computer.

Part of composing a text successfully involves envisioning the whole text as it develops from your prewriting materials. Here is one more template file which will help you complete the planning for a text. When you are ready to begin the drafting of your text, call up this template and complete it to use as a guide to your development:

Intention Template

My thesis is:

My intention in this text is to:

The text which will result from my drafting will be:

	[ ] expressive	or	[ ] transactional
	Choose one:		*Choose one:*
	( ) personal narrative		( ) explanatory text
	( ) opinion text		( ) analytical text
			( ) persuasive text

Expressive Writing Tasks

This chapter presents opportunities to try three kinds of writing tasks: to begin a writing journal, and to experiment with the personal narrative and the opinion text. In Chapter 13 you will discover writing tasks that center on the processes of explaining, analyzing, and persuading. Both chapters contain readings from professional and student writers that help to illustrate these writing tasks and provide you with ideas for your own.

THE JOURNAL

You may think of the journal as a repository of your ideas, impressions, dreams, memories—anything that you want to capture verbally. Your journal may be an actual notebook of some kind, or it may be a diskette which you have reserved just for compiling your thoughts. Your instructor may want you to keep a journal as an additional source of writing practice, or as an additional inventing tool to which you can turn for topic ideas for papers. The journal is for your eyes only: say what you think—do not censor anything or tone anything down. In your journal, tell yourself what you really think. Don't be timid.

If you choose pen and paper to record your journal thoughts, you will want to keep them with you at all times so that you will not miss opportunities for capturing any of your ideas. And you will probably want to take your journal along to any composing sessions on the computer, to jog your memory and stimulate your imagination.

If you use the word processor to keep your journal, you will use it as a "free-writing" record, capturing there your ongoing intuitions and your reflections on daily events and conversations. Below is a journal entry written by one of my students. You will note that she placed the date at the top of her file. After she entered her thoughts she scrolled back to the date and typed in a short phrase that captured the gist of her recorded ideas.

8 January 1987: anticipation spoils

I went to Matt's birthday party—a big letdown. He pretended that I wasn't even there most of the time. That's what you get when you anticipate a great time and end up with a fair one. I should have learned long ago that anticipation spoils the real thing when it comes.

9 January 1987: Too much TV

I never noticed how much TV I've watched since coming to Shaffer dorm. Last night after the evening news I watched a made-for-TV movie, a sitcom about two black families living in Macon, GA, and a police story about a crooked judge who let criminals go without bail all the time. I can remember almost every detail verbatim but I can't quite recall the reading assignment for tomorrow's recreation and parks class.

To get started in keeping a journal—on paper or on the VDT—you may use the following suggestions as stimuli:

1. Describe the most colorful person you encountered today. Why did this person stand out? Did you have a conversation with him or her? What sensory images do you have in remembering this person: visual, smell, taste, touch, sound? Don't leave anything out.

2. Discuss the course or subject matter you are finding most challenging this semester. Is it challenging because of the instructor or because of the material? Do you expect to do well in the course? Have you had a course in this subject before? What have you learned in the course so far?

3. What one thing would you tell a high school senior who is considering coming to your college? What do you wish you would have known before you came? Do you have any regrets about enrolling in the program you're in? How do you feel about living in your present housing?

4. What makes you angry? Is there a particular person who is giving you a hard time? Is there a difficult relationship with which you are struggling? Are there circumstances at home, at a job, or in school that make you lose your temper? Explore the source of your anger— get it all out!

5. Where would you like to be right now if you could be anywhere else? Why? What makes this other location special or attractive to you? Describe its features, atmosphere, unique qualities that draw you to it. What would have to happen to make your visit there a reality and not just a daydream?

THE PERSONAL NARRATIVE

If you chose to write about your own writing process in response to the writing task in Chapter 2, you already have some insights into how a personal narrative works. The personal narrative encourages readers to share your experiences for what they may reveal to the readers themselves. The personal narrative may be autobiographical or may simply be your reflections on relationships, hopes, dreams, or situations which you—or others you know—have faced. The personal narrative starts with the impulse to express what is inside the writer. It may "tell a story" but it does so for the reader's benefit and not the writer's alone.

Composing a personal narrative begins with reflection. A writer remembers a formative event from the first years of college or looks wistfully back on a childhood relationship with a grandparent or unravels the impact of a recent encounter with mortality in the death of a friend. It is "about" the writer in a direct, unassuming way: either an exploration of the writer's life or the writer's response to events and relationships he or she has been a part of, even vicariously. Yet, in being personal, the successful personal narrative does not become merely idiosyncratic rambling, incoherent to the reader.

The writer of a personal narrative must take care, then, to choose subject matter and approaches to that subject matter that remain accessible and meaningful to the reader.

Fig. 12.1 Components of a successful writing process.

COMPONENTS OF A SUCCESSFUL WRITING PROCESS

- *Write to Discover:* Use template files to discover and explore your ideas in search of a topic and thesis.

- *Write to Understand and Communicate:* Write a discovery draft, search for thesis and intention, and analyze the special needs of your audience.

- *Write to Develop and Organize:* Put your ideas into textual form according to your plan and intention.

- *Determine Revising Strategies:* Decide what needs to be done to your text to make it more effective.

- *Write a Second Draft:* Put your revising strategies into action.

- *Evaluate and Revise Again.*

- *Determine if Your Next Draft Is a Final Draft:* If so, proofread and edit it for your reader; if not, revise and draft again.

Obscurity, triviality and irrelevancy are the enemies of the personal narrative writer. Since personal narratives "narrate" or tell a story, you will want to pay particular attention to the way you order the events that you choose to discuss. Keep your readers informed about the direction and purpose of your narrative as you move from event to event and person to person. Be sure to use vivid, concrete language as you describe people, places, and events so the reader can share the same line of sight as you do.

WRITING TASK

Write a personal narrative which explores for your reader a formative experience in your life. Choose an event or a relationship that has affected your life ever since it occurred or began. Select something that has truly had an impact on your life—either for good or for ill—but something that you feel comfortable writing about for "public" consumption. Such experiences might range from the sober (the death of a loved one; the loss of a job), to the sublime (a victory over a handicap; the discovery of a special talent), or to somewhere in between (the first time you heard rock n' roll; your first visit to a zoo).

ACTIVITIES
(AT THE VDT OR ON PAPER)

1. Writing to Discover
    a. *Inventories:* List some experiences and relationships which you regard as formative. Out of this list, choose one or two to explore with further inventories. Or, use a journal entry which seems suitable for further development and exploration.
    b. *Freewriting:* Select one of these experiences and engage in at least two or three freewriting sessions of ten minutes each, focused on the experience you have selected.
    c. *Topoi and TIP:* Use at least one of these structured prewriting tools to explore this experience and narrow the topic for your text.
2. Writing to Understand
    a. *Write a discovery draft:* Expand and explore the topic you identified during your prewriting sessions.
    b. *Discover a thesis:* Sift the discovery draft you've written for a reasonable thesis.
    c. *Discover an intention:* Consider your topic and thesis and determine what purpose your personal narrative has. Is it to teach a lesson? present an insight? report an intrinsically interesting or entertaining event? explain some quality or ability you have?
3. Writing to Communicate
    a. *Consider your audience:* Who are you writing to? What details will be controversial? difficult to explain? need more elaboration?
    b. *Use outlining or nutshelling* to help you discover a plan or structure for organizing your next draft.

4. Revising and Editing

    a. *Compose the next draft of your text.*

    b. *Examine your draft and determine and execute appropriate revision strategies* to make it suitable for your intended readers, using the techniques presented in Chapters 6 through 9. If necessary, repeat steps 2 and 3.

    c. *Proofread and edit your text,* using the techniques presented in Chapter 11 to put your text into final manuscript form.

Sample Texts

The following are two personal narratives. "God's Spy," by Virginia Stem Owens, begins as a reflection upon a mundane incident—sipping coffee in a corner diner—and evolves into a thoughtful consideration of nature, time, and a person's role in making her fellow human beings more aware of life's potential for meaning.

    The second essay, "Bilingualism and Childhood's End," by Richard Rodriguez, is a poignant narrative about a Mexican-American, a holder of a Ph.D. in literature, and his childhood struggle with learning English and its impact on his family relationships and cultural heritage.

    Read each essay carefully as an example of an effective personal narrative. After you have read them, answer the questions that follow in preparation for classroom discussion.

God's Spy[1]
Virginia Stem Owens

(1)   My companion and I sit by the window in a coffee shop, watching snowflakes spin and drift to the solid sidewalk, where they dissolve upon a touch. Faces float past outside the glass wall that separates us from the cold; we scrutinize these visages for the several seconds it takes for them to struggle against the wind and pass out of sight again. We are watching the patterns that the snowflakes, drifting and dissolving, and the faces, intent against the wind, make through this slit in the wall and in time. This space and this moment effloresce before our eyes. We drink them in with our coffee and metabolize the vision in our brains, storing up the images from the refracted light as engrams, memories to ponder, perhaps forever. The crystals of ice, the formulations of faces become transmuted through our attention into other chemical structures swimming in our craniums.

(2)   Essential information is imprinted on both the faces and the snowflakes. That is why we pay our attention, why we watch so closely. Information essential to what makes up the world floats and drifts past the window. A cross-section of the cosmos presents itself for our inspection. Six-sided crystalline frames of ice-stars, a finite shape falling in infinitudes of variations from the leaden sky; the faces, themselves locked within the limitations of their form, yet, like the flakes, never replicated.

---

[1]Excerpt from Virginia Stem Owens, *And the Trees Clap Their Hands,* 2–9. Copyright © 1983 by Wm. B. Eerdmans Publishing Co. and used by permission.

(3)   And something more. The mystery of things. Something we cannot quite see, any more than we can see the six individual sides of each snowflake or the molecules oscillating within the faces. Something else the flakes and faces struggle against as it batters them, impels them, almost without respite, at each moment and at every turn.

(4)   For years my friend and I have both been trying to see this thing like the wind. We observe its effects: the hollows and grooves it has incised across the sheer, reflecting surfaces of faces and into the intricacies of the unresisting snow. But the thing itself eludes our direct vision. Just as the eye of man is made in such a way that it can never behold a bare electron, not even with amplified optical aids, but must rely on the tracks such particles leave behind for any knowledge of their nature, so we can only trace the markings this motion leaves in its wake as it races down sidewalks, down skies, through bloodstreams and brains.

(5)   That is why we sit in coffee shops and scan faces as they filter by unawares on the sidewalk. We are collecting, sorting, storing the data. But we do not call ourselves scientists; we cannot make controlled experiments. In life there can never be a control group. There is only what is—or what presents itself, at any given moment, for our perusal. And we, with our own limitations, can only be in one place and one time at any moment. For this reason we call ourselves spies, for we must strike a trail and stick to it. We must catch as catch can, life being no laboratory, spreading our senses wide and drawing them in again to study what we have managed to snare in the wind.

(6)   We have several covers, my companion and I, business we appear to be about while we are actually always watching for signs of the invisible prey, which is our primary occupation. He, for example, balances church budgets, counsels divorcées and delinquents, writes sermons. But beneath it all is a constant watchfulness, a taking note. Even as he stands in the pulpit, he sifts the faces of the congregation for those fine grains, no larger than the dust of pollen, that carry the spoor of the trail he's on.

(7)   And I sit among them there, internally knitting them up like Madame Defarge, listening, recording, watching, remembering. Softly, softly. The clues one must go on are often small and fleeting. A millimeter's widening of the eye, a faint contraction of the nostrils, a silent exhalation, the slight upward modulation of the voice. To spy out the reality hidden in appearances requires vigilance, perseverance. It takes everything I've got.

(8)   Forty years ago it came easy. Absolutely nothing got by me then. Even now a name, a color, an aroma will come back to me from those early years with extraordinary vividness. These first sensations were not the blunted surface impressions made on a dull brain. They went deep; they sunk in. My neurons must have leapt, exploded, gyred, oscillated in constant reciprocation with phenomena.

(9)   For the child, newborn, is a natural spy. Only his inherent limitations impede him from consuming all the clues of the universe fitted to his perceiving capacities. Sent here with the mission of finding the meaning buried in matter, of locating the central intelligence, he goes about his business briskly, devouring every detail within his developing grasp. He is devoted to discovery, resists sleep in order to absorb more data. Never again will he seek to unearth the treasure buried in the field with such single-mindedness. He has to learn the world from scratch, but the task seems nothing but a joy. Yet gradually, over time, something goes wrong.

(10)   The spy slowly begins to forget his mission. He spends so much time and effort learning the language, adopting the habits and customs, internalizing the thought patterns flawlessly, that somehow, gradually, imperceptibly, he becomes his cover. He

forgets what he's about. He goes to school, grows up. He gets a job, collects his pay, buys a house, waters the lawn. He settles down and settles in. He wakes up each morning with the shape of his mission, what brought him here in the first place, grown hazier, like a dream that slides quickly away. He frowns and makes an effort to remember. But the phone rings or the baby cries, and he is distracted for the rest of the day. Perhaps he forms a resolution to remember; still he seems helpless to keep the shape, the color of his mission clear in his mind. Then one morning he wakes up and only yawns. It must be there somewhere, buried in the brain cells, but at least superficially the memory is erased. The spy goes native.

(11)   I know that over the years I've grown more skilled at analyzing my information. I sort it, sift it, arrange it in various kaleidoscopic patterns until I come up with something I can actually log as significant. Still, I can't help thinking that if I could only regain that early perspicacity—that sharp sight, that ear for inflection, that scrupulosity of scent—I would indeed be in on some central secret, easily and effortlessly, with no need for laborious analysis.

(12)   But living in exile as I do, I must maintain my double existence at all costs. I cannot afford to forget my mission. Forget who you are and you cease to be. You sink down, like the girl in Andersen's fairy tale, beneath the marsh slime into the stifling darkness of a newt-like existence. Blind and barriered.

(13)   There are those who will think they have caught me out. They imagine they have discovered my ruse, that I am using something like allegory, casting myself in the role of spy to make a point. But this is not the case. When I say I am a spy I am in earnest. I intend no coy figure of speech. I am playing no literary tricks.

(14)   My friend and I do indeed sit by the window in the coffee shop. We watch the faces and the snowflakes melting on the sidewalk with just the intensity I have tried to describe. I consider this spying. All the world rushes by and has no idea what we are about, while bits of the central secret of the universe glint from the sidewalk, glance from the liquid surfaces of water and eyes, beat upon my skin.

(15)   I am trying to adjust, as precisely as possible, the focus on this picture of two people sitting at a window. I have falsified nothing in order to make a point—not the setting, not the characters, nothing. This story is not an allegory. I want to tell you what is actually going on here, all around you, instead of the bleared apparition you think you see.

(16)   I give every appearance of being only another unit of the populace. I was verified in the last census. Innumerable times on countless forms for employment, taxes, and credit, I have had to list my occupation, my education, the number and age of my children, where I live. I live in a house indistinguishable from thousands of others across the undulating land. I eat the food, wear the clothes, drive the cars it produces. Nevertheless, I am an alien. My allegiance lies elsewhere. I live in a constant state of treason, disguised.

(17)   I intrigue daily to keep alive my double existence. The effort required is enormous; the pressure to capitulate, unremitting. One is surrounded by those who already have defected, who have either forgotten or renounced the mission that makes them.

(18)   The name of this country we all live in is Time. It is my mission, and that of those who are also implicated in this intrigue, to colonize Time, to salvage what portions we can, to haunt it with memories of its origins, to subvert the population who were all, at one time, spies.

(19)   The life of one in such exile is inexpressibly sad. The Babylonian lament echoes

everlastingly: *How shall we sing the Lord's song in a strange Land? If I forget thee, O Jerusalem, let my right hand forget her cunning.* The threat that hangs over the spy in an alien land is not discovery or persecution, but forgetting Jerusalem, erasing the memories of a distant home, so that he comes to believe that this bleared Babylon is all there is, and nothing lies beyond its borders.

(20)   We all forget to some degree. It seems impossible to maintain a bright and undimmed vision of the Eternal City in the wasting atmosphere of Time. The acid rains of despair wash it, etching away the edges. The image fades, becomes only a figure of speech. We allow ourselves to be convinced that it is less than a memory, a mere wish.

(21)   I spoke of my early years, when I was fresh on the field. That, too, was no figure of speech, no clever attempt to describe childhood. It was a way of escaping Time's perversion of truth, of describing our actual situation here.

(22)   Consider these startling bits of information. A newborn child comes into the world with the apparatus for sight, but not knowing how to use it. Over a period of a few weeks he must learn the skill of seeing. Initially, the bright blurs that strike his retinas have no meaning at all as "things." Yet despite his limited capacities, his primitive equipment for dealing with our Time-bound world, he quickly learns to discern discrete objects. He figures out the fact of three dimensions, that there is more to the world than, literally, meets the eye: that there is another side to all he grasps; that, though invisible, the other side of his ball is round and solid like the side he can see. Most often this knowledge is a delight. He drinks in the world of time and space gladly.

(23)   Compare this eager response of the newborn to that of adults, however, or even older children, who through surgical processes are allowed to see for the first time after a life of blindness. They are most often totally disoriented and almost always terrified by their new sight. It takes not months but years of painful training to do so much as distinguish simple shapes. They seem unable to assimilate the visual information that assails them and make sense of it. Far from learning to see easily and naturally as the newborn does, welcoming each new apparition, they are frightened, often to the point of withdrawal, and beg for the bandages to be replaced over their eyes.

(24)   How to account for the difference? Obviously, the older surgical patients have gotten used to dealing with the world through their other senses. Any change of a long-embedded habit, especially one so basic, is frequently painful. The agony itself is understandable. But the difference in sheer *ability* to learn to perceive visually remains unexplained. Why do those persons fresh to this world learn to see quickly, effortlessly, and exactly, while those with vastly more sophisticated knowledge of its operation, those who are at home here, those who even have language to aid them, find it next to impossible to see?

(25)   The newcomers, of course, still know what they're about. They devour time and space with a voracious appetite. They suck all the world they can hold into their own little sensory vortices and transform it instantly into meaning, for only in the imagination of man does matter become meaning, an even more marvelous transaction than the constant shimmer of matter transmuting into energy and back again. The baby's bath water splashes and drips, the light fractures on its surface, motes dance in the sunbeam—the neurons of the baby's brain map it all ceaselessly, even before a word appears to index the experience.

(26)   God spoke being itself into time. He opened his mouth and out tumbled ions, trees, moons. The newcomer still perceives in the same mode. Directly, immediately,

the accent and syntax of things being-in-themselves. Who else finds water so funny as a baby in his bath? Who else is so absorbed by its amazing properties to disintegrate and fall back together again? Who else is driven to such an extravagance of tears at the yawning hunger of his interior? Sent here to redeem the time—indeed, the entire cosmos—an infant goes about it with a vengeance.

(27)   Years later he won't know what you're talking about. What's so funny about water anyway? He's got a word for it now, and that word "means" water, whereas water itself means nothing at all. He turns aside the questions of his own children as primitive misunderstandings of how the world works. He accepts a cut-rate, impoverished view of himself and all his experience. It all becomes merely—merely matter, merely motion, merely mind, merely water and light and sky. And himself the merest, most trivial part of all. It is hardly his place to go about tearing out raw hunks of time-space, devouring them and converting, contemplating them into meaning. He's no image of God. In fact, his primary occupation, so primary as to be almost unconscious, is to narrow his scope upon the world, to be aware of less and less, to ward off as much sensory experience as possible, and to get whatever he is forced to absorb second-hand, already mediated and masticated for him.

(28)   Instead of colonizing Time, instead of becoming a funnel through which Time flows into Eternity, he is himself colonized, devoured by Time. And Time, unredeemed, is death's dominion.

(29)   It is this fearful possibility of capitulation that the spy labors under. In the midst of apparent, even practiced, insignificance, he must maintain a sense of the value of his mission. Those around him do not feel this burden, this focusing of the cosmos through the lens of their perception. They yawn, they shrug, they turn away. They have a living to make, they say, and rarely consider the import of those words.

(30)   The spy stands among them, indistinguishable and unmarked, no one paying him any mind. Yet against all appearances and the weight of the general inertia, he preserves his infusion of purpose. He knows his mission is urgent.

(31)   Incarnation is not an abstraction, not some distant theological principle. It is reality itself. *Res;* things. Accessible to everyone. It starts with fragrant infants' flesh, blood, breath, and tears, and radiates from that single point to include the whole world. Straw, mites, dung steaming in the chill night air, eyes, stars, smells, songs.

(32)   It is the spy's purpose to raise this actuality to consciousness, to give a tongue to this truth, not because it will not be truth unless he tells it, but because there is no light in a truth untold, and no joy. In apprehending the flying photons, the electrical charges the world is made of, the spy becomes the film emulsion that traces the signs of their passing. And more than that. In the spy's mind, the passings become pattern. He is an anemometer that scores the will of the wind that creates the world. And only when it whistles through such caverns of comprehension is the movement of the spirit recognized as will. For the spy to fail in this mission is to fall himself into a broth of unapprehended being; to fail is to subject creation to futility.

QUESTIONS

1. How does Owens create a vivid picture of what she saw from the coffee shop window? Why is it important that she present these concrete images to the reader?

2. What is it that Owens and her companion are trying to "see"? Why does she say that the two of them are not "scientists" but "spies"?

3. In paragraph 9, Owens suggests that a newborn is a "natural spy"? What does she mean by this? How does this "spy" forget his mission, according to Owens?

4. Toward the climax of the essay (paragraph 28), Owens suggests that the spy eventually is "devoured by Time." In Owens's view is this a positive or negative experience?

5. In the last paragraph, Owens seems to be summing up the point of her essay. What is the spy's mission.

6. What do you think is Owens's intention in relating her personal experience? To convince the reader to become a "spy"? To explore her own struggle with living a "meaningful life"? Does the essay end on an upbeat note in your opinion?

Bilingualism and Childhood's End[2]
Richard Rodriguez

(1)   Supporters of bilingual education today imply that students like me miss a great deal by not being taught in their family's language. What they seem not to recognize is that, as a socially disadvantaged child, I considered Spanish to be a private language. What I needed to learn in school was that I had the right—and the obligation—to speak the public language of *los gringos*. The odd truth is that my first-grade classmates could have become bilingual, in the conventional sense of that word, more easily than I. Had they been taught (as upper-middle-class children are often taught early) a second language like Spanish or French, they could have regarded it simply as that: another public language. In my case such bilingualism could not have been so quickly achieved. What I did not believe was that I could speak a single public language.

(2)   Without question, it would have pleased me to hear my teachers address me in Spanish when I entered the classroom. I would have felt much less afraid. I would have trusted them and responded with ease. But I would have delayed—for how long postponed?—having to learn the language of public society. I would have evaded—and for how long could I have afforded to delay?—learning the great lesson of school, that I had a public identity.

(3)   Fortunately, my teachers were unsentimental about their responsibility. What they understood was that I needed to speak a public language. So their voices would search me out, asking me questions. Each time I'd hear them, I'd look up in surprise to see a nun's face frowning at me. I'd mumble, not really meaning to answer. The nun would persist, "Richard, stand up. Don't look at the floor. Speak up. Speak to the entire class, not just to me!" But I couldn't believe that the English language was mine to use. (In part, I did not want to believe it.) I continued to mumble. I resisted the teacher's demands. (Did I somehow suspect that once I learned public language my pleasing family life would be changed?) Silent, waiting for the bell to sound, I remained dazed, diffident, afraid.

(4)   Because I wrongly imagined that English was intrinsically a public language and Spanish an intrinsically private one, I easily noted the difference between classroom language and the language of home. At school, words were directed to a general audience of listeners. (''Boys and girls.'') Words were meaningfully ordered. And the point was not self-expression alone but to make oneself understood by many others. The teacher quizzed: ''Boys and girls, why do we use that word in this sentence? Could we think of a better word to use there? Would the sentence change its meaning if the words were differently arranged? And wasn't there a better way of saying much the same thing?'' (I couldn't say. I wouldn't try to say.)

(5)   Three months. Five. Half a year passed. Unsmiling, ever watchful, my teachers noted my silence. They began to connect my behavior with the difficult progress my older sister and brother were making. Until one Saturday morning three nuns arrived at the house to talk to our parents. Stiffly, they sat on the blue living room sofa. From the doorway of another room, spying the visitors, I noted the incongruity—the clash of two worlds, the faces and voices of school intruding upon the familiar setting of home. I overheard one voice gently wondering, ''Do your children speak only Spanish at home, Mrs. Rodriguez?'' While another voice added, ''That Richard especially seems so timid and shy.''

(6)   *That Rich-heard!*

(7)   With great tact the visitors continued, ''It is possible for you and your husband to encourage your children to practice their English when they are home?'' Of course, my parents complied. What would they not do for their children's well-being? And how could they have questioned the Church's authority which those women represented? In an instant, they agreed to give up the language (the sounds) that had revealed and accentuated our family's closeness. The moment after the visitors left, the change was observed. ''*Ahora*, speak to us *en inglés*,'' my father and mother united to tell us.

(8)   At first, it seemed a kind of game. After dinner each night, the family gathered to practice ''our'' English. (It was still then *inglés*, a language foreign to us, so we felt drawn as strangers to it.) Laughing, we would try to define words we could not pronounce. We played with strange English sounds, often overanglicizing our pronunciations. And we filled the smiling gaps of our sentences with familiar Spanish sounds. But that was cheating, somebody shouted. Everyone laughed. In school, meanwhile, like my brother and sister, I was required to attend a daily tutoring session. I needed a full year of special attention. I also needed my teachers to keep my attention from straying in class by calling out, *Rich-heard*—their English voices slowly prying loose my ties to my other name, its three notes, *Ri-car-do*. Most of all I needed to hear my mother and father speak to me in a moment of seriousness in broken—suddenly heartbreaking—English. The scene was inevitable: One Saturday morning I entered the kitchen where my parents were talking in Spanish. I did not realize that they were talking in Spanish however until, at the moment they saw me, I heard their voices change to speak English. Those *gringo* sounds they uttered startled me. Pushed me away. In that moment of trivial misunderstanding and profound insight, I felt my throat twisted by unsounded grief. I turned quickly and left the room. But I had no place to escape to with Spanish. (The spell was broken.) My brother and sisters were speaking English in another part of the house.

(9)   Again and again in the days following, increasingly angry, I was obliged to hear my mother and father: ''Speak to us *en inglés*.'' (*Speak.*) Only then did I determine to learn classroom English. Weeks after, it happened: One day in school I raised my hand

to volunteer an answer. I spoke out in a loud voice. And I did not think it remarkable when the entire class understood. That day, I moved very far from the disadvantaged child I had been only days earlier. The belief, the calming assurance that I belonged in public, had at last taken hold.

(10)   Shortly after, I stopped hearing the high and loud sounds of *los gringos*. A more and more confident speaker of English, I didn't trouble to listen to *how* strangers sounded, speaking to me. And there simply were too many English-speaking people in my day for me to hear American accents anymore. Conversations quickened. Listening to persons who sounded eccentrically pitched voices, I usually noted their sounds for an initial few seconds before I concentrated on *what* they were saying. Conversations became content-full. Transparent. Hearing someone's *tone* of voice—angry or questioning or sarcastic or happy or sad—I didn't distinguish it from the words it expressed. Sound and word were thus tightly wedded. At the end of a day, I was often bemused, always relieved, to realize how "silent," though crowded with words, my day in public had been. (This public silence measured and quickened the change in my life.)

(11)   At last, seven years old, I came to believe what had been technically true since my birth: I was an American citizen.

(12)   But the special feeling of closeness at home was diminished by then. Gone was the desperate, urgent, intense feeling of being at home; rare was the experience of feeling myself individualized by family intimates. We remained a loving family, but one greatly changed. No longer so close; no longer bound tight by the pleasing and troubling knowledge of our public separateness. Neither my older brother nor sister rushed home after school anymore. Nor did I. When I arrived home there would often be neighborhood kids in the house. Or the house would be empty of sounds.

(13)   Following the dramatic Americanization of their children, even my parents grew more publicly confident. Especially my mother. She learned the names of all the people on our block. And she decided we needed to have a telephone installed in the house. My father continued to use the word *gringo*. But it was no longer charged with the old bitterness or distrust. (Stripped of any emotional content, the word simply became a name for those Americans not of Hispanic descent.) Hearing him, sometimes, I wasn't sure if he was pronouncing the Spanish word *gringo* or saying gringo in English.

(14)   Matching the silence I started hearing in public was a new quiet at home. The family's quiet was partly due to the fact that, as we children learned more and more English, we shared fewer and fewer words with our parents. Sentences needed to be spoken slowly when a child addressed his mother or father. (Often the parent wouldn't understand.) The child would need to repeat himself. (Still the parent misunderstood.) The young voice, frustrated, would end up saying, "Never mind"—the subject was closed. Dinners would be noisy with the clinking of knives and forks against dishes. My mother would smile softly between her remarks; my father at the other end of the table would chew and chew at his food, while he stared over the heads of his children.

(15)   My *mother!* My *father!* After English became my primary language, I no longer knew what words to use in addressing my parents. The old Spanish words (those tender accents of sound) I had used earlier—*mamá* and *papá*—I couldn't use anymore. They would have been too painful reminders of how much had changed in my life. On the other hand, the words I heard neighborhood kids call *their* parents seemed equally unsatisfactory. *Mother* and *Father; Ma, Papa, Pa, Dad, Pop* (how I hated the all-American sound of that last word especially)—all these terms I felt were unsuitable, not really terms of address for *my* parents. As a result, I never used them at home.

Whenever I'd speak to my parents, I would try to get their attention with eye contact alone. In public conversations, I'd refer to "my parents" or "my mother and father."

(16)   My mother and father, for their part, responded differently, as their children spoke to them less. She grew restless, seemed troubled and anxious at the scarcity of words exchanged in the house. It was she who would question me about my day when I came home from school. She smiled at small talk. She pried at the edges of my sentences to get me to say something more. (What?) She'd join conversations she overheard, but her intrusions often stopped her children's talking. By contrast, my father seemed reconciled to the new quiet. Though his English improved somewhat, he retired into silence. At dinner he spoke very little. One night his children and even his wife helplessly giggled at his garbled English pronunciation of the Catholic Grace before Meals. Thereafter he made his wife recite the prayer at the start of each meal, even on formal occasions, when there were guests in the house. Hers became the public voice of the family. On official business, it was she, not my father, one would usually hear on the phone or in stores, talking to strangers. His children grew so accustomed to his silence that, years later, they would speak routinely of his shyness. (My mother would often try to explain: Both his parents died when he was eight. He was raised by an uncle who treated him like little more than a menial servant. He was never encouraged to speak. He grew up alone. A man of few words.) But my father was not shy, I realized, when I'd watch him speaking Spanish with relatives. Using Spanish, he was quickly effusive. Especially when talking with other men, his voice would speak, flicker, flare alive with sounds. In Spanish, he expressed ideas and feelings he rarely revealed in English. With firm Spanish sounds, he conveyed confidence and authority English would never allow him.

(17)   The silence at home, however, was finally more than a literal silence. Fewer words passed between parent and child, but more profound was the silence that resulted from my inattention to sounds. At about the time I no longer bothered to listen with care to the sounds of English in public, I grew careless about listening to the sounds family members made when they spoke. Most of the time I heard someone speaking at home and didn't distinguish his sounds from the words people uttered in public. I didn't even pay much attention to my parents' accented and ungrammatical speech. At least not at home. Only when I was with them in public would I grow alert to their accents. Though, even then, their sounds caused me less and less concern. For I was increasingly confident of my own public identity.

(18)   I would have been happier about my public success had I not sometimes recalled what it had been like earlier, when my family had conveyed its intimacy through a set of conveniently private sounds. Sometimes in public, hearing a stranger, I'd hark back to my past. A Mexican farmworker approached me downtown to ask directions to somewhere. "¿Hijito . . . ?" he said. And his voice summoned deep longing. Another time, standing beside my mother in the visiting room of a Carmelite convent, before the dense screen which rendered the nuns shadowy figures, I heard several Spanish-speaking nuns—their busy, singsong overlapping voices—assure us that yes, yes, we were remembered, all our family was remembered in their prayers. (Their voices echoed faraway family sounds.) Another day, a dark-faced old woman—her hand light on my shoulder—steadied herself against me as she boarded a bus. She murmured something I couldn't quite comprehend. Her Spanish voice came near, like the face of a never-before-seen relative in the instant before I was kissed. Her voice, like so many of the Spanish voices I'd hear in public, recalled the golden age of my youth. Hearing Spanish

then, I continued to be a careful, if sad, listener to sounds. Hearing a Spanish-speaking family walking behind me, I turned to look. I smiled for an instant, before my glance found the Hispanic-looking faces of strangers in the crowd going by.

(19)   Today I hear bilingual educators say that children lose a degree of "individuality" by becoming assimilated into public society. (Bilingual schooling was popularized in the seventies, that decade when middle-class ethnics began to resist the process of assimilation—the American melting pot.) But the bilingualists simplistically scorn the value and necessity of assimilation. They do not seem to realize that there are *two* ways a person is individualized. So they do not realize that while one suffers a diminished sense of *private* individuality by becoming assimilated into public society, such assimilation makes possible the achievement of *public* individuality.

(20)   The bilingualists insist that a student should be reminded of his difference from others in mass society, his heritage. But they equate mere separateness with individuality. The fact is that only in private—with intimates—is separateness from the crowd a prerequisite for individuality. (An intimate draws me apart, tells me that I am unique, unlike all others.) In public, by contrast, full individuality is achieved, paradoxically, by those who are able to consider themselves members of the crowd. Thus it happened for me: Only when I was able to think of myself as an American, no longer an alien in *gringo* society, could I seek the rights and opportunities necessary for full public individuality. The social and political advantages I enjoy as a man result from the day that I came to believe that my name, indeed, is *Rich-heard Road-ree-guess*. It is true that my public society today is often impersonal. (My public society is usually mass society.) Yet despite the anonymity of the crowd and despite the fact that the individuality I achieve in public is often tenuous—because it depends on my being one in a crowd—I celebrate the day I acquired my new name. Those middle-class ethnics who scorn assimilation seem to me filled with decadent self-pity, obsessed by the burden of public life. Dangerously, they romanticize public separateness and they trivialize the dilemma of the socially disadvantaged.

(21)   My awkward childhood does not prove the necessity of bilingual education. My story discloses instead an essential myth of childhood—inevitable pain. If I rehearse here the changes in my private life after my Americanization, it is finally to emphasize the public gain. The loss implies the gain: The house I returned to each afternoon was quiet. Intimate sounds no longer rushed to the door to greet me. There were other noises inside. The telephone rang. Neighborhood kids ran past the door of the bedroom where I was reading my schoolbooks—covered with shopping-bag paper. Once I learned public language, it would never again be easy for me to hear intimate family voices. More and more of my day was spent hearing words. But that may only be a way of saying that the day I raised my hand in class and spoke loudly to an entire roomful of faces, my childhood started to end.

QUESTIONS

1. What is Rodriguez's quarrel with the supporters of bilingual education? Is it the intention of his essay to attack bilingualism?

2. Rodriguez's essay contrasts the "public language" of the school with the "private language" of home and family. What does each represent to him? What is lost in acquiring the "public language," English?

3. How do Rodriguez's anecdotes about his school experience heighten the reader's identification with him? What is his purpose in spelling out the Anglo pronunciation of his name as *Rich-heard Road-ree-guess?*

4. Paragraph 7 recounts an incident which Rodriguez recalls as "heartbreaking." Why was this such a traumatic experience for him?

5. What was the ultimate effect of Rodriguez's mastering English on his parents and his relationship with them? Does he indicate that the cost was too high?

6. In the last paragraph, Rodriguez suggests that a particular linguistic episode convinced him that his childhood was ending. What was the incident? Why did it have such an impact on him?

THE OPINION TEXT

Most of us read the opinion columns and letters-to-the-editor of newspapers and magazines, for in them people share their direct, honest opinions. An opinion text is probably the purest form of written self-expression in that it declares to the world what you're thinking about a topic, yet it couches your opinion in a way that the reader can understand. An opinion text lets writers "sound off" on a particular topic in order to clarify an issue, declare support for one particular position in a debate, or simply to align themselves with a point of view.

An opinion text, thus, expresses the writer's opinion on a given topic or issue. Though the opinion text most often is found in the op-ed pages of a newspaper—in an editorial or column—people find it important to express their opinions in other forums as well, such as in letters and speeches that require a writer to take a stand.

What distinguishes an opinion text from a persuasive text? Simply this: the writer of an opinion text is primarily concerned with expressing his or her viewpoint, and not—necessarily—with winning people to the writer's views. In other words, the impulse for an opinion text is not to persuade readers to act in certain way or accept a certain proposition, but simply to voice one's personal perspective on an issue or topic.

An opinion text usually concerns the writer's response to a current issue, set of circumstances, or problem. Such texts are frequently impassioned and offer counterarguments to existing or majority sentiments on an issue. For instance, you might write an opinion text in order to express support for—or opposition to—a point of view, a candidate, a course of action, or an existing circumstance. Likewise, you might write an opinion text to clarify the true nature of an issue, separating it from false issues or drawing attention to faulty reasoning.

What makes an opinion text effective? In the opinion text, you must declare your views unambiguously yet compellingly for the reader. The text should be dynamic, direct, and responsible. In one sense, as the writer you do not care what readers "think" about your opinion; your motive is primarily expressive. The style of the text should be lively, provocative, and interesting to read. On the other hand, you want to leave the reader with the impression that your opinion is well-thought out and tempered with reason, judgment, and personal experience. As the writer of an opinion text, you have your reasons—and these reasons should convince the reader of the sincerity and meaningfulness of the opinion stated. Like an effective persuasive text, even the opinion text should avoid distortion of an issue or topic and blatant appeals to prejudice or questionable authority.

WRITING TASK

What campus or community issues start your blood boiling? Are there national issues—social or political—for which you have a provocative, seldom-expressed viewpoint? Select a topic you feel strongly about and craft an opinion text which expresses your viewpoint forthrightly and vigorously, but also in a manner that impresses your reader with its careful reasoning and coverage of the topic's component parts.

ACTIVITIES
(AT THE VDT OR ON PAPER)

1. Writing to Discover
   a. *Inventories:* Make some inventories of issues and beliefs that you feel strongly about. Out of this list, choose one or two to explore with further inventories. Or, use a journal entry which seems suitable for further development and exploration.
   b. *Freewriting:* Select one of these issues or beliefs and engage in at least two or three freewriting sessions of ten minutes each, focused on the one you have selected.
   c. *Topoi and TIP:* Use at least one of these structured prewriting tools to explore this issue or belief, and narrow the topic for your text.
2. Writing to Understand
   a. *Write a discovery draft:* Expand and explore the topic you identified during your prewriting sessions.
   b. *Discover a thesis:* Sift the discovery draft you've written for a reasonable thesis.
   c. *Discover an intention:* Consider your topic and thesis and determine what purpose your opinion text has. Will it declare your support for a person, issue, or course of action? Will it attack the reigning opinion on the subject? Will it attempt to place the issue in a clearer context for debate?
3. Writing to Communicate
   a. *Consider your audience:* Who are you writing to? Will your topic be controversial? difficult to explore? require a special approach?
   b. *Use outlining or nutshelling* to help you discover a plan or structure for organizing your next draft.
4. Revising and Editing
   a. *Compose the next draft of your text.*
   b. *Examine your draft and determine and execute appropriate revision strategies* to make it suitable for your intended readers, using the techniques presented in Chapters 6 through 9. If necessary, repeat steps 2 and 3.

c. *Proofread and edit your text,* using the techniques presented in Chapter 11 to put your text into final manuscript form.

Sample Texts

The following presents two opinion texts. The first was written by George F. Will for his column in *Newsweek.* His essay, "The Indignation Industry," demonstrates his mastery of the brief opinion text. Will presents a pungent, direct thesis, followed by a consideration of an opposing viewpoint and his strong rebuttal.

The second text was written by Chris Abels, one of my students. Chris wrote her text as a letter to the Cleveland *Plain Dealer* in response to an editorial in that newspaper on the topic of teaching creationism in the schools. I have included that editorial at the head of Chris's letter. Chris was concerned that the editorial's tone excluded a thoughtful consideration of an alternative—which she intended her letter to offer.

Read each essay carefully as an example of an effective, provocative opinion text. After your reading, answer the questions that follow in preparation for classroom discussion.

The Indignation Industry[3]
George F. Will

(1)　　　Richard Lamm's thick shock of hair was gray long before he said that dreadful thing, but the reaction to what he said was enough to bleach white anyone's hair. And the reaction illustrated a recurring, growing and dismal aspect of public discourse. The phenomenon is indignation exhibitionism.

(2)　　　America spends a large and growing portion of its wealth on medical care, much of it in the final months of patient's lives. So last year Lamm, then 48, meeting with some health lawyers, said society has ethical questions to answer about prolonging life. It should not automatically allocate scarce resources and technological miracles to produce short extensions of life for persons who are terminally ill. He said we all have "a duty to die and get out of the way with all of our machines and artificial hearts and everything else." He could have given this issue a wide berth. Or he could have touched it with soft, round-edged language that would have caused neither contention nor, of course, reflection. Instead, refusing to prettify things, he used the stern word "duty." What he produced was a Krakatau of indignation.

(3)　　　Part, but only part, of the problem was that he was misquoted as saying the terminally ill and elderly should get out of the way. (One headline was: LAMM TO ELDERLY: DROP DEAD.) The misquotation was quickly corrected and the correction was quickly forgotten, lest it spoil the fun of the folks who were reeling about and acting scandalized. By raising a difficult problem Lamm was exercising leadership. He was rewarded with the stigma of "insensitivity."

(4)   **Blistering Stuff:** Washington is home for many advocacy groups and has an unreasonably high ratio of television cameras to human beings. In Washington when an official says something that might ignite some advocates (for the poor, the teachers, the trout and trees ...) the camera crews fan out, knocking on doors, collecting statements of outrage. The statements come not from the unorganized masses. (Lamm's mail indicated that most elderly Americans think he spoke common sense.) Rather, the really blistering stuff comes from people who specialize in strong feelings, persons whose job is to advocate. No advocate, nervously looking around him, can dare to seem less indignant than the other advocates, lest he seem insufficiently sensitive.

(5)   Do you remember when Ed Meese said there is no hunger in America? No, you do not because he did not say that. He said some people go to soup kitchens because they prefer not to pay for food, and he said he had not seen ''any authoritative figures'' establishing that there are hungry children. Now, he could have raised the issue he wanted to raise—that there is more passion than precision in arguments about poverty; that compassion can stand to be leavened with information—more delicately. But we were off and running in the sensitivity sweepstakes. Many Americans earn their living by striking moral poses. They make neither shoes nor butter nor poetry. They are participants in an unending moral Olympics, a competition in spiritual preening—the more-sensitive-than-thou event. For a week or so Meese's words were a public-works project, providing work for the indignation industry.

(6)   This advisory panel, said Jim Watt jokingly, has ''a black, a woman, two Jews, and a cripple. And we have talent.'' One reason for the firestorm that followed was that Watt was being playful with a piety—with the ethnic and sexual spoils system that has grown behind the euphemism ''affirmative action.'' But his cardinal sin was the word ''cripple.'' Handicapped people understandably do not like that word. But in this case there was not even an opening phase when people pretended that the issue was substantive. It was sensitivity, all the way, which brings us all the way to Bitburg ...

(7)   Whoa! Do not throw this magazine across the room. I raise the wrung-out subject of Bitburg to put that controversy into a pattern. The two low points were when the president suggested we should somehow put the Holocaust behind us and when he seemed to say that many German soldiers were not just victims but as much victims of Nazism as Jews were. His problem was not mere insensitivity, it was stark intellectual chaos. But by the time he got to Bitburg he and his writers had put down on paper, as precisely as the language makes possible, the truth: we should work at remembering the ghastly consequences of Nazism, including the fact that for thousands of young Germans Nazism meant only ''a brutal end to a short life.''

(8)   However, an hour later a leader of the American Jewish Committee was on network television declaring that Reagan ''seems again to be equating the nature of the deaths and the nature of the killings between those who died fighting for Hitler and those who were the victims of Hitler.'' That was simply and flagrantly false: Reagan had done no such thing. Perhaps by then nothing he could have said—he could have spoken as eloquently as Pericles; he could have read a Pizza Hut menu—would have prevented some persons, impelled by the momentum of indignation, from insisting that he had repeated his blunder. It was almost as though Reagan had done something unfair by correcting himself. He had no *right* to recover.

(9)   **Institutional Gridlock:** Our addiction to indignation is going to compound the problems of governance. Already we have institutional gridlock; soon we may have intellectual paralysis. As the inability to write a budget demonstrates, the government

is bound down by thousands of thin but cumulatively immobilizing threads. The government among the client groups is like Gulliver among the Lilliputians. If the trafficking in indignation continues, public discourse is going to become more and more bland and homogenized. Everyone in public life may eventually practice too much self-censorship, lest any thought give some hair-trigger group a pretext for the fun of waxing outraged. The result will be timid, frozen, boring thought.

(10)   On an old radio program a character used to say, "If it makes you happy to be unhappy, then be unhappy." The character was admirably broad-minded, but it is not easy to be so placid about people who, luxuriating in indignation, are infecting public life with a moralism that is shrill, sterile, perfunctory and unconvincing.

QUESTIONS

1. Will opens with an example (Richard Lamm's infamous "duty to die" quotation; paragraphs 1–3). How does this help illustrate the problem he is addressing?

2. What seems to be Will's thesis and intention? Where and how does he reveal it to the reader? How does he establish a frame of reference for the reader?

3. What incidents or individuals does Will choose to help further his intention in the text? Are they relevant and effective?

4. How much of a "presence" is Will in his text, that is, how "objective" or dispassionate does he try to be? Is it distracting for the reader to have Will at his "elbow"?

5. Toward the end, Will argues that our ultrasensitivity makes it harder for officials to govern (paragraphs 9–10). Does this follow from the kinds of evidence that he has presented?

6. What do you believe is Will's stance toward his audience? Does he seem to believe they will be hostile, neutral, or indifferent? Does Will seem to care, in the end, if he convinces the audience, or is he more interested in getting them to think about the issues he has raised?

7. Perhaps Will's text is effective—whether we end up agreeing with him or not—because it is entertaining to read. At what points does Will rely on his wit to keep his reader involved?

Deep in the Books of Texas[4]
Cleveland *Plain Dealer,* Editorial

(1)   When the Texas Board of Education repealed a ruling that effectively had restricted references to evolution in school textbooks throughout the country, it was a fine, albeit belated thing to do. By requiring texts to discuss evolution as "one of several explanations of the origin of man"—the other major one being creationism—Texas had arrogantly challenged science itself, and wrongly influenced the education of millions of pupils.

[4]Reprinted with permission from *The Plain Dealer,* April 17, 1984.

(2)   By nature of economics, the Texas requirement diluted science education across the nation. Texas is one of the largest textbook markets in the country. Publishers eager to win contracts there altered their texts, some so radically that the word "evolution" never even appeared. By doing so, an unknown but surely huge number of children never learned about Darwin and the Beagle, and therefore never learned the foundations of modern biology. That's not education, that's selective revisionism.

(3)   The line between spiritual and temporal theory is not so fine that Texans cannot recognize it. Yet it was only the threat of a lawsuit that caused the board to change its mind. You might presume, therefore, that Texas still favors the creationist cause, which is too bad, because boards of education come and go, while science and religion remain locked, it seems, in eternal battle. It took the Catholic Church some 350 years to recognize the legitimacy of Galileo's theories of astronomy. How long will it take the fundamentalists to recognize Darwin?

(4)   The Texas case reflects a disturbing tendency to confuse belief and fact. Perhaps a good rule of thumb, therefore, is to presume that if a school is not parochial, it should be resolutely secular. Such schools should not be forced to snarl science and theology. Just the opposite is true: They must be defended from religious advocacy with equal vigor. Teaching creationism—or, alternatively, belittling evolution—violates that principle, and consequently violates the right of pupils to receive the best possible education.

Reply to the *Plain Dealer* Editorial[5]
Chris Abels

18 April 1984

To the editor:

(1)   The recent editorial regarding the Texas Public Schools and the teaching of evolution exemplifies the kind of paranoia with which the media meets the idea of "scientific creationism." It is surprising to see so many otherwise rational and considerate spokespersons use a sledge hammer to express their views on what is a fairly innocent concern of many parents and educators. Have we reached a point in time when "belittling evolution" is akin to attacking some ancient, sacred creed? In this case, the editorialist seems as defensive as the most ardent creationist could ever be.

(2)   It is a naive view, in my opinion, to suggest, as your editorial does, that "science" is a settled body of facts, beyond question, and that "religion" is a collection of myths. No one familiar with the work of contemporary scientists like Thomas Kuhn or Michael Polanyi could so facilely equate science with "factuality" and religion with mere "wishful thinking." Science, we now know, has its own mythology, its own metaphors for explaining nature. Research in quantum mechanics has left physicists dazzled with the complexity and variety of the physical world—a world ever more mysterious and mystical, and ever more difficult to describe with so-called "objective

---

[5]Reprinted by the author's permission.

language.'' And to read a work like *The Tao of Physics* is to read a religious book, even though it is written by a trained research scientist. Darwin's reputation itself is now in eclipse in most scientific circles.

(3)   The fact is, our public schools do not give our children a choice between ''the way things really are'' (''Science'') and ''the way a certain percentage of people want it to be'' (''Religion'') as your editorial implies. Instead, our kids really face a choice of two religions. You see, science is itself a religion of sorts, with its own priests (like, say, Carl Sagan), its own saints (like, say, Darwin), and even it own rituals (like, say, its inductive method of research), just as the creationist tradition, rooted in Judaism and Christianity, has. The question becomes, using the language of your editorial, ''Which religion do we want to 'protect' our children from?''

(4)   There is a middle ground in all this, though many believers and committed secularists are not inclined to seek compromise. Let our children at least hear this much when they enter the hallowed halls of their sixth-grade science class or the tenth-grade biology lab:

> Historically, most cultures have believed that the world and the universe was created, and the western heritage, of which we are part, has traditionally accepted the Judeo-Christian creation story as its ''Genesis.'' Science is, however, primarily concerned with what presently *is* and can only offer speculation about origins and destinies. Science provides us with tools for research and methods of analysis. Your conclusions about how the universe originated and what lies ahead must come from your personal value system. No scientist can tell you that.

(5)   Let science put on a somewhat more modest face, for once.

Sincerely,

Chris Abels

QUESTIONS

1. What seems to be Chris's intention in replying to the editorial? What issue in the editorial is she reacting to? Does she want to refute the editorial? clarify the issues involved? offer an alternative view? Which paragraphs in the editorial do you think she is addressing most directly?

2. How does Chris's first paragraph set an appropriate context for what follows? That is, how does it forecast what the rest of the letter will be about?

3. In paragraph 2, Chris refers to two scientists and a certain book by name. Why does she do this? Even if you have never heard of these two scientists or the book, how does this lend credibility to her opinion? How does this second paragraph shift the focus to ''science'' as a ''religion''?

4. Paragraph 3 seems to bring Chris's opinion to the surface. What is her opinion about public schools and the teaching of creationism? Can you tell from this paragraph whether

or not Chris herself is a "creationist"? How effective is her depiction of science as a "religion"?

5. What is the purpose of the final paragraph, with the extended statement of what Chris thinks students should "hear" when they enter the science classroom? What is the meaning of the last sentence?

6. How would you describe the overall tone of Chris's letter? Is it calm and matter-of-fact, or arrogant and snide? Do you believe Chris has succeeded in presenting a clear—and provocative—response to the substance of the original editorial?

CHAPTER 13

Writing to Explain, Analyze, and Persuade

This chapter presents three transactional writing tasks. These tasks are "transactional" because they engage the reader directly, as the writer attempts to put aside purely personal points of view and experience in order to present clear, factual information that the reader can believe and act upon. In writing an **explanatory text,** writers try to explain something clearly and informatively so that their readers can understand it and use it for their own purposes. In writing an **analytical text,** writers try to break a topic into its component parts or evaluate its merits so that their readers can understand how it works or make informed judgments about its usefulness to them. In writing a **persuasive text,** writers try to convince their readers that the evidence they present validates the position or claim their text makes.

THE EXPLANATORY TEXT

You may remember from the discussion of John Bebb's composing process that an explanatory text is one that explains something—its present features, how it works, its effects, its future status and so on. The writer of an explanatory text is generally, then, not preoccupied with sharing personal experience or with advocating specific positions. Rather, the writer's task is to present information inobtrusively so that it can be processed and understood easily by the reader.

Typical explanatory texts include texts that explain how something works, the effects of a particular historical event, the reasons behind a particular decision, the facts behind a certain political situation, and so on. Exposition is the key mode of development used since a writer is inquiring into the nature, history, future, component parts, etc., of a person, object, event or relationship. The explanatory writer is involved in defining terms, classifying and dividing a topic into its various parts, and comparing and contrasting a topic with items like it to "expose" its essential core.

The information readers receive allows them to better understand some aspect of life, provides useful facts that will enable them to make a decision, or simply entertains them by revealing the background of some topic they have been interested in. Usually, the personal experience and qualifications of the writer are irrelevant to the information being presented and explained, since it is the information itself which is central to an explanatory text. Texts entitled *Joe's History of the World* or *Barb's Explanation of the Bay of Pigs Invasion* would suggest somewhat outrageously personal accounts uninteresting to the reader—unless the reader has some compelling interest in Joe's or Barb's views.

The writer's challenge is to remain objective. Unlike personal narrative or opinion texts, explanatory writing is not "about" the writer, but about the central topic of the text. The writer's views of the subject should be kept distinct—and distant—from the information presented. Thus, the explanatory text must be oriented to its readers and their needs in selecting details, organizing and structuring the information, and in the format of the text itself. In regard to the latter, many explanatory texts depend heavily on the use of graphics and special print effects (e.g., boldface) and such textual cues as "headers" to present the information economically and clearly to the reader. Writing with a microcomputer gives the explanatory text writer a number of tools to use in addition to the traditional rhetorical ones. Printing in more than one column, using headers and subheaders for each section of your text, and emphasizing special words or concepts with boldface or italics may be useful to you in crafting your explanatory text.

WRITING TASK

Select a topic that interests you or that you have some experience with, and craft an explanatory text which engages your reader with an interesting and informative presentation. This might be something you know how to do ("Scuba Diving"), some event you have researched ("The Leadership of Anwar Sadat"), some process you can explain ("How to Reupholster an Old Couch"), or some historical circumstance you have an interest in ("Why We Dropped the Bomb on Hiroshima"). Your text should present information objectively, clearly, and directly, and should provide your readers with content that is fresh, relevant, and informative.

ACTIVITIES
(AT THE VDT OR ON PAPER)

1. Writing to Discover
   a. *Inventories:* List some topics you would be interested in as topics for an explanatory text. Out of this list, choose one or two to explore with further inventories.

    b. *Freewriting:* Select one of these experiences and engage in at least two or three freewriting sessions of ten minutes each, focused on the topic you have selected.

    c. *Topoi and TIP:* Use at least one of these structured prewriting tools to explore this topic and narrow the topic for your text.

2. Writing to Understand

    a. *Write a discovery draft:* Expand and explore the topic you identified during your prewriting sessions.

    b. *Discover a thesis:* Sift the discovery draft you've written for a reasonable thesis.

    c. *Discover an intention:* Consider your topic and thesis and determine what purpose your explanatory text has. Will it explain a process so the reader can perform it? Will it detail the circumstances which led to a particular historical circumstance, giving readers insights they can use in interpreting similar events? Will it survey the component parts of some natural phenomenon? Can you answer the question, ''I am explaining x so that the reader can . . .''?

3. Writing to Communicate

    a. *Consider your audience:* Who are you writing to? What details will be controversial? difficult to explain? need more elaboration?

    b. *Use outlining or nutshelling* to help you discover a plan or structure for organizing your next draft.

4. Revising and Editing

    a. *Compose the next draft of your text.*

    b. *Examine your draft and determine and execute appropriate revision strategies* to make it suitable for your intended readers, using the techniques presented in Chapters 6 through 9. If necessary, repeat steps 2 and 3.

    c. Proofread and edit your text, using techniques presented in Chapter 11 to put your text into final manuscript form.

Sample Texts

Following are two explanatory texts. The first essay, ''The Value of Theory Building,'' by Kenneth L. Pike, explains the nature of ''theory'' and discusses why theory is an important and relevant concern of even the most practical person.

    The second essay, ''A Computer Writing Project at a Liberal Arts College,'' by M. Elizabeth Wallace, is a classic explanatory essay; the essay introduces a special program the author initiated in Baltimore public schools to train teachers to use computers in the classroom. Wallace's essay explains how she set up the project and the results that came from it.

    Read each text carefully as an example of an effective, provocative explanatory text. After your reading, answer the questions that follow in preparation for classroom discussion.

The Value of Theory Building[1]
Kenneth L. Pike

(1)   ''Why study theory? Why not just be practical?'' So speak those who fail to realize that the line between theory and practice is blurred—that in many situations only an approach to theory will allow practical results to be obtained in reaching one's goals. Today's practicality is often no more than the accepted form of yesterday's theory.

Value of a Theory

(2)   A theory is like a window. The intellect, in order to get outside itself and to interpret the sense data impinging on the body, needs in advance some kind of idea of the way in which the data may turn out to be organized. Then it can search for pattern. A theory in this sense is *directional*. By looking out of a south window we get one view, but out of a north window a different view. Both lead to partial insight into one's surroundings, but in different directions. Sometimes, however, the same view may be seen through two different windows. Similarly, different theories may each contribute insight into the nature of patterns of language. If we look at the same data through different theories, we may see different aspects of a pattern.

(3)   A theory must be *simpler* than reality if it is to be helpful. It attempts to strip away from attention those items which are not important to the observer *at the moment*. In this way it helps obtain answers to particular questions on a narrow front by simplifying the task of investigation. Only if a theory is simpler than that reality which it is in part reflecting is it useful.

(4)   In physical situations, a model may be physical—a construction, to scale, which can be destroyed or distorted. The model is less expensive to destroy than the real thing would be. Conceptually, on the other hand, a mathematical model may allow one to manipulate in more detail and more extensively some of the characteristics of reality without interference by other characteristics not built into the model. The relation of two plus three does not need apples—or bridges—to clutter the addition process.

(5)   It follows, therefore, that a model allows more *exhaustive* and *systematic* tests for relationships between certain variables than can be handled or isolated with ease in reality itself. By exhausting possibilities of *certain* relationships one can test certain implications of those relationships without the expense involved in trying to test them when other factors interfere.

Weaknesses of a Theory

(6)   Any theory may have a weakness at the point of its greatest strength. Since a theory looks in a particular direction, as in the window illustration, it may tell us nothing about data or characteristics of reality which must be seen from some other vantage point. A scientific theory is good only if it *leaves out wisely* those materials which are relevant to other questions but not to those immediately being answered. But the necessary valuable simplicity of a particular thoery can destroy its usefulness if it happens to leave out data which are in fact at that moment important. Unfortunately, the observer cannot always be sure what is important; a mistake here will hurt him.

(7)   All theories eventually are doomed to be outmoded. A useful theory investigates

---

[1]Reprinted from *Linguistic Concepts: An Introduction to Tagmemics*, by Kenneth L. Pike, by permission of the University of Nebraska Press. Copyright 1982 by the University of Nebraska Press.

a point of interest to a particular observer at a particular time. If the theory is successful, that particular problem will have been solved by it. Interest then switches to other problems, requiring further theory. But these other problems are of the deepest kind only if they involve data deliberately or unintentionally left out by the otherwise successful theory. The next stage of investigation requires a model which is more inclusive. When that one, in turn, has made its contribution, it needs to be replaced by another with wider, or different, perspectives which cover other parts of the physical or conceptual universe.

(8)　　A good theory is like a smooth, clean window. A bad theory may allow us to see, but with excessive distortion, blurring, or a filtering out of some useful information relevant to the task at hand. A window which has wavy glass may distort reality. Nevertheless, if one wishes to look out of a room, one had better have a glass window which is wavy than have no window at all. A dirty window allows one to see something, even though what one sees may be blurred. To have a poor theory is better than having no theory at all.

Selection of a Theory

(9)　　In trying to choose or to build a theory we should seek an organized, systematic arrangement of general principles which will help us to *understand* something about our physical or conceptual world. We wish for insight into the nature of the setting of our lives, our behavior, and the things with which we must cope.

(10)　　Since we want a theory to help us, a theory may be viewed as a conceptual tool. A good theory is a *useful* one. Usefulness, in turn, is relevant to some purpose, to some goal. This implies that theories may be good or bad, relative to the sociological setting in which they are found. A dentist's drill and a steam shovel both are useful for excavation, but not at the same spot. Einstein's theory of relativity may not comprise the most profitable mathematics for designing a culvert—but most of the world's traffic at some time rolls over culverts, whether on rails or at an airstrip.

(11)　　The freight which a linguistic theory may be called on to carry may include the refinement of techniques for teaching foreign languages, the preparation of an alphabet for a preliterate culture, the teaching of freshman composition, and the provision of frames of reference to help us understand the relation of language to culture, of language to psychology or philosophy, or of language to life and action.

(12)　　A theory is most likely to be useful if its results, or predictions, can be easily *tested.* In general, this can be done by two radically different methods: the inductive one works *from* the data toward the theory, and the deductive one works from the theory *toward* the data. Both are useful and effective. In the inductive approach, some available data may be carefully classified as elements appropriate to parts of a guessed-at larger pattern. To test the accuracy of the guess, more data are taken; the analyst then tries to fit these into the pigeonholes of the pattern. If all goes well, one knows he is right—until he is proved wrong.

(13)　　In a deductive, formal approach, one guesses, to reach an idea of a larger pattern, without worrying how that pattern was arrived at. Then, to test the hunch, a formal theory is built and used. Such a theory can be thought of as a kind of intellectual machine with three parts: an initial set of axiomatic sentences containing primitive terms, not defined by the theory; secondly, an interpretation, preferably through mathematical formulas which look from these initial statements toward the observed data; and, third, specific predictions about data to be found. This time one knows one is right—until proved wrong—if a satisfactory number of the data not in hand at the start, but now checked, are just those which the machine predicted should have been there.

(14)   A part of the world which we wish to investigate may be likened to a mysterious old castle. One boy may enter it by scaling the high walls; another, by smashing through a sagging door; a third, by crawling through an old escape tunnel. Their first-stage excited reports to each other seem to describe different, unconnected buildings. Later, after they have met somewhere inside the castle, it becomes clear that each *can* find all the areas reported by the others. Each avenue of entrance, however, has its own peculiar directness. To the dungeon? Use the tunnel!

(15)   While working with data, all scholars from time to time utilize parts of various underlying theories, not just one. They differ in the proportion of energy devoted to each. In publication, on the other hand, a scholar often, but not always, presents all of his conclusions from just one viewpoint. Logical consistency may appear to him to be desirable in the presentation of results, even if it is impossible during the stages in which the data are being *found* and analyzed.

QUESTIONS

1. How does Pike begin his explanatory essay? Is this an effective way to start? What do you think are Pike's assumptions about his audience? When does it become clear what his essay will be about?

2. How carefully does Pike define his terms? Does he leave the reader any doubt about what he is talking about? How does he illustrate the definitions he employs?

3. Pike uses several headers in his text: ''Value of a Theory,'' ''Weaknesses of a Theory,'' ''Selection of a Theory.'' What are their purpose in the essay? How do they guide the reader in understanding Pike's thesis and intention?

4. In staying clear of the information he wishes to present, Pike himself is not ''present'' in the text. Is this effective or not? Upon what ''authority,'' then, does the information of this text rest?

5. At the end of his essay, Pike uses the analogy of an old castle. Is this an effective way of drawing his essay to a close? Would more analogies like this one help or hurt the reader's understanding if they were employed throughout the essay?

A Computer Writing Project
at a Liberal Arts College[2]
M. Elizabeth Wallace

(1)   The KayPro Writing Project (KWP) began the day a physics major, the worst writer in my freshman composition class at Gettysburg College, turned in a completely rewritten, freshly-typed essay two hours after the morning's class. He had not simply

---

[2] From *T.H.E. Journal*, 12 (Oct., 1984), 111–115.

edited his essay, supplying missing commas and correcting misspellings; he had eliminated whole paragraphs and written new ones, had presented his argument more coherently and climactically, had moved related details into the same paragraph and had presented his most telling evidence last.

(2)   "How did you do this?" I gasped, leafing through what was obviously a carefully proofread and flawlessly typed manuscript.

(3)   "Oh, I use the Burroughs mainframe in the basement to do all my essays," he replied. "Then when you ask for a rewrite, it's easier to add stuff and move stuff around and then print it out again."

(4)   Suddenly I knew that my methods of teaching composition were obsolete.

(5)   This was in the Spring of 1981. A year later, rather than renewing my contract in the Gettysburg English department, I left to take a graduate course in computer programming. What I hoped was that I could learn enough to be able to one day set up a computerized writing lab and train teachers how to use such a facility. To do so, however, would require a grant. My efforts to obtain a grant, as well as my experiences with the project I finally launched, may be of interest to others.

(6)   I first submitted a preliminary proposal to the National Endowment for the Humanities (NEH), but the final verdict there was that the project did not have enough humanities content. If we would have students write about Shakespeare, for instance, NEH might be interested, but writing by itself would not suffice. A second proposal, to the National Institute of Education, also failed to meet our needs.

(7)   At this point, two other people got involved in the project, despite the fact that I had not yet obtained funding. Dr. Hermine Saunders, chair of the English Department at Randallstown Senior High School, Baltimore County Public Schools, walked into one of my Catonsville Community College word processing classes. We became friends and, after learning of my grant proposal and sharing my enthusiasm, Dr. Saunders put me in touch with Donna Flynn. Flynn is Baltimore County Public Schools Facilitator of Project Basic, which administers the functional literacy tests required for graduation in the state of Maryland.

(8)   A doctoral student at the University of Maryland, Flynn was looking for a dissertation topic for her Ph.D. During the Spring of 1983, she presented our computer writing project as an ideal research task to her dissertation advisor. She defined the primary research question thus: "Will students failing the statewide writing exam learn to write more effectively in a review composition course with access to the computers, or without them?" Control groups of students in high schools similar to Randallstown, studying in review composition courses under the same curriculum but without computers, would take the writing exam for the second time at exactly the same time as the Randallstown students—who would use computers under our project. The testing instrument was already established and approved as a basis for comparison, before and after.

(9)   In August of 1983, having given up on government funding that apparently would not grant us permanently the equipment we needed, I sent a grant proposal to the KayPro Computer Corp. in Solano Beach, Calif., because the KayPro II was, in my experience, the most cost-effective computer for sophisticated word processing.

Equipment Grant Requested

(10)   I asked for an outright grant of 20 computers, to become the property of Baltimore County Public Schools after the two-year project was completed. Dr. Saunders wrote

one page of the proposal describing the student population at Randallstown Senior High School. Donna Flynn wrote two pages defining the primary research questions for her proposed dissertation on the project, and suggesting further research questions for which other graduate students or Maryland Writing Project personnel might want to collect data.

(11)   Two weeks after I submitted the 12-page proposal, KayPro responded in a positive manner.

(12)   Naively, I thought it was going to be that simple. But from September 1983 until April 1984, I fought to give those 20 computers to Baltimore County Public Schools. Writing a contract that everyone would be willing to sign was an ideal task for a word processor—the contract was rewritten at least five times. I later discovered that Baltimore County Public Schools, one of the 20 largest school systems in the United States, has frequently been offered free computers by various companies wanting the school system to try their wares. However, Baltimore County had always resisted the idea of taking computers for which there was no clearly defined use or curriculum, and approved our project primarily because we had an exact vision of what these computers might make possible in the classroom.

(13)   The structure of the Writing Project is not complex. Authority in matters of staffing and curriculum is entirely in the hands of Baltimore County Public Schools and its office of English Language Arts. An Advisory Council serves as a forum for all those institutions participating in the project—KayPro Computer Corp.; Basically Computers, Inc., their local retailer; Baltimore County Public Schools; Western Maryland College; and Randallstown Senior High School. The Advisory Council also includes experts in related fields and writing program directors in Maryland colleges.

Teacher Training and Project Objectives

(14)   Training teachers for such a project is a ticklish business. The grant proposal required a three-hour graduate course for all participants. Our proposed training course was approved last Spring by the Graduate Affairs Committee at Western Maryland College, a private liberal arts institution of 1,300 undergraduates which also offers graduate work in education. Dr. Saunders wrote a successful grant proposal to the state of Maryland asking for funds to cover tuition for 20 Baltimore County teachers and English supervisors who took the month-long course this past Summer. The class met for two hours each morning in the newly established computer writing lab at Randallstown Senior High School, and was entitled Computers and the Teaching of Writing.

(15)   Several of the teachers who signed up for the class owned their own computers; some had taken programming classes and felt quite comfortable with computer terminology and with BASIC programming. Others were terrified of computers. So the first problem was figuring out how to avoid leaving anyone behind while not boring anyone else or insulting their intelligence.

(16)   Class size for the pilot course was established at 20 teacher trainees per writing class—a size that will be difficult for Randallstown to implement for its high school students. Consider that each teacher has at least five classes daily, and the problem becomes apparent. If only one essay is required per week, the average instructor would be faced with 125 to 150 essays to grade weekly. At the nearly impossible speed of ten minutes per essay, working at peak concentration with no distractions, an instructor would be facing a minimum of 20 hours of paper-grading per week on top of class preparation and eight-hour work days.

(17)   The coordinator of English Language Arts in Baltimore County, Jean Kuhlman, was understandably concerned about the content of the course, which I was to teach; she wanted to know what the texts would be and wanted me to stick to explaining computers, not stray into telling her professionals how they should teach writing. On the other hand, the purpose of the course was to discuss how writing is taught and how it could be better taught with a new tool available—the microcomputer.

(18)   I asked myself what I would find most valuable if I were a high school teacher spending my precious summer hours in the classroom: I would like to improve my own writing; I would like to become more articulate about my own teaching methods and curriculum; and I would like to take away with me lesson plans, detailed ideas for improving curriculum, and a sense that what I do—teaching students to think and write clearly—is important and that I should keep on doing it.

(19)   Based on these considerations the course objectives for each participant were defined as follows:

(1) To master a suitable word processing program, using it for all aspects of class writing assignments—pre-writing, composing, and rewriting—and to observe its effect on these processes.

(2) To write a clear, succinct account of his or her present composition curriculum and then suggest ways a computer could enrich and extend that curriculum.

(3) To prepare some practical, detailed lesson plans for the introduction of word processing to high school students in the context of a writing lab.

(4) To learn how to organize and maintain a computer writing lab.

(5) To work with and evaluate available software for proofreading, editing and instruction in English, and to develop clear guidelines for evaluating or writing educational courseware.

(6) To read a few current texts on writing theory and discuss them with colleagues, weeding out unsound or impossible suggestions and embracing useful or challenging ones, particularly as they might affect the integration of the computer into the classroom.

(7) To share the results of the course with local public school and college administrators and faculty.

Numerous Goals Considered

(20)   Although these may seem to be too many objectives for one three-credit course, it should be noted that they overlap and reinforce one another. Our approaches to achieving some of these objectives deserve description.

(21)   Our attempt to meet our third objective, to formulate detailed lesson plans for introducing word processing and for integrating its capabilities into English curricula, was strengthened by presentations from guest speakers. Two college professors who have already experimented with word processing technologies in the writing classroom were invited. Dr. Leroy Panek of the Western Maryland College English Department described his use of terminals on the college mainframe, a Prime computer with an editor called EMACS, in his freshman composition class. He discussed the problems his students encountered with the new technology, and problems we might expect to run into ourselves. Dr. Larry Bielawski, academic computing coordinator at Frostburg State College in Maryland, spoke about the text he wrote and the accompanying CAI (computer-assisted instruction) pre-writing program he developed to help improve student writing.

(22)   The fourth objective governed the class structure from the first meeting. On the first day, the 20 computers were sitting in their cardboard boxes on the writing lab floor when we arrived. The teachers and supervisors each unpacked and set up their own computer, and assumed responsibility for it for the duration of the course. This was done so that in the event the unit developed odd quirks, they would have learned how to run diagnostics on it, how to check cable connections and software to eliminate common problems and how to describe more unusual problems coherently to a technician. They learned how to use the operating system of the machine to make backup copies of disks, and how to install a program so that it ran properly with a particular computer and printer.

Classes Unusually Hardware-Dependent

(23)   Teaching classes on computers is an unusually hardware-dependent exercise, one for which even the most avid devotee of audio/visual equipment may not be prepared. One student, stuck somewhere in a software program or baffled by a computer failure, can hold up an entire class for a half hour if the teacher is not prepared for such occurrences or doesn't know how to diagnose them quickly. Computer manuals are notorious for not describing what to do when you press the wrong key instead of the one the manual told you to press. A teacher has to know when a problem is minor and solvable, and when to ask for technical help. Thus, a major goal of the course was to give each teacher that sense of control and authority over the computers they would be using in their own classes.

(24)   Objective number five may please teachers even more than students. Many programs exist for checking spelling errors, typos, punctuation mistakes or usage problems. Teachers may at first resist such programs, feeling it is morally weak for a student not to look up his or her own misspellings. However, programs like the Word Plus, SpellStar, Perfect Speller, and the Random House Proofreader allow the teacher for the first time to require papers to be completely rid of typos and spelling errors before they are submitted.

Texts Illustrate Limitations

(25)   The sixth objective, to read a few current texts in writing theory and discuss them with colleagues, not only stimulated our thinking about the teaching of writing, but also helped us understand the limitations of certain computer programs as writing tools. One program we used was Punctuation and Style, part of which is a routine called Phrase that matches a list of approximately 500 overused phrases in its phrase dictionary against those in the essay. If it finds any matches, it will display them and may make a suggestion about eliminating or rewriting the phrase. The manual states that the program is based in part on Richard A. Lanham's book, *Revising Prose,* and on the paramedic method he describes for revising "the Official Style," which is wordy, roundabout, jargon-ridden and euphemistic. Therefore that book was one of our texts, and one of our goals was to establish how faithfully a mechanical program can translate Lanham's skill into action.

Reading of Manuals Is a Skill

(26)   Obviously, there were a few other texts in the course—computer reference and training manuals. Learning how to use a computer manual is a skill in and of itself, and several teachers found themselves overpowered by the desire to rewrite all the

manuals. Certainly, learning firsthand the difficulties inherent in documenting software will benefit some of these teachers as they design new courses in technical writing. One such course has now been initiated at Randallstown that takes advantage of computers not only for writing assignments but for preparing charts and graphs to accompany technical reports.

(27)   Finally, the seventh objective, to share our results with local administrators, was achieved by a local conference held during the last week of class for college and public school faculty and administrators. Members of the KWP Advisory Council were invited to see demonstrations of how the computer was to be used in the writing classroom, and to hear papers on current writing theory and how it might both welcome and resist this new technology. Our hope is to hold a similar conference in the Spring of 1986 near the close of this two-year project to report on its actual success or failure in the classroom, on Donna Flynn's research findings and on remaining research questions.

Three Certainties Emerged

(28)   We have only been able to work out the details that we foresaw; all sorts of unexpected difficulties may crop up in other such courses. There are a few things that are certain, however.

(29)   First, the computer can only do so much. It is a mechanical tool. It can never replace the trained intuition of a good teacher or the instincts of a good writer.

(30)   Second, whether or not student writing improves as a result of this two-year project, teacher morale will have been raised. Not only can proper use of computers reduce or eliminate much of the drudgery associated with painstakingly marking student papers; the mere presence of 20 computers in an English department can provide encouragement to writing teachers who may have felt neglected and undervalued by society.

(31)   Third, as a result of this project, I have come to understand more clearly the problems and challenges of teaching writing in public high schools. I know that through meetings of the Advisory Council and through project presentations at local colleges and high schools, a network of faculty committed to the teaching of writing at both the high school and college levels can evolve to sustain and encourage us all in the important work we do.

(32)   Finally, I believe that whatever the official results on the Maryland State writing exam may be, the thousands of dedicated writing teachers across this country deserve the best tools available for the strenuous and crucial work they do.

QUESTIONS

1. Wallace uses a personal anecdote to begin her explanatory essay. Is it effective or does it distract the reader from what will become her main thesis and intention?

2. Wallace chose to inform the reader about the origins of her project using a narrative of the steps that led up to her writing project. Was this effective? Why is this information relevant to the overall purpose of her essay?

3. Like Pike, Wallace uses "headers" to define different sections of her text. Do these seem particularly useful in her essay, or are they just for show? How do they make the text easier or harder to read?

4. Unlike Pike, Wallace is clearly present in her essay; she uses first-person throughout. Does this detract from the authority of her text? When is it useful, even crucial, to write in first person in an explanatory essay?

5. What is the purpose of Wallace's concluding section? That is, why doesn't the essay end earlier, before the section headed "Three Certainties Emerged"?

6. As a result of reading Wallace's essay, what information do the readers have? How can they use this information?

THE ANALYTICAL TEXT

An analysis surveys a topic, issue, or phenomenon, providing a breakdown of its essential nature, its origins, its component parts, and how they interrelate. Often the writer evaluates the topic according to specific criteria and presents an interpretation or judgment. Analytical texts are often written to assess something's value, to guide the choices of individuals, or to offer an account of how something reached its present status. Thus criteria used in an analytical text must be clearly delineated so that readers understand the premises with which the writer is working. Writers of analytical texts may use both exposition and argumentative structures in organizing and developing the texture of their essays. (Chapter 5 discusses four modes of development, including exposition and argumentation.)

An analytical text has much in common with explanatory texts in that the writer intends to present information to the reader; in fact, the analytical text is a particular *kind* of explanatory text. The analytical text also shares certain similarities with a persuasive text, in that you, as the writer, attempt to persuade the reader of the validity of your analysis, of your strategies for conducting the analysis, and of your criteria for evaluating your data.

The analytical text does differ in one respect from the kind of explanatory text discussed earlier. Analytical texts not only present information—"facts" and "data"— they also explicitly present an *interpretation* of those facts and data. That is to say, analytical texts directly and unapologetically present the results of an analysis and interpret those results for the reader. An *explanatory* text about a novel might describe its main characters, plot, length, how much money it brought to its author, and so on. An *analytical* treatment of a novel, on the other hand, would not merely describe elements of it; it would probe deeply into the effect each of these component parts has on each other, and would interpret the text in terms of theme and significance. The analytical text is not content with the simple presentation of information. It explicitly offers an interpretative context for understanding how each part of something (the novel) works, and how each part effects everything else.

While all explanatory writing unavoidably involves the writer's interpretation of facts, an analytical text brings the interpretative task of the writer to the surface and makes it central to the text. Analysis involves breaking things apart and examining their component parts. It means getting to the heart of what something consists of, what makes it tick, what makes it what it is. It is the opposite of *synthesis*, the process of putting things together to see how they fit, which is a key component of much explanatory writing.

In crafting an analytical text your reader will expect you to (1) make the object and purpose of the analysis clear; (2) explain the strategies and criteria used to analyze and evaluate the subject; and (3) provide a convincing defense of your interpretation of the analyzed data, well supported with meaningful evidence.

WRITING TASK

Choose a topic to treat in an analytical text. It might be a favorite musical group and their latest album, or a movie you have particularly enjoyed or disliked. Or you might choose a controversial historical event, such as the assassination of President Kennedy, and attempt to analyze and interpret the facts surrounding the event (for example, How many assassins were there in Dallas?). Or you might analyze the impact of a particular incident, such as the effect of the Three-Mile Island nuclear disaster on America's enthusiasm for building other nuclear-power plants.

Will your topic require a particular kind of research? Is your analysis manageable within the page length your instructor has set? Craft a text that presents a clear analysis of your topic and interprets the analysis according to relevant and meaningful criteria.

ACTIVITIES
(AT THE VDT OR ON PAPER)

1. Writing to Discover
   a. *Inventories:* List some topics which would interest you as subjects for an analytical text. From this list, choose one or two to explore with further inventories.
   b. *Freewriting:* Select one of these topics and engage in at least two or three freewriting sessions of ten minutes each, focused on the topic you have selected.
   c. *Topoi and TIP:* Use at least one of these structured prewriting tools to explore the topic and narrow the topic for your text.
2. Writing to Understand
   a. *Write a discovery draft:* Expand and explore the topic you identified during your prewriting sessions.
   b. *Discover a thesis:* Sift the discovery draft you've written for a reasonable thesis.
   c. *Discover an intention:* Consider your topic and thesis and determine what purpose your analytical text has. What will your reader be able to do with the analysis and interpretation you have provided? Select a different kind of car? Determine not to invest in a certain stock? Decide to read all of the works by the author you've examined?
3. Writing to Communicate
   a. *Consider your audience:* Who are you writing to? What details will be controversial? difficult to explain? need more elaboration?

b. *Use outlining or nutshelling* to help you discover a plan or structure for organizing your next draft.

4. Revising and Editing

    a. *Compose the next draft of your text.*

    b. *Examine your draft and determine and execute appropriate revision strategies* to make it suitable for your intended readers, using the techniques presented in Chapters 6 through 9. If necessary repeat steps 2 and 3.

    c. Proofread and edit your text, using techniques presented in Chapter 11 to put your text into final manuscript form.

Sample Texts

The following presents two analytical texts. The first, "Cool Cops, Hot Show," by *Time Magazine*'s Richard Zoglin, attempts to analyze the success and popularity of the NBC police drama, "Miami Vice." Explaining how "Miami Vice" is put together and what fans find unique about the show, Zoglin paints a vivid portrait of a television phenomenon.

The second essay, "Jackson Browne: Rock Artist as Pop Prophet," was written by one of my students, Pam Day. Pam analyzes what was then Jackson Browne's latest album, *Lawyers in Love,* and places it in the context of his previous releases. She wrote her essay for an audience familiar with Browne's work but not necessarily aware of his basic themes. Her text is an attempt to portray Browne as a "conscience" in the contemporary music scene.

Read each of these two essays carefully as an example of an effective analytical text. After your reading, answer the questions that follow in preparation for classroom discussion.

Cool Cops, Hot Show[3]
Richard Zoglin

(1)   The rat-a-tat sound of machine gunfire resolves into a pulsing electronic rock beat. Staccato images flash by. A flock of pink-plumed flamingos. Bikini-clad girls on the beach. Race horses bursting from the starting gate. The ocean speeding by under the bow of a boat. And, of course, the familiar art deco logo, glowing in vibrant turquoise and pink.

(2)   If viewers are not sufficiently hopped up by the credit sequence of NBC's *Miami Vice,* chances are they will be before the hour is over. The plots whiz by with a minimum of exposition, the dialogue is tough and spare, the rock music almost nonstop. Characters may be shot in lyrical long shots or bathed in moody lighting or framed against semiabstract pastel backdrops. The local color of South Florida is augmented

by the local colors: flamingo pink, lime green, Caribbean blue. *Miami Vice* has been filmed under what may be the strangest production edict in TV history: "No earth tones."

(3)   A year after its debut on NBC, *Miami Vice*, TV's hottest and hippest new cop show, is reaching a high sizzle. Scheduled on Friday nights opposite CBS's popular *Falcon Crest,* the show languished in the bottom half of the Nielsens for its first few months on the air. But viewers gradually began to take notice of its high-gloss visual style and MTV-inspired use of rock music, its gritty South Florida ambience and the cool charisma of Don Johnson and Philip Michael Thomas, who star as Miami Detectives Sonny Crockett and Ricardo Tubbs. Since the end of May, the show's reruns have finished in the Nielsen Top Ten for ten of eleven weeks. Following the pattern of another innovative cop show that caught on during its first summer of reruns, *Miami Vice* is poised to become TV's next breakthrough hit. "Like *Hill Street Blues* before it, *Miami Vice* has redefined the cop-show genre," says Brandon Tartikoff, programming chief of NBC, the former last-place network that is suddenly doing everything right.

(4)   *Miami Vice* already seems to have supplanted *Hill Street* as the darling of one segment of the TV audience: the Emmy Awards committee. The program has garnered a record 15 Emmy nominations (compared with *Hill Street's* eleven), including ones for best dramatic series and best actor (Johnson). No matter how it fares at the awards ceremony on Sept. 22, the show is changing the way TV looks and sounds. Two new series debuting this month, ABC's *The Insiders* and *Hollywood Beat,* each feature a pair of young crime fighters and a pounding rock score, à la *Miami Vice*. Other *Vice* imitators are currently in the works.

(5)   Perhaps more important, the innovative visual style of *Miami Vice* has helped show TV executives that there are alternatives to the cookie-cutter blandness of most network fare. Says Joshua Brand, a co-creator of *St. Elsewhere* who is co-producing Steven Spielberg's new series *Amazing Stories:* "The success of *Miami Vice* shows that people *do* notice production values, lighting and what comes out of those little television speakers."

(6)   Nor has the show's impact been limited to the TV screen. This month MCA Records will release a *Miami Vice* album containing the show's theme music, several songs used in last season's shows, and three new numbers recorded for the coming season by Glenn Frey, Chaka Khan and Grandmaster Melle Mel. Meanwhile, the show's tropical-chic fashions (especially Don Johnson's typical ensemble of Italian sport coat, T shirt, white linen pants and slip-on shoes) have begun to catch on. "The show has taken Italian men's fashion and spread it to mass America," says Kal Ruttenstein, a senior vice president of Bloomingdale's. "Sales of unconstructed blazers, shiny fabric jackets and lighter colors have gone up noticeably." After Six formal wear is bring out a *Miami Vice* line of dinner jackets next spring, Kenneth Cole will introduce "Crockett" and "Tubbs" shoes, and Macy's has opened a *Miami Vice* section in its young men's department. TV cops have never been so glamorous. Says Olivia Brown-Williamson, who plays Undercover Detective Trudy Joplin on the show: "Who wanted to look like Kojak?"

(7)   The flash and dash of *Miami Vice* has not been universally welcomed. Some critics have objected that the show makes violence alluring by dressing it up in pretty photography; others complain that coherent stories and fully drawn characters have been junked in favor of visual flourishes and a rock beat. Some of the show's creators

admit there is a certain laxness about narrative matters. Says Lee Katzin, who earned an Emmy nomination for his direction of the episode *Cool Runnin'*: "The show is written for an MTV audience, which is more interested in images, emotions and energy than plot and character and words."

(8)   Even the show's much vaunted stylistic breakthroughs can be overrated. Flashy visuals and rock music on the soundtrack were hardly invented by *Miami Vice*—or by MTV, for that matter. They have been staples of artfully directed feature films for a couple of decades. "We haven't invented the Hula Hoop or anything," admitted Michael Mann, the show's executive producer and stylistic guru, in an interview with *Rolling Stone*. "We're only contemporary. And if we're different from the rest of TV, it's because the rest of TV isn't even contemporary."

(9)   Yet at its best, *Miami Vice* has brought to TV a swift and evocative mode of visual storytelling. Points are made through looks, gestures, music, artful composition. In one of the season's best episodes (written by Playwright Miguel Piñero and directed by Paul Michael Glaser, the former co-star of *Starsky and Hutch*), Glenn Frey's song *Smuggler's Blues* both enhances the mood and comments on a tense story in which Crockett and Tubbs pose as drug dealers to set a trap for a vicious kidnapper. In the climactic sequence, the cops race to defuse a bomb that has been wired to Trudy, the detective who has served as bait. After a narrow escape, the culprit is revealed to be a police lieutenant gone bad. "I can smell 'em but I can't understand 'em," says a federal agent involved in the case, as Frey's lyrics chime in: "It's the lure of easy money/It's got a very strong appeal/It's a losin' proposition . . ." In a subtle and moving final shot, the agent drifts out of the frame to reveal Tubbs and Crockett comforting Trudy, the forgotten victim of this dirty but necessary operation.

(10)   In another episode, Crockett's infatuation with a new girlfriend is distracting him from a case involving a gang of murderous youths. One morning he fails to show up for surveillance duty with Tubbs, who as a result is beaten up by a pair of thugs. No words are spoken between the partners; everything is conveyed by looks of recrimination and guilt. Indeed, the pair say nothing at all to each other until Crockett's redemption at the episode's end, when he comes to Tubbs' aid in a tight spot. Again there are no heavy-handed closeups or explicit dialogue, just an understated shot of the pair walking away from the camera arm in arm and a terse final exchange. Crockett: "Want to go fishin'?" Tubbs: "I'd rather go trollin'."

(11)   With its rich, almost operatic texture and stripped-down story lines, *Miami Vice* has brought TV's cops-and-robbers genre back to its roots: the mythic battle between good and evil. Such battles were once commonplace on TV, in westerns like *Gunsmoke* and *The Rifleman,* and in an earlier generation of police shows, from *Kojak* to *The Streets of San Francisco.* In recent years, however, these hard-nosed cops have been replaced by a new band of lighthearted crime fighters, from Tom Selleck in *Magnum, P.I.,* to Angela Lansbury in *Murder, She Wrote.* Even the few "serious" police shows on TV, notably *Hill Street Blues* and *Cagney & Lacey,* are less about black hats vs. white hats than about ordinary folks coping with the stress of extraordinary jobs.

(12)   It took a few episodes for *Miami Vice* to hit its stride. The earliest segments were sprinkled with predictable character exposition and comic relief. Crockett, for instance, was an ex-college football star with a wife suing him for divorce and a "funny" pet alligator named Elvis. Two mid-season changes were crucial. The alligator, along with most of the comic relief, was dropped. And a riveting new character, the brooding Lieut. Castillo (played with remarkable power by Emmy Nominee Edward

James Olmos), joined the show. Castillo, Tubbs and Crockett bear less resemblance to other cop-show protagonists than to classic western heroes—men, in the words of critic Robert Warshow, whose "melancholy comes from the 'simple' recognition that life is unavoidably serious."

(13)   *Miami Vice* is the most intensely serious cop show on TV. The drug smugglers, mob bosses, psychotic youth gangs and smut peddlers who emerge from the underworld each week are the most vividly portrayed evildoers on TV since Eliot Ness squared off against Frank Nitti on *The Untouchables.* Even more striking, however, is the show's depiction of the temptation that evil presents to basically good men. It is no accident that Crockett and Tubbs frequently go undercover, and seem to blend in perfectly when they do. Moreover, the show's most powerful episodes deal with law-enforcement officials who have gone over to "the other side."

(14)   The seeds of this new cop show were planted in mundane TV fashion, in the Burbank, Calif., office of NBC's Tartikoff. Trying to figure out how the network might cash in on the success of rock videos, he had jotted down a few notes to himself; one read simply, "MTV cops." Tartikoff presented the notion to Anthony Yerkovich, 34, formerly a writer and producer for *Hill Street Blues,* who related a movie idea he had been mulling, about a pair of vice cops in Miami. Yerkovich went to the typewriter and turned out the script for a two-hour pilot, originally called *Gold Coast* and later *Miami Vice.*

(15)   Yerkovich (who supervised the first five episodes after the pilot, then left to develop film projects for Universal) was fascinated by South Florida as a setting for his new-style police show. "Even when I was on *Hill Street Blues,* I was collecting information on Miami," he says. "I thought of it as sort of a modern-day American Casablanca. It seemed to be an interesting socioeconomic tidepool: the incredible number of refugees from Central America and Cuba, the already extensive Cuban-American community, and on top of all that the drug trade. There is a fascinating amount of service industries that revolve around the drug trade—money laundering, bail bondsmen, attorneys who service drug smugglers. Miami has become a sort of Barbary Coast of free enterprise gone beserk."

(16)   If Miami was an ideal setting for this new-wave Casablanca, Don Johnson and Philip Michael Thomas were inspired choices as the defenders of law and order. Both were picked only after the network had auditioned dozens of candidates and had twice delayed shooting the pilot. NBC had particular doubts about Johnson, 35, a journeyman actor who had appeared earlier in several unsuccessful pilots. A Missouri native, Johnson made his movie debut at age 20 in *The Magic Garden of Stanley Sweetheart,* and later starred in such films as *A Boy and His Dog* and the TV mini-series *From Here to Eternity.* He has also dabbled in songwriting, collaborating on two numbers that were recorded by the Allman Brothers in their 1979 album *Enlightened Rogues.*

(17)   Johnson's offscreen life has been more eventful. At 22 he began a four-year liaison with 14-year-old Melanie Griffith, the daughter of Actress Tippi Hedren, with whom he had appeared in the movie *The Harrad Experiment.* Later Johnson plunged into drugs and alcohol. "I never drank or did drugs while I was working," he told *People* magazine. "But brother, when they said 'Wrap,' I would try to set the land speed record." Johnson rehabilitated himself with help of his current mate, Actress Patti D'Arbanville, and *Miami Vice* has put him in the fast lane to stardom. Among his upcoming projects are a starring role in next month's NBC mini-series *The Long Hot Summer.*

(18)   For Thomas, 36, *Miami Vice* also marks a career breakthrough after a variety of stage, screen and TV roles. Part Irish, German, American Indian and black ("I'm American gumbo"), Thomas writes poetry, markets a line of women's clothing and peppers his conversation with upbeat spiritual homilies ("If you love anything enough it will give up all its secrets"; "I replenish myself by giving, and it comes back"). Easygoing and exuberant, he is a sharp contrast to Johnson, who is described as meticulous and demanding on the set. "We're like night and day," says Thomas. "Don's like a truck driver, and I'm like an angel that sits up there and watches over everything. Don is real intense; I'm more intuitive. He maps out the way he wants to go. I just do it."

(19)   The most driven performer on the show, however, may be Olmos, who plays the stone-faced Lieut. Castillo. The Los Angeles-born actor won a Tony nomination in 1979 for his supporting role in the play *Zoot Suit* and produced and starred in the 1983 film *The Ballad of Gregorio Cortez.* He has an unusual nonexclusive contract with the series, which enables him to do other work during the season. Yet Olmos approaches his role with almost mystical dedication. "One of the things I have found most exciting about *Miami Vice* is that they have allowed me to play this character the way I wanted to play him," he says. "Castillo is very disciplined, very obsessive in his routines. He is a Ninja warrior. In order to be a very good combatant of crime you have to understand crime. So Castillo walks a very thin line."

(20)   Even a Ninja warrior might have a hard time competing for attention with what many consider the real stars of *Miami Vice:* the music and the visual pyrotechnics. Both are largely the contributions of Michael Mann, who joined the show as executive producer when NBC decided to turn Yerkovich's pilot into a series. Mann had directed the stylish film thriller *Thief* and the TV movie *The Jericho Mile,* as well as creating the TV series *Vega$.* But *Miami Vice* marked his first opportunity to bring a cinematic eye to the small screen.

(21)   "There is a very definite attempt to give the show a particular look," says Bobby Roth, who directed a *Miami Vice* episode last season and is now executive producer of the new ABC series *The Insiders.* "There are certain colors you are not allowed to shoot, such as red and brown. If the script says 'A Mercedes pulls up here,' the car people will show you three or four different Mercedes. One will be white, one will be black, one will be silver. You will not get a red one or a brown one. Michael knows how things are going to look on camera. A lot of it is very basic stuff that has never been applied to TV. For example, Michael carried a water truck around with him on his movie *Thief,* watering the streets down. So I decided to water the streets at night in my episode of *Miami Vice.* You get a different look, a beautiful reflection of moonlight off the pavement."

(22)   With virtually all filming done on location in Miami (at an average budget of $1.3 million per episode, compared with $1 million for a typical cop-show episode), the show goes to unusual lengths to find the right settings and props. "I found this house that was really perfect," says Roth, "but the color was sort of beige. The art department instantly painted the house gray for me. Even on feature films people try to deliver what is necessary but no more. At *Miami Vice* they start with what's necessary and go beyond it."

(23)   The show's directors are encouraged to look for creative ways to use music. "What I wanted to do was not to use music as just background but as psychological subtext, if you will," says Thomas Carter, who directed the pilot episode. "What I

felt was happening to Crockett at one point was he had lost touch with reality. His marriage had fallen apart, and he had discovered that his ex-partner was leaking information to the bad guys. So I said, 'I want to do a sequence with Crockett and Tubbs in a car, lay some music over it, and I think they should drive somewhere.' I came up with the idea of using a Phil Collins tune, *In the Air Tonight.*" The song, combined with striking shots of the street lights glinting off the detectives' sleek black Ferrari, gave the scene a mournful resonance. Says Carter: "That is probably the prototypical *Miami Vice* sequence."

(24)   Unlike other TV shows that have utilized rock music, *Miami Vice* can spend more than $10,000 per episode buying the rights to original recordings, rather than using made-for-TV imitations. The selections have ranged from '50s hits like the Coasters' *Poison Ivy* to recent numbers from Todd Rundgren, U2 and Frankie Goes to Hollywood. The rest of the show's bracing musical score is supplied by Jan Hammer, a Czech-born composer, using sounds stored in a digital computer synthesizer. Working in a state-of-the-art studio in his 150-year-old colonial home near Brewster, N.Y., Hammer composes the score for each episode from a rough cut sent to him by network courier. That is another break with TV tradition. "The old style was for the composer to sit in production meetings, and someone would say, 'Let's put something here,' or 'Let's put something there,'" says Hammer. "We have managed to bypass all that. The only occasional talk with Michael is when he wants even more music."

(25)   The same attention is lavished on the show's fashions. On a typical episode, Crockett and Tubbs wear from five to eight different outfits—always in shades of pink, blue, green, peach, fuchsia and the show's other "approved" colors—from such chic designers as Vittorio Ricci, Gianni Versace and Hugo Boss. "The concept of the show is to be on top of all the latest fashion trends in Europe," says Costume Designer Bambi Breakstone, who has just left for a trip to Milan, Paris and London to pick outfits for the coming season.

(26)   Back in Miami Beach, the show's crew has taken up semipermanent residence in the Alexander Hotel, where the walls are painted peach, the carpet has a magenta stripe, and even the lines in the parking garage have been repainted pink. Some civic leaders were originally unhappy at the prospect of a network-TV series blaring the city's crime problems into living rooms across the nation. But *Miami Vice's* success has quieted most of the naysayers. Miami officials estimate that the production contributes $1 million per episode to the city's economy, and the show may even be boosting the tourist trade. "I like *Miami Vice*," says Mayor Maurice Ferre. "It shows Miami's beauty." Adds William Cullom, president of the Greater Miami Chamber of Commerce: "It has built an awareness of Miami in young people who had never thought of visiting Miami." Since its debut last September, *Miami Vice* has been the No. 1-rated network show among local viewers.

(27)   If summer trends extend into fall, the series may be poised for a long reign in the national Top Ten as well. The two-hour fall premiere episode, shot in New York City and scheduled for Sept. 27, will feature such guest stars as Gene Simmons of Kiss and Peter Allen. The show is also playing a major role (along with such new series as *Amazing Stories* and *The Twilight Zone*) in attracting writers and directors who have previously avoided television. "The old stigma against TV is gone now," says Bobby Roth. "A lot of shows are going to sound better, and they are going to look better. And I think *Miami Vice* is a big reason for that."

(28)   Not everyone is so enthusiastic about the direction *Miami Vice* is taking TV.

"*Miami Vice* is a cop show—very well done and stylish, but still a cop show," says Bruce Paltrow, the executive producer of *St. Elsewhere.* "It's hip and glib, but not very deep." Concedes Creator Yerkovich: "In the long run you can only rely so much on color coding and Bauhaus architecture and the Versace spring catalog." Yet *Vice* may be revving up to move beyond such trendy props. "As soon as they get a handle on the script situation," says Yerkovich, "the show is going to burn rubber." With Crockett and Tubbs at the wheel of their Ferrari, designer jackets whipping in the wind, the TV world had better run for cover.

QUESTIONS

1. Why is Zoglin's beginning paragraph an effective way to start an analysis of a television show like "Miami Vice"?
2. How much knowledge of the show does Zoglin assume his audience has? What does his selection of detail indicate about his sense of audience? Who would be most likely to read and enjoy an article about "Miami Vice"?
3. If you were to list the features of "Miami Vice" that comprise Zoglin's analysis, what would you include?
4. Why does Zoglin bring in discussions of the show's actors? How is this relevant to an understanding of the success or popularity of "Miami Vice"?
5. Other television shows are mentioned in passing in the essay. What purpose does the mention of these other shows serve in the analysis?
6. What, ultimately, sets "Miami Vice" apart as unique, according to Zoglin?
7. If readers were not familiar with the show, what kind of impression would they have of it? If readers *are* familiar with the show, what new information, insights, or appreciation would they have for it?

Jackson Browne:
Rock Artist as Pop Prophet[4]
Pam Day

(1)   Jackson Browne's seventh album, *Lawyers in Love,* reestablished him at the forefront of introspective, brooding rock-and-roll. In the past decade, no rock artist has peered more deeply into the American soul or indicted its materialism and its listlessness more scathingly than Browne. *Lawyers in Love* renews a lyrical tradition begun with his 1972 debut album, *Jackson Browne,* and which continued through such searing audio documents as *The Pretender* (1976) and *Running on Empty* (1977). This tradition was interrupted somewhat by his upbeat but paradoxical 1980 release, *Hold On.* Nevertheless, the emotional tenor of his work has always tilted toward the somber and sardonic. Throughout his eleven-year recording career, Browne has been preoccupied as the poetic chronicler of a cut-flower generation, a reader of the signs of the times, a pop prophet of the road and the sky.

[4]Reprinted by author's permission.

(2)   Browne's six previous releases were filled with apocalyptic visions about the spirit of the age—how our times have drained us and maimed us psychologically and spiritually. He confronts our epidemic of disillusionment with poignant initiation tales, using the weapons of the poet: the dark biblical imagery of the end-times. He leads us through the graveyard of popular culture's optimism, its shallow preaching about war and ecology, love and sex, commitment and revolution.

(3)   Browne's first single, "Doctor, My Eyes," revealed our post-60s syndrome in which we took indifference and irrelevance for granted. "The Road and the Sky," from his second album, captured the ambivalence of a generation which had supposedly avoided the hypocrisy of their elders but lacked the will to behave differently. But the most sustained attack on our moral malaise occurred in Browne's masterful *The Pretender*. Battered and harassed, "caught between the longing for love and the struggle for legal tender," the narrator of the title song from that album asks rhetorically, "What became of the changes we waited for love to bring?"

(4)   If it sounds as if Browne is a humorless artist, moralistic in tone, sermonic in delivery, this is not too far from the truth. At times he is almost unbearably melancholy, yet his songs rarely disintegrate into cheap sentimentality. Browne writes and sings as an "exile in paradox," one who is not at home on planet earth, but who has nowhere else to go. As he characterized it in one memorable lyric, our age is "running on empty," running "blind," running "behind"; breathless, desperate, trying to catch up to some vague standard but not knowing why.

(5)   These are Browne's perceptions of a crumbling culture, and few theologians or preachers have penetrated to the heart and soulessness of our times as authentically as Browne has. No one in our times has painted more vividly the trauma of facing a technological and nuclear future. And this brings me to *Lawyers in Love*.

(6)   If there is any disappointment in this audio document, it is that there are only eight cuts. After Browne's three-year absence from the recording studio, eight songs seems a meagre crop. Still, among the eight are some of Browne's best—and certainly some of his most poignant. Musically, Browne experiments very little, though there is a harder edge to his instrumentation and the synthesizer plays a larger role. In all this, *Lawyers in Love* is vintage Jackson Browne lyrically. He is still asking the hard questions and pointing out the contradictory impulses inherent in our culture.

(7)   Three of the new cuts cover familiar Browne territory: resiliency in love affairs ("On the Day You Fall in Love"); the risks of commitment ("Tender Is the Night"); and the bitter-sweet, cold-hearted world ("Knock on Any Door"). None of these songs comes close to matching the power of Browne's earlier composition, "Here Come Those Tears Again," in confronting these themes. A fourth cut, "For a Rocker," is an unabashed party song, tinged with Browne's familiar melancholy. The rock beat and festive atmosphere of the song hardly disguise the narrator's recognition that the party-goers "exist for one thing only/To escape living lives of the lonely."

(8)   The remaining four cuts represent Browne at his best. "Downtown" is an ode to city life, its syncopations and its symphonies. Reminiscent of his earlier song, "Boulevard," "Downtown" plays a playful tribute to Petula Clark's older tune while celebrating the ambivalence of the city: "The Bible screamers, the plasma donor/Buses, car horns, ghetto blasters/The shouts, the cries of the human disasters." "Cut It Away" is a suitable anthem for our times. Its narrator cries for release from his fruitless search for something beyond the superficial and the tawdry. His is a "desperate heart," whose desire is to cut away "the crazy longing" for "the dream he wanted life to be."

(9)   Finally, there are Browne's two most political songs: "Lawyers in Love" and "Say It Isn't True." The former is a bitter indictment of America's complacency and contentment with coldy materialistic values, "human beings in designer jeans" who are "tuned into Happy Days/Waiting for World War III while Jesus slays/To the mating calls of lawyers in love." "Say It Isn't True" is a chilling song, antinuclear in genre, apocalyptic in tone. One need not be an antinuclear sympathizer to be chastened and rebuked by this song, which implicitly calls upon each listener to "repent" and evaluate his or her own soul in troubled times.

(10)   In the end, Browne and other artists, like Bruce Springsteen, capture the despair and loneliness of the age as effectively as the writer of Ecclesiastes, the biblical book that declares that "all is vanity," unless a person has a reason to live. By his blunt denunciation of our fallen values, Browne is a voice in the wilderness trying to be heard above the clatter of selfish "yuppiedom." For those who have ears to hear, the message could change their lives—and save a world.

QUESTIONS

1. How does Day use the first three paragraphs to set up a frame of reference and focus for her analysis of Browne's new album? Is this opening information crucial, or could it be omitted without damage to the coherence of the essay?

2. Day cites a number of Browne's earlier songs and interprets them for the reader. How do these brief discussions establish the criteria and context for her later analysis of "Lawyers in Love"?

3. Day quotes from portions of the songs she is analyzing. How effective is this? Would a paraphrase of the song work equally as well? What does the reader gain with the presentation of Browne's actual lyrics?

4. What seems to be the purpose of Day's analysis? Does she want the reader to buy Browne's album? Or, is it for listeners who already know a great deal about Browne and wonder whether this album is like his others? How does her intention manifest itself in her selection of details and organization?

5. Throughout her essay, Day focuses on the "prophetic" tone of Browne's song lyrics. If you don't know such words as "apocalyptic," "paradoxical," "listlessness," "melancholy," look them up. How are these words useful to Day in describing Browne's music?

6. Day mentions Bruce Springsteen in the final paragraph. What is the purpose of this mention? Is it relevant to her comments or a distraction?

7. Is Day ultimately successful in her analysis of Browne's album? That is, when readers finish this text do they have a concrete notion about Browne's work and how it fits into the contemporary music marketplace?

THE PERSUASIVE TEXT

The persuasive text—in contrast to the opinion text discussed earlier—is centered in the writer's intention to convince a reader that his or her viewpoint should be accepted. In an opinion text, you as the writer simply wish to express your viewpoint; whether or not your claims are convincing to a reader is much less important. In the persuasive text, however, your primary aim is to convince the reader of your proposition's validity.

The persuasive text is thus designed by the writer to change readers' viewpoints, move them to action, or solidify their support of a particular proposition. As the writer, you want not merely to express a view, but to convince readers that your viewpoint is valid and should be adopted by the readers themselves. A persuasive text is effective when the readers are challenged to consider their own beliefs and are motivated to consider the writer's viewpoints seriously.

Audience analysis is important to any writing task, but it is particularly crucial to effective persuasion. As much as possible, you should anticipate your readers' reaction to the topic, your approach to the topic, your selection of supporting evidence and argumentative strategies, and your own credentials or qualifications for making the case in the first place. In addition, as the writer you need to be aware of your readers' own experiences with the topic and vested interests in the conclusion. Arguing the case that Social Security should be abolished takes on a different character depending on whether your audience is a group of nursing home residents over the age of 62, or a group of midlevel managers in a large corporation.

Much could be said, of course, about argumentative strategies making a persuasive text effective. For example, we could discuss types of fallacies; inductive and deductive argumentation; and Aristotle's notions of ethos, logos, and pathos. For our purposes here, however, the following principles will suffice to guide the writer of a persuasive essay:

1. *The persuasive writer needs to find common ground with his or her reader.* To persuade readers that you should be listened to and taken seriously, you need to establish that you and your readers have a common goal—for instance, the resolution of a particular problem, the determination of a specific course of action, or the election of a certain candidate. In other words, readers need to be assured that they and you have something in common and that you understand, at least somewhat, the point of view that the readers hold.

2. *The persuasive writer needs to state his or her proposition(s) unambiguously and articulate them effectively with supporting detail and definition.* Much of the task of persuasive discourse deals in outlining and defining what is really at issue. As a persuasive writer, you thus must secure the boundaries of the issue you are debating and make sure that readers, whatever their disposition toward the issue, know where you stand. This may require discussion of the history of the issue or circumstance, what others have said or done about it, and how your argumentation fits into that context.

3. *The persuasive writer needs to support his or her proposition(s) with effective, meaningful evidence that emerges from careful research or relevant firsthand experience.* That evidence should be presented to readers in as direct a fashion as possible. In addition, the character of the evidence should be above board: no appeals to questionable authority, blatant prejudice, or unreliable testimony. Likewise, you should avoid personal testimony unless it is compellingly relevant to the issue at hand, and you should disdain altogether what can be called ''bandwagon'' evidence (''Everyone thinks this way . . .'').

The effective persuasive text thus articulates clearly the writer's proposition(s), supplies adequate evidence, and leaves the reader with a clear choice to make, for or against, to act or not to act, to trust or to distrust.

WRITING TASK

What issue or topic interests you? What could you craft a persuasive text about? The issue need not be current. Any debatable topic will do, though something that is currently in the news or is particularly relevant to you or your eventual audience may prove easier to write about. Select something which you can easily garner information about. What will your sources be?

ACTIVITIES
(AT THE VDT OR ON PAPER)

1. Writing to Discover
   a. *Inventories:* List some issues or propositions about which you have a settled position to defend or explore. Out of this list, choose one or two to explore with further inventories of experiences and relationships which you regard as formative.
   b. *Freewriting:* Select one of these issues or propositions and engage in at least two or three freewriting sessions of ten minutes each, focused on the one you have selected.
   c. *Topic and TIP:* Use at least one of these structured prewriting tools to explore this issue of proposition and narrow the topic for your text.
2. Writing to Understand
   a. *Write a discovery draft:* Expand and explore the topic you identified during your prewriting sessions.
   b. *Discover a thesis:* Sift the discovery draft you've written for a reasonable thesis.
   c. *Discover an intention:* Consider your topic and thesis and determine what purpose your persuasive text has. Is it to prompt the reader to a particular action? To convince the reader of your proposition's validity? To clarify the issue in a confusing debate? To suggest an alternative to an already proposed piece of legislation?
3. Writing to Communicate
   a. *Consider your audience:* Who are you writing to? What details will be controversial? difficult to defend? Will you proceed deductively or inductively?
   b. *Use outlining or nutshelling* to help you discover a plan or structure for organizing your next draft.
4. Revising and Editing
   a. *Compose the next draft of your text.*
   b. *Examine your draft and determine and execute appropriate revision strategies* to make it suitable for your intended readers, using the techniques presented in Chapters 6 through 9. If necessary, repeat steps 2 and 3.
   c. Proofread and edit your text, using techniques presented in Chapter 11 to put your text into final manuscript form.

Sample Texts

The following presents two sample persuasive essays. The first, ''Nothing to Look At: Perversity and Public Amusements,'' by Joseph Sobran, tackles the issue of pornography and its effect on society. Sobran, a widely read columnist, argues the proposition that pornography is a detriment to society which eventually wears down its fabric and destroys the family unit.

The second essay was written by Joan Redmond for a faculty newsletter at a large southern state university. Her task was to remind—and persuade—her colleagues of the value of teaching students about their historical heritage without letting the past be consumed or distorted by the present.

As you read the following essays, note carefully the way the authors argue their points and attempt to persuade readers of the validity of their positions. After your reading, answer the questions that follow in preparation for class discussion.

Nothing to Look At:
Perversity and Public Amusements[5]
Joseph Sobran

(1)   For some centuries England was notorious for the cruelty of its entertainments. Two of the most popular amusements were cock-fighting and bear-baiting. In the former, two or more cocks were placed on a large table with sharpened beaks and spurs attached to their legs; in the latter, a blinded bear was typically tied to a stake and fierce dogs were set on him, until he had torn them, or they him, to death. There were variants: in *The Age of Voltaire,* Will Durant quotes an eighteenth-century advertisement promising "a mad bull to be dressed up with fireworks" in a ring, "a dog to be dressed up with fireworks over him, a bear to be let loose at the same time, and a cat to be tied to the bull's tail." Durant also writes of "a game called 'cock throwing' [in which] a cock was tied to a stake and sticks were thrown at it from a distance until it died."

(2)   Public executions too were festive occasions. One diarist, a physician named John Knyveton, recounts an excursion to Tyburn for "some diversion," the hanging of a woman who had stolen three loaves of bread. In his entry for November 4, 1751, Knyveton wrote in part:

On taking our seats [we] found a crowd already gathered, such occasions being quite a holiday for the poor people who live in Oxford Street, and also for those in the village of Paddington and the hamlets along the road leading to Edgeware. A number of the gentry [were] present, standing on the roofs of their coaches, both the gentlemen and the ladies very fine, the bucks dressed as for a rout and the ladies all powdered and patched, monstrous pretty with their scarves and great hats and flowered pannier skirts.

The gallows a big one, to take four at once; but this day only the woman [is] to be hanged, and with her a boy who is to be half hanged and then cut down and whipped through the town as a warning to him against begging. [My friend] George Blumenfield [is] very merry and quizzing the ladies on the coaches, and Mr. Pope kindly sends out to a drawer for cans of liquor for us all, which puts us quite happy to watch the Turning Off. The woman arrives after we had waited some twenty minutes—a young wench,

[5]Reprinted with permission from *Single Issues,* by Joseph Sobran (The Human Life Press, 1983; copyright 1983 by the Human Life Foundation, Inc.).

not ill-favored, driven in a cart tied on to a board so that she might not leap over the side; the hangman greeting her with much cheer and she answered him in kind, so that the crowd and the gentry were Highly Diverted (one buck near me with a vast wig I thought would swoon with mirth), and so she to the Tree and the hangman makes her mount upon a bucket, she being a Vagabond and of no importance, and then fastens the rope about her neck, and she blowing him a kiss, his assistant pulls away the bucket and she fell with a force that must instantly have deprived her of Her Higher Faculties. Was intrigued to see how the body did jerk so that I thought the rope would break.

Then the boy aforesaid, who had been brought there very early so that the execution might prove of instruction to him, was taken up, he squalling in a fashion that made the gentry cry Shame upon his Cowardice and, proving near frantic, the hangman did not trouble to tie him to the tree but threw him to the ground and, encouraged by the shouts from the crowd, did kneel upon his chest and strangle him with a cord, removing same before the boy was dead. Then the rogue was pulled to his feet and a bucket of water splashed over him, and so he was taken to the cart in which the woman came and tied to its tail, two gentlemen nigh our window shouting themselves hoarse with admiration; and the hangman's assistant takes up his whip and the cart moves on, the assistant wielding the rope right shrewdly. The woman was cut down and delivered to her father who had been waiting for her corpse with a barrow; and so the crowd disperses and the gentry drive off, one lady laying her whip about the ears of the father with his barrow for not being out of the reach of her coach. And so to dine with my friends and a very pleasant hour of music and talk afterwards on divers topics. Did learn that the woman hanged was the mother of the boy aforesaid, which I trust will be a lesson to him on the Penalties of An Evil Life.

(3)   "The puritan objected to bear-baiting," wrote Macauley, "not because it gave pain to the bear, but because it gave pleasure to the spectator." Reading Knyveton's diary entry, one feels the maligned puritan had a point. The severity of the law that killed a young woman for petty theft and tortured her son for begging is bad enough. What is really shocking, I submit, is that it should be made a sensational entertainment. "Severity" somehow seems to be the wrong word: it is not the severity but the mad jollity of the proceedings that offends—the smug insensibility that can relish such a spectacle and sum it up as "the Penalties of An Evil Life." The *kind* of pleasure it affords is, or ought to be, beneath humanity.

This would be so even if the poor wretches fully deserved the treatment they received, or even if their suffering was merely simulated. We do not, after all, regard the routine butchering of animals for our food as immoral, but we would hardly consider it proper fare for public viewing either. A few people—mostly philosophers, of course— have inferred from this that we are hypocrites who are ashamed of our treatment of animals; so Jeremy Bentham thought, and he looked forward to the day when men would be civilized enough to acknowledge that animals have rights. "The question," he said, "is not, Can they *reason?*, nor Can they *talk?* but, *Can they suffer?*"

(4)   For Bentham, the relevant criteria of ethical behavior were pleasure and pain, and he explicitly refused to make qualitative distinctions among *kinds* of pleasure and pain: pushpin was as good as poetry, he insisted. This position rules out any classification of pleasures as humane (that is, proper to human nature as such) or bestial. In its views pleasures are only more or less intense. It survives today in what we may call the orgasm ethic: whatever turns you on! And a surprising number of people seem

unable to talk back to the argument that sexual practices or displays of all kinds are legitimate, so long as they occur between (or among) "consenting adults." This line of thought has considerable rhetorical authority, that is, it is deferred to; it represents a sentiment to which most people can't assent, but to which they are too inarticulate and too diffident to offer a serious rebuttal. It wins in public discussion as it were by default.

(5)   Let us consider an extreme case. Let us suppose that one man receives extreme pleasure from seeing another man in extreme pain. Perhaps, on some Benthamite scale, the two sensations cancel each other out; there is no preponderance of good over evil, or of evil over good. But suppose two men receive pleasure from seeing the one in pain; does that justify the infliction of torture? Perhaps the Benthamite will reply that no legitimate pleasure can be taken in another's pain: not in the sense that such a kind of pleasure is wrong, for if pleasure is itself the sole standard of good then it cannot be criticized by any other standard, but in the simple sense that we postulate (let us waive the question on what grounds) that no pleasure should be taken by means of anyone's pain. Still, the evil of inflicting pain would be mitigated, rather than aggra- vated, in proportion to the number of people who took pleasure in it. To put it another way, we might admit that torturing a child could never quite be justified; but as long as sheer pleasure and pain are our coordinates, we should have to say that the evil of doing it would be offset, to some extent, by the fact that a great number of spectators enjoyed seeing it. If through the miracle of television the whole world could enjoy it, so much the better.

(6)   Such reasoning is violently contrary to the ordinary sentiments of moral people. If the whole world could enjoy such a sight, we feel, the whole world would be degraded, and not worth living in. It would make little difference to our disgust if we learned that the agony was simulated, or that the spectators had all witnessed it by accident, turning their sets on fortuitously just as the event occurred so that they were not complicit, as consumers, in producing it.

(7)   For we know that there are certain occurrences which are changed in their nature by the participation of observers; they don't merely "happen" to be seen. What is natural to be done alone becomes affectation under the pressure of self-consciousness before onlookers. To some extent, therefore, the spectator may be by his presence a determinant of what happens before him. The conventions of the theater are obviously based on this fact. All the utterances of characters in a play are intended to be overheard, even when a character is talking to himself. But the essence of a play involves the knowledge that it is mimetic, and we take pleasure not in supposing that it is "for real" but in the excellence of the imitation *as* an imitation. The pleasure of watching a hanging, on the other hand, is vitiated by the suspicion that is not actually occurring.

(8)   Pornography, like displays of torture, depends for its effect on apparent authen- ticity and the absence of stylization. What it shows has to be real. Hence pornographic films are obliged to show males ejaculating, and the more respectable pornographic magazines try to show nude photos of celebrities—people whose identities are known. Hence too the affinity between pornography and cruelty, which appears increasingly in movies of sado-masochism (advertised, by the way, even in the New York *Times*). One can hardly feel respect or affection for people in a film or magazine to whom we are related only by our having a desire to see someone, anyone, stripped of privacy and hence of individuality. As children and adolescents we may have a certain curiosity to see what people look like undressed, but that soon is appeased, and can hardly be

sustaining the multibillion-dollar porn industry. As the increasing tendency to feature women and even children in debased and deviant activities suggests, the appetite for pornography is in large part an appetite, and an insatiable one, for human indignity, for the tearing away of protective veils and manners, for the violation of personality. Human beings can't be fully or rightly known in their immediacy: they must be properly introduced by the multitudinous and complicated ceremonies of civilized societies, with all their attendant restraints. The more you see of someone at a glance, the less of him there is to see. Privacy is based on the presumption that there are recesses in our being to which a too-hasty exposure is an injustice. Obscenity wants to deny this; it is assertively reductive, and it is essential to the kind of pornography that we are flooded with that it have as much verisimilitude as possible. Otherwise its destruction of properly human attributes is fake, too weak for the malignant appetite for dehumanization. Even the anonymous wretches who appear in the stuff must be really depraved, or the customer isn't getting what he paid for. But it does require a certain depravity even to perform an intimate act before strangers. Obscenity isn't simulated, though intercourse may be. Obscenity simply *is*. Its reality is identical with its seeming. It can only authenticate itself by means of generous detail, which means ever-increasing variations in perversity.

(9)   Acts, therefore, which might between lovers alone be expressive of mutual interest, are, as spectacle, inadequate. The "lovers" in a pornographic film aim to gratify not themselves or each other, but the spectator, with whom they are in fact performing an unnatural sex act. They must "prove their love" for him by retaining as little of their privacy, autonomy, and self-respect as possible. In a sense making a pornographic film is the ultimate act of altruism, though not of charity. It is the sacrifice of one's own personality to another's ego.

(10)   It might be thought that pornography might take a higher road and simply record an act of genuine love between a man and his wife. But again, the presence of an observer destroys the intimacy intrinsic to such an act and makes it, so to speak, three-cornered. It becomes, under the circumstances, a different act by virtue of occurring in a different medium: sight.

(11)   Decency for the most part has to do with what is seen. It is concerned with veiling things not because they are evil but because they do not belong to the eye. They must be known in a deeper context of significance. This applies, of course, to many non-sexual matters. One reason public executions would be undesirable is that most people, in a given instance, could not fully know the crime for which the criminal was paying with his life, and so could not apprehend his punishment *except* as a grisly spectacle, which must be either repulsive or, what is worse, morbidly attractive.

(12)   To say that nothing is obscene or indecent may sound like an affirmation of the goodness of all things. But it is really tantamount to saying that nothing is private; or, to put it a little differently, that there are no levels of significance beyond the surfaces of things. Ironically, the "new morality" began with claims based on the right to privacy; now it is hardly possible to pass a newsstand without having one's sense of privacy rudely assaulted. All this goes on in the name of freedom of expression; but although the gift of expression is among man's distinctive attributes, we should be suspicious when we hear it invoked as a slogan by those whose principal contribution to public discussion is to make it crude and gross. We know from personal experience that people express themselves most richly and subtly through their costumes, though of course most intensely in the buff; and it is refinement rather than intensity that we

aim at in our civic life. Public nudity doesn't liberate us; it merely cheapens and trivializes us. And the pleasure it affords is a different kind of pleasure from that we take in the nakedness of a spouse—a low and promiscuous kind, unrelated to affection and devotion.

(13)   Thus there is a very simple reason why we should discourage pornography: its tendency is to lower the tone of society. It is cynical in itself and, we may fairly surmise, the cause of cynical behavior. The common objection, endlessly repeated by social scientists and official commissions, is that we cannot prove a connection between pornography and sexual crimes. That may be. But there are two clear answers to it, either of which is sufficient in itself.

(14)   In the first place, people who make this objection, as John Sparrow has recently pointed out, demand a kind of demonstration that can hardly be made in principle, and which is seldom required in other areas of life in which we nonetheless act on what we think probable. As Aristotle never tires of reminding us, the educated man does not demand a degree of certitude beyond what the subject matter admits of. We cannot prove that anyone ever acted more wisely or nobly for having read *King Lear,* but we don't on that account hesitate to prescribe it for college students. The general presumption is that people's behavior is influenced, one way or the other, however indirectly, by the things they read. That is why we have formal education. Nobody, not even a presidential commission, has called, on similar principles, for the abolition of the liberal arts curriculum. Pornography may even be thought of as an illiberal education.

(15)   This brings me to the second answer. We are concerned with something more than just sex crimes; we must also have regard to the general tone of our society. To make us love our country, Edmund Burke reminds us, our country ought to be lovely. He wasn't talking about beautification campaigns. He was referring to a habitual sense of the fitness of things that ought to infuse our minds and manners: "the unbought grace of life," he called it, in the absence of which we tend to look on each other with selfish contempt. This kind of thing has practical and tangible effects. It would be simplistic to look at our soaring rates of divorce, promiscuity, abortion, rape, and general sexual anomie as the direct effect of allowing the sale of *Playboy* and *Hustler.* But it would be preposterous to suppose that our manners, including our tolerance of aggressive and doctrinaire boors, have no cumulative impact on our attitudes and, ultimately, on our behavior. Life imitates art, as Oscar Wilde quipped. First we put up with the mass-production of degraded images; then we become fatalistic and callous toward the view of women, and the relation of men to women, which they represent; and finally, by degrees, we ourselves sink a little toward the level of the antisocial models and precedents we see on every side. Ceasing to hold our fellow citizens responsible, we find ourselves tempted, even if we possess unusual fortitude, to slacken in our own responsibilities. From the perception that pleasure may be taken anywhere with relative social impunity and with no great disgrace, we advance to the feeling that cheating on a wife is only a minor betrayal; and so a principle bond of social loyalty is weakened. Even if we do not proceed to violate it, there are secondary effects, including a subtle decrease in reverence for it that lets us become more restive and irritable with our spouses rather than invest the energy we should into sustaining the little household harmonies. Many a marriage is poisoned when one of the partners begins to think he owes himself an innocent fling. In such ways the prevalent circumambient levity sows petty discords even when the formalities are kept and no actual

adultery is committed. These tensions simply can't be anticipated in detail. The only way to prevent them is to maintain good sexual manners in daily life. This is what is meant by tone, which society plays its part in supporting. The constant presence of good principle in the modes of esthetics and etiquette trains us to respond graciously in the immediate and unforeseen situation.

(16)   The influence of pornography is not of a sexual nature only, any more than is the love of a husband or wife. It extends to civic relations in general. Various levels of society have their own codes and manners—family, school, club, office, all suggest models of behavior, and tolerate only a certain range of deviations from it if they are to maintain their cohesion. The same is true of the larger social framework within which they exist. Citizens, strangers to each other, must be united by a kind of civic amity (to use John Courtney Murray's phrase); a mutuality of respect based on a somewhat elevated opinion of one another as co-participants in civil society. This requires for its sustenance many delicate conditions, not least among them a decorous code of public conduct carrying in its ordinary gestures and restraints the sense of common human dignity. One word for it is civility. We still recognize as offensive the ultimate symbolic incivility of exposing one's genitals in public; in that area, at least, there seems no hesitation to apply and enforce the sanctions of law, even though the familiar abstractions could as easily justify that sort of thing as the rest of the smut that obtrudes on us. We still do, then, have a consensus, hard as it may be to remind ourselves of that fact. The law might fairly and prudently narrow the limits of tolerance in keeping with both the real consensus and the requirements of civic amity. What is most needed is not a huge crackdown, but an affirmation that there are in fact standards recognized by those who govern. While sufficient legislation already exists, the dithering of its putative enforcers demoralizes those who look to the state for some reflections of ethical norms.

(17)   The moment one proposes legal action in this area one meets several objections. One is that it is not the proper business of the state to legislate morality. That is true enough. But neither is it proper for the state to ignore or militate against the common moral code of its citizens. Various levels of government have differing purviews, but all of them must have reference to right and wrong. In a republican system we do not have paternalistic government creating moral standards where none have existed before. But where a standard of decency has traditionally prevailed, the law should support the public code of its citizens. Of course those citizens themselves, in their capacities as parents, teachers, neighbors, and so on, do most to set the tone. Their political rulers should not be eager to make the community much different from what it collectively makes itself. The state exists to back up society, not to transform it against its grain.

(18)   It is further objected that anti-pornography legislation is unconstitutional. The Supreme Court has never said so, and has frequently held the contrary; but its tendency has been such that people on both sides of the issue regard a totally libertarian ruling as something like the fall of the other shoe. Of course we are always at the mercy of the Court's unpredictable juridical impulses. But the First Amendment has historically co-existed with many inhibitions on absolute free expression: libel laws, truth-in-advertising laws, citations for contempt of court for insolent witnesses, and so forth. As a matter of fact, the intention of the Framers of the First Amendment was very (one might say shockingly) narrow, especially by our present standards. According to Leonard Levy, it was more nearly to preserve a parliamentary privilege than to confer a civil right. In any case, that provision was passed in a world without photographs, let alone motion pictures. If we are entitled to any confident surmises about the intent of

the men who passed it, it is that they would have objected violently to the application of their words to protect the fare of our "adult" cinemas and bookstores.

(19)   But perhaps the most fundamental objection of all is simply that freedom of expression is the most precious of our freedoms, and that no avoidable restriction should be placed on it. The answer to this, if there is one, is that speech, like anything else, is subject to realistic limits, and that displays, especially commercial displays of nude human bodies, are at several removes from speech.

(20)   But I think there is a larger principle to be affirmed here. The discussion of pornography has tended too much, in my judgment, to shuttle between the poles of license and suppression, reflecting a merely negative concern with what may be permitted or tolerated. Surely a civilized society's first concern is not how much uncivilized expression it can put up with, but what kind of expression it should actively favor. The good society, as I think most of us conceive it, consists of men and women who address each other with attention and respect, treasuring the conventions of civility because they treasure each other and the public life they share. And a healthy public life depends on the maintenance of private standards; public life, in fact, is rooted in private life and private morals. The notion that these two can be divorced, that sexual levity is no more serious than tickling, is given the lie by the violence and sadism against women and even children that is now becoming prominent in pornography. When sex is cheapened, life is cheapened; when civility is flouted, humanity is flouted. To suppose that these affronts to manners, manners in the deepest sense of the morality of appearances, can have no great effect on behavior, is merely doctrinaire. Common sense says otherwise. The argument that we can't *prove* a correlation between crime and what a less barbarous age would have called barbarous manners is irrelevant, and rings as hollow as the tobacco producer's argument that we can't *prove* a causal nexus between smoking and cancer. The correlation is there; we have a reasonable certainty of that. No more can be expected.

(21)   Society, after all, is based on love. The family can't survive without the intense loves necessary and proper to family life. The larger society not only cannot survive, it cannot be said truly to exist, without certain more general, though less passionate, loves among its members—particularly that "civic amity" we have mentioned. There is no simple way to keep this alive. But the toleration of gross forms of prurient and violent exploitation—in pornography, bear-baiting, public execution, and what Tom Wolfe has called "pornoviolence"—should never be confused with the humane tolerance of people who care enough about each other to accept, among themselves, conscientious differences. A merely negative permissiveness is no kin to patience rooted in charity, and can signify only a weak and indifferent contempt for those who are insulted, abused, and brutalized by gross indecency. We must not be too dogmatic about drawing lines that can only be charted by prudent judgment. But to shirk altogether the duty of carefully approximating standards is an abdication of civility, and a betrayal, at the civic level, of humanity.

QUESTIONS

1. Sobran begins his essay with a survey of "public amusements" once popular in England. What is his purpose in doing so? How does it set a frame of reference for the central issue of his essay?

2. Sobran takes issue with the "whatever turns you on" ethic of pleasure. What are his reasons for opposing this view? How does he attempt to classify and define "proper" sources of pleasure?

3. In paragraph 12, Sobran broaches the subject of pornography and suggests that it is immoral because it strips the people of their privacy and individuality. How is this classification and definition useful to his overall argument and intention? What does he mean when he says that the appetite for pornography is "an appetite . . . for human indignity"?

4. To what extent does Sobran try to deal with possible objections to his views? How seriously does he treat alternative viewpoints? Is this a strength or weakness in his argument?

5. What, ultimately, seems to be Sobran's intention in writing this essay—that is, of what does he want to convince the reader? That pornography is immoral? That those who oppose pornography should be applauded? That arguments in favor of pornography are weak? Or something else?

6. What assumptions does Sobran make about his audience? Is he writing to the already converted, the indifferent, or the openly hostile? What elements of the essay reveal his sense of audience?

7. Describe Sobran's concluding paragraph. Is it effective? Does it merely repeat his earlier arguments? Or does it offer a rounded summary of his main points?

Backwards to the Future[6]
Joan Redmond

(1)   A friend of mine recently had me review a proposal he had written for a new history course that would be required of all students. Too many of our students, Bob argued, come to college without a core "cultural literacy" that would serve them in understanding their intellectual heritage, including literary allusions to, say, Oedipus's mother or Coleridge's albatross. Bob hoped he could drum up both student and faculty support for a "Challenges of Civilization" course while offending none of the potentially offendable special interest groups represented on campus.

(2)   Who could object to such a course? Plenty of folks, it seems. As Bob explained with concern, "Their objections might be paraphrased like this: To study the 'great ideas' of civilization is to say that some writers, some texts, some ideas are more important than others. To do that is to celebrate and legitimize centuries of oppression, superstition, and chauvinism. To read the past in and of itself without a corrective balance added from the contemporary world is to endorse a literature and a culture dominated primarily by one gender, one culture, one worldview."

(3)   Reduced to its essence, this argument amounts to an undisguised attack on our Western cultural heritage, equating westernness with a particular set of antivirtues. Proponents of this view believe that students reading Plato or Augustine or Rousseau without being reminded that they were part of an elite class—or that they were all

[6]Reprinted by author's permission.

males—might mistakenly believe that something they said was true. But, to my mind, if a course is to deal with the past, then it has to *deal with the past*. If a reader is constantly interrupted and reminded of how much the past is inferior to the enlightened views of the present, she can never quite see what it is that the past has to say, right or wrong.

(4)   Critics of the new course seem to be saying that unless we admit that we are all biased and that something called the "Western view" is at best flawed and at worst oppressive, we cannot really be educating our students about the past. I disagree. While I believe every student arrives at college with a somewhat distorted view of the world which must be challenged and probed, I do not share the view that, therefore, the remedy to this problem is to jettison the preceding 20 centuries or to hold that all worldviews are equally valid or equally interesting. I believe some things are right or wrong no matter who may be looking at them.

(5)   Our finiteness as human beings need not always imply that what we believe is erroneous *in and of itself.* It *does* imply that we all need to be checking our cultural compasses to see whether we—or our culture—is out of step. But it is the peculiar delusion of our era, it seems to me, that if its perspective on a current issue conflicts with one from the past, the past must be wrong.

(6)   I am, perhaps, overly sensitive to the rampant revisionism of our era—the attitude that says now is better mainly because it is now and not then. My hopelessly bankrupt appreciation for and dedication to reading and understanding the past *qua* the past no doubt qualifies me for a number of pejorative epithets. To remark that the "past is slanted," as some of my colleagues do, is only to imply that it is slanted according to a *particular* viewpoint—presumably that of the present—which in turn implies that the present consensus must be the superior of the two, else how could one call the past "slanted"?

(7)   Logically, too much is being smuggled in when one argues that one perspective is "slanted"; the shorthand ("the past is slanted") may too facilely veil an agenda that should be made explicit. Ironically enough, part of the implicit argument for advancing the "cultural literacy" of our students is that we believe we can recognize and transcend the particular slants and mindsets of our own culture precisely by knowing and calling in question the past—and the present in light of the past. Anything less inevitably yields political and philosophical determinism.

(8)   But such a critique is possible only when we let the past speak for itself. That we feel compelled or obliged to call in question ideas of the past does not mean that we have license to make an archaeological trek into the anatomy or psyche of the author in order to dismiss any text *a priori*. The fact is, we live too often chained to the present and mortgaged to the future—captives of twentieth-century dogma about roles, about political platforms, about the "good society."

(9)   I confess that I find the twentieth century remarkable in its arrogance toward the past. The most attractive feature of the proposed "Challenges of Civilization" curriculum for me is that it might assist us in overcoming our "chronological snobbery," our tendency to equate currently popular beliefs and philosophies with the ultimate truth about humankind and its destiny. If the last fifteen years are any measure, we have become a people prepared to embrace any social current, any religious impulse, any political action as long as it has no roots in the past.

(10)   In the end, Bob's proposal for a course to teach students about the foundations of their culture is an audacious one in modern education precisely because it dares to

say that the past is as important a part of the present as anything said or done in the last twenty minutes. Only free, unencumbered contemplation of the past and its texts—free, that is, from ideology imported and imposed from the present—can liberate us from sacred cows and cherished notions that perhaps need to be challenged.

(11)   My students seem to know this intuitively. After spending some time with my colleagues, however, I am shocked to discover that it is not just one's students that live unexamined lives.

QUESTIONS

1. What claim does Joan Redmond wish to argue in her essay? How does she attempt to create a common ground with the reader?

2. What does Redmond mean by "westernness"? How does she feel it is under attack? What evidence does she offer? Does she seem to be fair in paraphrasing the arguments of those who are critical of the "Challenges of Civilization" curriculum?

4. In paragraph 9, Redmond refers to "chronological snobbery." What does she mean by this term? Why is it a threat to learning about the past?

5. As you see it, what kind of audience does Redmond seem to be addressing—those who would already agree with her? Those whose minds are not already made up? Those who would oppose her views? How do you think faculty would respond to her views? What about the students she seems to be defending?

6. According to Redmond, why must the past be allowed to "speak for itself"? What attitude is she confronting here? What does she think the consequence will be if her colleagues don't allow the past to speak?

7. Redmond calls her piece, "Backwards to the Future," an obvious take-off on a popular movie from recent years. How does this choice of title indicate or underscore the thesis of her persuasive essay?

8. How do you read the conclusion? Is she praising students or criticizing faculty? Why do you think she ended the essay this way?

CHAPTER 14

The Research Paper

INTRODUCTION

The larger purpose of most introductory writing courses is to teach apprentice writers how to write transactional texts with clarity and economy. Research writing is often a part of such courses, and it is itself a special kind of transactional writing. Research writing engages the writer in gathering information about a topic by investigating various information bases and reporting that information in an appropriate form for a selected audience. By investigating "information bases," I mean such activities as personal interviewing; the combing of library catalogues, reference works, and bookshelves; and the surveying of national and regional data bases accessed by computer.

You may have written a research paper in the past which was primarily a library exercise intended to acquaint you with the basic steps in using a card catalogue, finding the reference section of a library, documenting sources, and so on. In such cases, you may have produced a paper consisting of quotations and paraphrases strung together and cited in proper footnote or bibliographic form—a watered down version of the more skillful and meaningful paper to be introduced in this chapter. Such exercises have their place and to the extent that they introduced you to the research process, they have served you well. The intent of this chapter, however, is not only to illustrate how one may use the library effectively but to demonstrate how to produce a documented research text which explains, analyzes, or argues a particular topic and thesis for a particular audience.

This process of researching and composing is best illustrated, I believe, by showing you the different steps one student used in prewriting, drafting and revising her own research text. By examining the composing process Sarah Scheinblum used in producing her paper—rather than merely reading lists of possible library sources or rules of documentation alone—you will be better equipped to draft your own research text.

Learning to write an effective research text is, finally, a matter of cultivating these skills, most of which you have already developed:

1. *Prewriting:* Finding a topic, thesis, and intention; gathering relevant materials from information bases: libraries, national and regional data bases; and conducting personal interviews with knowledgeable spokespersons.

2. *Planning and Drafting:* Selecting from one's research the most relevant and important information; plotting the paper as a whole, and drafting it coherently with its intended audience in mind.

3. *Revising and Documenting:* Documenting the information presented in the text honestly and appropriately for one's field of study in order to authenticate the research done.

4. *Editing:* Appropriately formatting bibliographical references to permit the reader to follow up cited materials.

This chapter presents an overview of the composing and documenting processes involved in research writing, featuring up-to-date, sample MLA reference and bibliographical formats. However, because different disciplines use their own peculiar formats for documentation, you will want to consult a handbook or research manual in your field which covers more extensively its documenting conventions.

Where is the "computer connection" in all this? While computers are increasingly helpful in permitting one to do extensive research without even leaving one's desk, academic research today remains primarily a library activity. As the computer revolution continues, it may be that soon writers will be able to call up every source they need from a personal computer. And it may be that in your library you already have access to the peripheral equipment—modem, phone lines, etc.—to do a data base search. (If so, you will want to consult the reference librarian in your library to see if such a search will be helpful to your particular research project.) In most cases, however, research writing still means library work, and learning how to use the various library components—catalogues, encyclopedias, indexes, and so on, effectively.

But, you may ask, "If I am primarily using the library books for my research, how can the microcomputer help me in writing a research paper?" In plenty of ways! First of all, your are already aware of how easy it is to compose and revise with a word processor. This greatly simplifies some of the more tedious work that research writing represents, including—especially—maintaining accurate bibliographical information about your sources.

Secondly, because research writing involves the writer in "meshing" quotations, paraphrases, examples, and illustrations with his text, the block copy/block move functions you have used previously become all the more useful. As you integrate the pieces of your research with the framework of your exposition, analysis, or argument, this word processing feature will be invaluable. Finally, since formatting is itself a major part of research writing—indentations, special margins, headers, quotation conventions—the word processor makes these format features so much more "do-able" than on a conventional typewriter.

The rest of this chapter is divided into these seven sections:

1. Sarah's Research Task: An Overview
2. Selecting a Topic

3. Gathering Information
4. Organizing Materials
5. Drafting a Text and Documenting Sources
6. Creating the Final Bibliography
7. Sarah's Final Draft

SARAH'S RESEARCH TASK: AN OVERVIEW

Sarah Scheinblum, along with the rest of her class, was assigned a research writing task by her instructor. Students were permitted to write an explanatory, analytical, or argumentative text. Along with various other stylistic regulations, the class was told that the final copy should be between 8–10 pages, and should follow the MLA Style guidelines for documentation and bibliography in the text.

Sarah's childhood interest in the *Chronicles of Narnia,* a series of seven children's books written by British author, C. S. Lewis, led her to investigate the life of Lewis and the circumstances surrounding the composition of these tales. After a brief period of prewriting at her microcomputer, she decided to write an explanatory research paper which would examine the origins of the Narnian tales, explaining how Lewis composed them.

Sarah spent approximately two weeks working on her paper. Here is her writing log, covering the length of her research project, ranging from the first day she brainstormed about possible topics to the final editing and printing of her text, "Imagining Narnia: How C. S. Lewis Composed His Never-Never Land."

Sarah's Writing Log

WEEK ONE:

Monday: Went to the computer lab and began freewriting about possible topics for the research paper. I kept thinking about the Chronicles of Narnia by C. S. Lewis. Always wondered about their origin and how Lewis composed them; so I decided to make him and the tales the object of my research. Have a tentative thesis and intention.

Tuesday: Did some preliminary scanning of possible library materials, starting with the subject card catologue and locating some books both by and about Lewis. Began to make bibliographical cards which listed all the pertinent information about the books and authors I was uncovering.

Wednesday: Began a periodical and newspaper search, using various indexes. I hoped to find some book reviews, critical commentary, or news items about Lewis more contemporary with the time of composition of the tales. Found a few items, but it looks like the books will be the most fruitful.

Thursday: Took a break!

Friday: Began to sift through the bibliography cards to determine which books and articles would be most relevant to my topic. Assembled the designated books and articles and began making up note cards which recorded relevant quotations or paraphrases of material I thought I could use.

Saturday: Back to the computer lab to begin putting some of my information on disk to make it easier to manipulate when I begin to compose the first draft. Made a hard copy of all my stuff and thought about my audience.

Sunday: Gave everything a once over: my thesis and intention; musings about audience; and my collected materials. Got ready for a try at a first draft on Monday.

WEEK TWO:

Monday: Roughed out a sentence outline on the computer and began planning the paragraphs. Eked out a short discovery draft of four pages.

Tuesday: Getting serious. Well into the second draft, decided I needed to read through a few more sources that I had put aside, thinking I had enough materials. Made a hard copy and went back to the library.

Wednesday: Settled on a few more helpful quotations and explanations and plugged them into the second draft where I had gotten stuck earlier. Completed second draft; made hard copy.

Thursday: Checked over the instructor's style sheet. With appropriate margins, etc., I'll have about eight pages; enough. Worked on local sentence- and word-level stuff.

Friday: Break! Final typing scheduled for Sunday-the day after the homecoming football game!

Saturday: Went over the documentation and bibliographical format and made notes in my hard copy about how to arrange the citations within the text.

Sunday: Typed in final copy; proofread; fixed typos; printed two copies. It's ready to hand in tomorrow!

As we examine the various components of research writing that Sarah performed, you will learn useful strategies for prewriting, drafting, and revising a research paper. Each section contains an ''Activity'' to guide you in using the same activities in pursuing your own research paper.

SELECTING A TOPIC

The task of writing a research paper begins much the way any of the transactional writing tasks we have discussed would begin: searching for a topic and thesis and then defining one's intention and audience. The prewriting skills you learned and practiced in Chapters 2 and 3 will assist you well in finding and narrowing a topic appropriately.

The distinctive emphasis in research writing is that the writer gathers and presents information usually available only by deliberate research and investigation. Like any transactional writing task, the research paper demands that the writer ''stay out of the way'' of the information presented so that the thesis of the text itself is the focus of the reader—not the personal opinions or judgments of the writer. The impulse for a research project comes from a writer's curiosity about a person, place, event, or idea; the writer wonders, ''How can I find out more about this?'' and ''Where do I go to look for sources?''

What, ultimately, does a research text try to do? It answers these kinds of questions:

When and how did X ever come about?
Why is it that X occurred/occurs?
What really happens in/at X?
Who is responsible for X?
What really happened during X?
What could have been done about X?
Who discovered X and how has it been used?

A research text may thus be explanatory (explaining how something has come into existence, what its nature is, how it works, etc.); analytical (analyzing a process, a historical event, the origin of an idea or set of circumstances, etc.); or argumentative (what likely will happen ''if''; what could have been done ''if''; why Mr. or Ms. X proved unsuccessful in a particular circumstance, etc.).

What sorts of topics make good research projects? Usually, something or someone who has been around long enough to generate an information base: books, articles, or other media treatments (such as video; audio recordings; movies). Something as hot as today's headlines may not be useful as a topic, since it forces you to rely on speculation, personal opinion, or sources so recent that their authority is in question. For instance, you might find it difficult to research the question of how drug use affected entries at this year's Kentucky Derby—not enough will have been written or said about it to permit a substantial project.

A writer of a research paper must be pragmatic; a topic must be ''researchable.''

Not only that, but the topic should be limited enough to be covered adequately in the space of 8–10 pages. The prewriting activities you used earlier will help you discover and analyze your topic. In her prewriting, Sarah eventually narrowed her quite general beginning topic, permitting her to devise a meaningful research project:

General: Literature $\longrightarrow$ Fiction $\longrightarrow$ Fantasy $\longrightarrow$ Children's Fantasy
Limited: 20th Century Children's Fantasy $\longrightarrow$ C. S. Lewis's Fantasy
More Limited: Lewis's *Chronicles of Narnia*
Even More Limited: How and Why Lewis Composed the Chronicles

Activity #1:
Discovering a Topic
and Thesis for Your Research Paper

Create the following template file. Then, answer its questions, and print a hard copy to guide your library research.

Finding a Research Topic

1. Inventories: What events, persons, ideas, are you curious about? (List at least five.)

2. Choose one of these and freewrite for five minutes.

3. Examine the information you have generated. What stands out? What questions can you form that could serve as useful research questions? What do you know about your topic? What would you like to know more about? What audience would be interested in your topic? If you get stuck, freewrite some more with one of the other items you listed in your inventory.

4. What do you need to know to pursue your research? What are the likely books, periodicals, etc., that would contain the information you need?

5. What will be a guiding intention in pursuing your research? Do you want to *explain, analyze,* or *prove* something in your text. Who will be your audience for the text? (Use appropriate prewriting and planning templates to pursue your research topic further.)

GATHERING INFORMATION

After the initial freewriting period, Sarah had a clearer idea of what she wanted to research, and had discovered as well a potential thesis. She knew that she wanted to know more about how and why C. S. Lewis wrote *The Chronicles of Narnia*. Her first try at defining her purpose took this form:

> In this research paper I want to examine the origins of C. S. Lewis's popular seven-volume series of children's novels, *The Chronicles of Narnia* in trying to discover what makes them successful and popular.

Sarah had a few research leads since she owned a biography of C. S. Lewis that contained a modest bibliography, but her first search stop was at the subject catalogue at the college library. Looking under both "Lewis, C. S." and "The Chronicles of Narnia," she found a number of books and pamphlets *about* Lewis and his work which looked useful. She spent an afternoon copying the essential bibliographical information for each source on 3 × 5 index cards. From here she moved to the author–title catalogue and again looked up "C. S. Lewis," discovering several works by Lewis that looked relevant for her research interests.

Her next library activity took her to the indexes in the reference room, where she sought articles and book reviews contemporary with the time of composition of the Narnian tales. Here she looked at *Book Review Index, Book Review Digest,* and *The Readers' Guide to Periodical Literature* among others. This search proved somewhat helpful, but not as helpful as she hoped. It appeared that most of her sources would come from the books she had located earlier.

Activity #2:
Using the Library to Locate Sources

If you are not already acquainted with your library, you will certainly want to schedule a tour with the reference librarian so you can discover the locations of materials you will need for researching your topic. Fortunately, you don't have to understand the whole library system to do effective research. The library is a vast information-retrieval network whose various indexes, catalogues, and reference works help you to get started and to locate the materials you will need for a successful research project.

You will want to get a library map and be able to locate these parts of the library: (1) stacks; (2) circulation desk; (3) reference section; (4) reserve desk; (5) periodical and newspaper room; (6) microforms section; and (7) the card or computer catalog.

The stacks are where books are shelved; these may be "open" (meaning you can browse freely among the shelves and select the books you need) or "closed" (meaning you must give the call number of the books you need to a clerk who will then find the book for you).

The circulation desk is where you may check out your books. The reference section houses books, usually indexes, bibliographies, encyclopedias, etc., which may only be used in the library. The reserve desk is where a library user may temporarily borrow books or periodicals in heavy use for a specified period of time, usually from 2 hours to overnight. The periodical and newspaper room contains both current and bound issues of various magazines, journals, and newspapers. The microform section houses all microfilm and microfiche materials which must be read using a special optical device.

Finally, the card catalogue is the central source of information about your library holdings. It contains author–title and subject cards that specify the kinds of information you need to locate specific works related to your research project. In many libraries, the "card" catalogue is now available on microforms or on-line for a quick computer search.

A TYPICAL SEARCH PATTERN

Sometimes if you get hold of even one recent book with a substantial bibliography, your work is half-done. In Sarah's case, her Lewis bibliography gave her some immediate help in locating helpful sources. But unless you already have a good bibliographical source for beginning your research project, you will probably follow a pattern like the one presented below.[1]

1. Start with the Subject Catalogue

Perhaps you have a clear sense of the key categories, persons, topics, and ideas that are related to your topic, and that will give you a good start in locating materials. If you do not, however, ask your reference librarian for the *Library of Congress Subject Headings* volume. Since it is extensively cross-indexed, the chances are that you will find many of the related terms and subject headings you need to do a competent search.

The subject catalogue contains cards which contain the information depicted below:

PR 6023 .E926 c534 1979	Lewis, Clive Staples 1898–1963 Chronicles of Narnia Hooper, Walter 　　Past watchful dragons.: The Narnian Chronicles of C. S. Lewis/ by Walter Hooper.—1st Collier Books ed.—New York: Collier Books, 1979. 141 p.; 18 cm. Includes bibliographic references and index.	SAMPLE SUBJECT CARD

---

[1]These search strategies and the bibliographic strategies in the next section are adapted from Frederick Crews, *The Random House Handbook* (New York: Random House, 1984), 374–427.

```
823.91        Lewis, C. S. 1898–1963.
L67
Z8G79ch       Green, Roger Lancelyn.

              C. S. Lewis; a bibliography [by] Roger
              Lancelyn Green and Walter Hooper.
              New York, Harcourt, Brace,
              Jovanovich [1974]

              320 p. 22 cm.

              1. English Literature—History and
              criticism—bibliography. 2. English
              Literature—biography—
              bibliography. 3. Authors, English—
              Biography—Bibliography. 4. American
              Literature—History and criticism—
              Bibliography. 5. American Literature—
              Biography—Bibliography. 6. Authors.
```

SAMPLE
SUBJECT
CARD

In addition to the coded information primarily directed to librarians, the subject card contains five kinds of information:

1. The call number of the book, enabling the user to locate it in the stacks;
2. The title of the book, its author's name, the place of publication, and the date of publication;
3. Physical features of the book: how many pages of preface material; how many main pages of text; whether it contains illustrations; and its height. This tells the user that the book is substantial in length and not just a short pamphlet;
4. Notes on the context and contents of the book that guide the reader's judgment of its usefulness;
5. A list of all the headings under which the book is filed in the card catalogue. Such information can suggest other avenues of research for the user.

2. Move to Author-Title Catalogue

After sampling a number of subject cards, the user might want to move to the author–title catalogue, especially if the research involves the work of a specific author. The author and title cards contain information similar to the subject card:

```
823.91      Green, Roger Lancelyn                            AUTHOR
L67              C. S. Lewis; a biography [by]               CARD
Z8G79ch     Roger Lancelyn Green and Walter
            Hooper.
            New York, Harcourt, Brace,
            Jovanovich [1974]
            320 p. 22 cm.

            1. Lewis, Clive Staples 1898–1963.
            I. Hooper, Walter. Joint author.
            II. Title
```

```
PR          Companion to Narnia                              TITLE
6023                                                         CARD
.E926       Ford, Paul F.
c533
1980             Companion to Narnia/Paul F.
            Ford; illustrated by Lorinda Bryan
            Cauley.—1st ed.—San Francisco;
            Harper and Row, 1980.

            313 p.: ill.; 24 cm. Includes index.
```

Note that there are two kinds of call numbers used. While most libraries are moving to the Library of Congress system, which uses a letter/number system to categorize and shelve books (see Title Card above), many libraries still have stacks ordered according to the Dewey Decimal System (see Author Card above). Check with your reference librarian to determine where each kind of volume is located in your library.

3. Check Indexes, Collections of Abstracts, and Other Sources

After you have checked systematically for books on your topic and have created bibliographical cards for them, you may wish to search for periodicals, journals, and/or newspapers for articles relevant to your research. "Periodicals" usually refers to popular-level magazines, like *Time, Psychology Today, National Review,* or *Ms.,* which contain current information written for a nonscholarly audience. Such articles rarely have footnotes or bibliographies and are generally suited to quick reference and overview reading. "Journals" usually refers to scholarly publications whose writers and editors are experts in their field. Their articles usually are heavily documented and permit the reader to pursue a topic further by examining the author's own sources. Journals are also heavily indexed, and thus accessible from a number of information bases, including some computer data bases. "Newspapers," of course, refers to daily or weekly publications which cover newsworthy current events. Newspapers may inform a researcher about the latest developments related to a topic, but rarely with any depth or development, and sometimes without the accuracy that a less recent treatment may offer.

There are a number of indexes to consult, depending upon the topic you are pursuing. Check with your reference librarian for the best places to start. I will mention two here, since they were the ones which Sarah consulted early in her search for materials about C. S. Lewis.

The Readers' Guide to Periodical Literature, published since 1900 and continually updated, will assist you in finding popular-level articles related to your topic. Since Sarah was interested in finding articles roughly contemporary with the composition and publication of Lewis's Narnian tales, she consulted the *Readers' Guide* for 1955, discovering an article entitled, "Finding God in Narnia," by C. A. Brady, which she tracked down in bound periodicals of her library:

LEWIS, Clive Staples (Clive Hamilton, pseud)
  Back to faith. C. Walsh. por Sat R 39:32-3 Mr
    3 '56
  Circular pursuit. M. Swenson. Nation 182:474
    Je 2 '56
  Finding God in Narnia. C. A. Brady. Amer-
    ica 96:103-5 O 27 '56
  Greatest divide. por Time 65:94 My 2 '55
  Love was the weapon. B. R. Redman. ii Sat
    R 40:15 Ja 12 '57
  Most dejected and reluctant convert. G.
    Paulding. Reporter 14:45-6 Mr 8 '56
  Not quite all. T. A. Gill. Christian Cent 73:
    585 My 9 '56
  Portrait
    Newsweek 49:104 Ja 21 '57
  Reluctant convert. por Time 67:98 F 6 '56
  Universe rang true when fairly tested. A.
    Fremantle. Commonweal 63:464-5 F 3 '56

The *Readers' Guide* indexes author, title, and subject and lists the publication, date, volume, issue and page numbers of the articles it cites.[2]

Sarah also consulted several book review indexes, including *Book Review Index* (1965–); *Current Book Review Citations* (1976–); and *The New York Times Book Review Index, 1896–1970;* and the *Book Review Digest,* to discover whether there was more current information about Lewis and Narnia available. She found several useful citations, including the following capsule review about Walter Hooper's pictorial biography of Lewis in the 1983 volume of *The Book Review Digest:*

HOOPER, WALTER. Through joy and beyond; a pictorial biography of C. S. Lewis. 176p il $15.75 1982 Macmillan B or 92
1. Lewis, C. S. (Clive Staples), 1898–1963 ISBN 0-02-553670-
2   LC 82-9884

    "Through Joy and Beyond is the title not only of this . . .
photographic record of Lewis's life, but also of the 1979 film
biography (coauthored and narrated by Hooper). This book [con-
tains] . . . unpublished photos, personal reminiscences by Lewis's
acquaintances from [various] walks of life, and Hooper's [com-
mentary]." (Choice) Bibliography of works by C. S. Lewis. Index.[3]

[2]Material from *Readers' Guide to Periodical Literature* reproduced by permission of The H. W. Wilson Company, publisher.

[3]*Book Review Digest* Copyright © 1983, 1984 by The H. W. Wilson Company. Material reproduced by permission of the publisher.

Before leaving the reference section, Sarah consulted several other indexes, some of which provide abstracts, or summaries, of the articles which it lists, including the *MLA Abstracts of Articles in Scholarly Journals* (1971–), *Religious and Theological Abstracts* (1958–), and the *British Humanities Index* (1962–). There are many other indexes and abstract sources for other fields of study and you will want to consult with your reference librarian on likely leads for your topic.

4. Check a Computerized Data Base

Increasingly, books, periodicals, journals, and newpapers are being cross-indexed and gathered in the form of data bases, or computer files that can be accessed from your library's computer system. Whether or not this would be a helpful step (or an economical step—many data bases charge fees for their services) in your research depends upon how well-defined your topic is, how extensively you want or need to search, and whether or not printed sources will be as convenient to consult as the data base. Your reference librarian or instructor can give you guidance in this area.

5. Consult General Sources

In addition to the books and articles which may focus directly on your topic, you may need to get a broader perspective on your topic provided in such reference works as encyclopedias, specialized dictionaries, handbooks, and general histories. Your reference librarian, again, can direct you to appropriate reference sources to pursue your topic.

6. Interview an Expert in the Field of Study You Are Pursuing

Is there someone on campus or in your community who is an expert in the field or discipline which your topic touches? For instance, if your topic is literary, perhaps someone in the English, Ethnic Studies, Women's Studies, or Foreign Language departments can be of help in answering your questions or locating sources. If your topic is something in the social sciences or the hard sciences, you may wish to inquire in the appropriate departments for someone who can field your questions about the topic. Many colleges and universities maintain a list of faculty and staff, as well as local citizens, who are knowledgeable in particular fields. This information can often be obtained in their Public Relations or Development offices.

Schedule an appointment with the person you select and beforehand make a list of the questions about your topic to which you would like answers. If the person you are interviewing cannot answer your questions, perhaps he or she can direct you to someone else or to a book or article which can.

ORGANIZING MATERIALS

Having assembled a number of bibliographical citations, it is important that the writer use these sources resourcefully, capturing the essential bibliographical information for later citation, and taking good, clear notes to guide the later use of these materials. It should go without saying that you should not trust your memory to help locate that "essential" book which too often becomes impossible to find later. As Sarah located the sources she wanted to consider, she created a bibliography card for each of them. A *bibliography card* is a 3 × 5 inch index card which contains the essential bibliographical information you need to track down your source and to identify it later when you want to cite it in your text or bibliography. In addition, the writer will want to create a set of *content cards* which contain key quotations, summaries, or paraphrases of the materials he expects to use. The samples employed in this section follow the MLA documentation format.

Each bibliography card should contain this information: (1) call number of the book (or, if an article in a journal, the appropriate information for finding it in the stacks or periodical room); (2) the author of the book; (3) the title of the book; (4) the publisher, the place and the date of publication; (5) a brief identifying "tag" to explain the relevance of the source later when you are looking at your references.

PR 6023 .E926 Z48 1985	Dorsett, Lyle and Marjorie Lamp Mead, Editors. *C. S. Lewis Letters to Children* New York: Macmillan Pub. Co., 1985. (Letters from Lewis about Narnia to American and British children)	SAMPLE BIBLIOGRAPHY CARD

When Sarah had completed her initial sweep of library materials related to her topic, and had assembled nearly 40 different bibliography cards, she then began a survey of these cards to determine which sources she should examine first. She scheduled an afternoon at the library just to sift through her various sources, locating books in the stacks, and sampling the journal articles in the periodicals room.

After this survey she separated her cards into three groups. Into the first group she placed those cards that she knew were her *prime sources of information,* directly related to her topic and thesis. Into the second group she placed those cards that she knew could provide helpful *backgroud information* to give context and support to her main line of inquiry. Into the third group she placed cards that were only *tangential to her research concerns,* but which still might be useful later to check the accuracy of the general information she gathered about Lewis's life and career.

Sarah's next task was to create *content cards,* based on her classification of her materials. She used a separate card for each individual quotation, summary, or paraphrase. A quotation is a verbatim transcript of another writer's or speaker's words. Care should be taken to capture the exact wording and punctuation of the quotation to avoid distortion or incompleteness. A summary is a brief condensation of the point or points of a passage, used by the writer for background information. A paraphrase puts a passage in the writer's own words while retaining the basic meaning and sense of the passage under consideration. Each kind of content requires documentation in a research text.

On each content card she placed four kinds of items: (1) an identification of the source by the author's last name (or the title *and* author if she used more than one source by the same author) and the page reference in the upper left-hand corner; (2) an indexing tag which identified the kind of information the card contained in the upper right-hand corner; (3) a direct quotation, accurately transcribed, a summary, or a paraphrase of the information she wanted to cite; and (4) a brief comment about how the card might be used in her text.

Dorsett and Mead, p. 92
                                                                                                    quote from
                                                                                                    Lewis about
                                                                                                    Narnia

"All I can tell you is that pictures come
into my head and I write stories about
them. I don't know how or why the pictures
come. I don't think I could write a *play*
to save my life. I am so glad you like the
Narnian books."

[Lewis wrote this letter to a young girl about
Narnia and how it occurred to him.]

TIPS ON USING BIBLIOGRAPHY AND CONTENT CARDS

• It is helpful to use a larger index card for your content cards (4 × 6), in order to distinguish them from the bibliography cards, and to give you more space to write on.

• Quotations should be handled carefully, maintaining all the spelling, punctuation, or emphasis which appear in the original.

• Be sure to use some system on the card for distinguishing between *your commentary* and a *direct quotation* or *paraphrase* of a source, either by putting your comments in brackets or placing your initials near your comment.

• Photocopy any sources that provide detailed and extensive information that spans several pages and would be inconvenient to copy by hand.

Activity #3:
Compiling Bibliography and Content Cards

1. After you have completed your search for materials about your topic, compile a separate, 3 × 5 bibliography card for each reference. Each should include this information:

- call number of the book (or, if an article in a journal, the appropriate information for finding it in the stacks);
- the author of the book;
- the title of the book;
- the publisher, the place and the date of publication;
- a brief identifying "tag" to explain the relevance of the source later when you are looking at your references.

2. After assembling your bibliography cards, classify each card in one of three categories: (a) those sources that will be most immediately helpful and directly related to your topic and thesis; (b) those sources which provide good background information; (c) those sources which only provide tangential support or interest to your topic and thesis. Select those cards most useful and create a set of content cards that capture relevant quotations or your own summaries or paraphrases of the material you will cite in your text. Each content card should contain this information:

- an identification of the book by the author's last name (or use the title and author if there is more than one book by the same author) and the page reference in the left-hand corner;
- an indexing tag which identifies the kind of information the card contains in the right-hand corner;
- a direct quotation, accurately transcribed, or a paraphrase of the information;
- a brief comment about how the card may be used in your text.

Activity #4:
Transferring Information to Disk

After finishing your bibliography and content cards, you may find it useful to transfer this information to a file which you can use later to compile your bibliography, and to weave quotations and paraphrases into your research paper. Of course, if you have a notebook-size portable computer you can take to the library, of if you have access to a computer within the library, you might want to compile bibliography and content files on-line to save this step of transferring your information to disk. In most cases, however, moving the information from cards to the disk will be a good refresher for you in organizing and developing your text.

Sarah brought her two sets of index cards to the computer lab and created several separate files. In her BIBLIO file she entered the information from each bibliography card in alphabetical order by the author's last name, conforming to the proper MLA bibliographic form, and included a brief annotation indentifying the kind of source it represented. When she was ready to compile her final bibliography, her list would be complete and she would then be able simply to delete any references she did not use. Here is an excerpt from her BIBLIO file:

```
Bibliography Data for Narnia Paper

Carpenter, Humphrey. The Inklings: C. S. Lewis, J. R. R.
     Tolkien, Charles Williams, and Their Friends.
     Boston: Houghton Mifflin Company, 1979.

     (Biography of Lewis and friends; a great number of
     anecdotes about the creation of Narnia)

Ford, Paul F. Companion to Narnia. San Francisco: Harper
     and Row, 1980.

     (Dictionary of terms used in Narnia with helpful
     notes about the composition of the books as well)

Green, Roger Lancelyn, and Walter Hooper. C. S. Lewis: A
     Biography. New York: Harcourt Brace Jovanovich,
     1974.

     (Full-scale biography of Lewis; many quotations
     about Narnia)

Hooper, Walter. Past Watchful Dragons: The Narnian
     Chronicles of C. S. Lewis. New York: Collier Books/
     Macmillan Publishing Company, 1979.

     (Extensive, key discussion of how the tales were
     written)

Lewis, C. S. On Stories and Other Essays on Literature.
     Edited by Walter Hooper. New York: Harcourt Brace
     Jovanovich, 1982.

     (Two key essays by Lewis in this book: "On Three Ways
     of Writing for Children" [pp. 31-44]; "It All Began
     With a Picture" [pp. 53-55])

----------. Surprised by Joy: The Shape of My Early Life.
     New York: Harcourt Brace and World, 1956.

     (Autobiography that presents interesting details of
     Lewis's childhood that prove his early interest in
     writing and children's stories)
```

Sarah also created several files to hold information she had compiled on content cards. She named each file according to the kind of information it contained and then entered the corresponding quotations and paraphrases into the file that she thought would be useful to her when beginning her draft. Here are excerpts from several of the files she created. First is an excerpt from LEWIS BIO file:

```
                     LEWIS BIO facts


    "As difficult as these years were [the years during
which his mother, grandfather and uncle died], something
positive came from it all. Decades later Jack [Lewis's
nickname] drew upon the memory of his mother's illness
when writing The Magician's Nephew. In this book Digory's
mother nearly suffered the same fate as Flora [Lewis's
mother], but Aslan intervened before it was too late."
Dorsett and Mead comments about Lewis's childhood.
In Dorsett and Mead, p. 15.
    _____


    Lewis read few "children's books" as a child, with the
exception of E. Nesbit's "Psammead" series. He preferred
to write his own, even as a child. Later in life he began
reading and enjoying fairy tales with great enthusiasm.
(My paraphrase)
    In Green and Hooper, pp. 236-237.
```

As you can see, Sarah distinguished verbatim quotations from summaries and paraphrases with her annotations. She also enclosed in brackets any information that was not part of the original quotation but which she needed to clarify information in the quotation. Here is another excerpt, this time from her NARNIA file:

```
                     NARNIA facts


    "All I can tell you is that pictures come into my head
and I write stories about them. I don't know how or why the
pictures come. I don't think I could write a play to save
my life. I am so glad you like the Narnian books. . . ."
Lewis, writing to a young girl in America, 2/5/60. In
Dorsett and Mead, p. 93.
    _____
```

> "The Chronicles of Narnia are, at present, the best-
> known and most influential works of a well-known and very
> influential writer. They outsell the rest of C. S. Lewis's
> works combined, at a rate now of several hundred thousand
> copies per year. Regarded as classics by many authorities
> on children's literature, they are read and loved also by
> college students and older adults."
> Schakel, commenting about the popularity of the tales. In
> Schakel, p. xi.

In all, Sarah had one BIBLIO file containing all of her sources, and ten different CONTENT files to hold her quotations and commentary about her sources.

She made a hard copy of these files and, when she was ready to draft her research text, she brought these copies with her to the lab. Whenever she was ready to insert a quotation, she opened up the appropriate file and block copied the appropriate quotation into place. Later, when she was ready to compile her "Works Cited" page, she copied her BIBLIO to the end of her text and deleted sources and annotations irrelevant to her needs.

1. Following Sarah's example, create a BIBLIO file, entering accurately and fully the bibliographical information you have compiled on your bibliography cards. Be sure to enter information in alphabetical order by author's last name. If you are not sure about how to record certain information, consult the discussion earlier in this chapter.
2. Create an appropriate number of files to contain the information you compiled on your content cards. Organize the information in your content cards by useful categories. Create separate files for each separate set of quotations, summaries or paraphrases.

DRAFTING YOUR TEXT
AND DOCUMENTING THE SOURCES

Having discovered a topic, thesis, and intention, and having done the necessary detective work to find appropriate sources and relevant information to support your thesis, it is time to plan a draft of your text. You may use the outlining and nutshelling techniques presented earlier or you may begin with a discovery draft that fleshes out the main ideas you want to articulate. However you begin, do not put too much emphasis on where to place quotations and how much documentation to use in your text; first explore the boundaries of your text and determine what you want it to do.

Sarah began by plotting a modest sentence outline at the VDT:

I. The Popularity of Lewis and the Narnian Tales

    A. C. S. Lewis has become a popular children's author in the past decade.

    B. His Narnian tales are a favorite of young and adult readers alike.

    C. This popularity and the critical success of these books are remarkable considering the author and the subject matter of the works.

II. How and When Lewis Wrote the Narnian Chronicles

    A. The Narnian tales were written during the 1950's.

    B. All were completed before even the first one was published.

    C. Lewis revealed a great deal about his composing process and his intentions for writing the Narnian tales in his letters to the children who wrote to him.

III. Analyzing the Success of the Narnian Tales

    A. The seven Narnian tales have great characterization and timeless themes.

    B. The style of the books transcends the gap between young readers and adult readers.

    C. The Narnian tales, finally, help young readers see beyond the limits of their experience and help adults recapture the imagination and wonder of their youth.

She followed this outline with a brief discovery draft:

Imagining Narnia: How C. S. Lewis
Composed His Never-Never Land
Sarah Scheinblum

Any book or set of books that sells millions of copies every year deserves our attention and inquiry. What makes it popular? Is it something about the author? Who is it who is buying these books? Do they appeal only to certain people or to all ages and groups? This is the case with the Chronicles of Narnia, a seven-volume set of children's books written by the British author and teacher, C. S. Lewis.

C. S. Lewis wrote the Narnia tales over a period of several years during the 1950's. Each book appeared successively during the middle and late 1950's and each became very successfully. During Lewis's lifetime, however, he did not see the explosion of interest in his work or reap the financial awards that his books have brought him.

When one knows more about Lewis, the success of the tales is even more surprising. Lewis was not a children's writer by profession but an Oxford don, that is, a professor of Medieval and Renaissance Literature at the famous Oxford University in England. He had no children of his own and wasn't even married until late in his life. Most of his other works are rather dry historical and critical works about English literature or theological works about Christianity. Besides his Narnian tales, he did write several science-fiction novels and another imaginative work, Till We Have Faces that is heard to classify.

This hardly qualifies Lewis, then, to write quality, popular children's works. How does one explain his success? Part of the answer lies in examining the way he went about writing these works. Any author's composing process is, of course, a mystery. But many people have a mistaken impression about how they do their work. Since there are some religious parallels in the Narnian tales to Lewis's own faith, some readers assume he started with a message he wanted to get across, and then he simply made up the characters and ideas that would push this message.

This is not true in Lewis's case. In his many letters to children and others, he claims that his work began with an image of a Lion who later became Aslan, the great hero of Narnia.

Lewis, in fact, wrote all seven Narnian stories before even the first one was published, The Lion, the Witch, and the Wardrobe being the first to be published. Though acclaim came to Lewis for these books (The Last Battle won an award for children's books), he could not have foreseen just how successful they would become. Why is this?

First, Lewis's books have great characterization and timeless themes. The style of the books transcends the gap between young readers and adult readers. And the Narnian tales, finally, help young readers see beyond the limits of their experience and help adults recapture the imagination and wonder of their youth.

In analyzing her discovery draft, Sarah knew there would be portions that needed a great deal of elaboration and definition. For instance, she felt that she would have to explain more about the Narnian tales themselves, earlier in the text, so the reader unfamiliar with them could follow her later discussion about how they were composed.

She also knew that she had used a number of obscure expressions that would need to be explained better or replaced by more accessible words and phrasing. Her major section, that which would explain the success of the tales, would require a great deal of amplification and illustration in order to be meaningful to her audience.

Despite all of this, Sarah was pleased that she had succeeded in fleshing out so much of the territory she would need to cover in her research text. She turned from this initial draft to a thorough survey of her sources. At this point her comment to herself is revealing: "I now know what I want to say and which sources will be the most helpful in documenting my ideas."

Activity #5:
Planning and Drafting Your Research Text

1. Spend some time at your microcomputer outlining or nutshelling the text you wish to write. Be sure to consider carefully the intention of your text and the audience to which it is directed. Your outline or nutshell can guide the writing of a discovery draft.

2. Write a discovery draft of your text. What are the main points your text will present? What is the best order for them? What kind of opening paragraph is best suited to the information and thesis you will be presenting? What points will need the most support or documentation in your text? *Mark places* in your text with an asterisk (*) or slash (/) that require a quotation or other citation of information to authenticate the point you are making. Later you will return to these markers and supply the appropriate information. Be sure to save your file to the disk on which your BIBLIO and CONTENT files are located. Make a hard copy for further revision and reference.

The Problem of Plagiarism

Once Sarah had her bearings on the shape and scope of her research text, she turned her attention to documenting her ideas in the text. Documentation means supporting one's assertions with appropriate quotations, summaries, or paraphrases from the sources that have been investigated. Sarah knew that though some readers would know who C. S. Lewis was and would have read or heard of *The Chronicles of Narnia*, most of her research text would require extensive documentation. The questions she faced confront every research writer: "What do I have to acknowledge?" and "What is the proper form for doing so?"

Plagiarism occurs when writers present the words and ideas of another writer as their own. The most extreme case occurs when a student literally buys a research paper or copies someone else's and submits it as his or her own work. But few student writers deliberately set out to borrow another's work and claim it as their own; plagiarism begins innocently enough as an attempt to "put in one's own words" the interesting or compelling facts found in a relevant source. Under the constraints of time and limited sources, a writer may be tempted to take shortcuts, taking poor notes and summarizing the content of a passage without detailing the appropriate bibliographical information. Even writers trying to avoid plagiarism may fail to document a source because they feel that the sense of a quoted or paraphrased passage is "common knowledge"—for instance, a famous historian's explanation of the causes of a particular event. These lapses of ethics may be understandable, but they do not excuse the plagiarism of the writer.

Consider the following source material and the ways Sarah might have used it in her text:

ORIGINAL SOURCE:
During those six most fulfilling years, Lewis's own health had been ominously deteriorating; when he married Joy, he was no longer well himself. His own medical facts were of no more interest to him than the facts of his financial affairs. The basic trouble was an enlarged prostate gland which cause irreparable damage to the kidneys. . . . That was the end of his country walking. (Kay Lindskoog, C. S. Lewis: Mere Christian. Downers Grove, IL: Inter-Varsity Press, 1981.)

VERSION A:
By 1960, Lewis's own health was ominously deteriorating. By the time he had married Joy Davidman, he was no longer well himself. Lewis cared no more about health than he did about the facts of his financial affairs. Because of his prostate problems, his kidneys were irreparably damaged. That was the end of his country walking that had inspired so much of the geography of his fiction, especially in the Narnian tales.

COMMENT: This is clearly plagiarism. There are several stolen phrases and the ideas, while somewhat in the public domain, belong to the original writer, not the researcher. Note that just because the writer interweaves her own introductions to certain sentences or adds a few of her own items here and there, she is not innocent of plagiarism.

VERSION B:
By 1960, Lewis's own health was ominously deteriorating. As Kay Lindskoog has pointed out, by the time he had married Joy Davidman, he was no longer well himself (1981: 21). Lewis cared no more about health than he did about the facts of his financial affairs. Because of his prostate problems, his kidneys were irreparably damaged. That was the end of his country walking that had inspired so much of the geography of his fiction, especially in the Narnian tales.

COMMENT: This passage is still plagiarism; the documenting of one particular passage does not absolve the writer from her overall borrowing of the original source's ideas and phrasing.

VERSION C:

```
        In 1960, Lewis was no longer writing fiction, and
by the time he had married Joy Davidman, his own
health was quite poor. As Kay Lindskoog has pointed
out, Lewis's "own medical facts were of no more
interest to him than the facts of his financial
affairs" (21). Because of recurring prostate
problems, his kidneys were severely damaged and
prevented him from taking those long walks in the
country that had inspired so much of the geography of
his fiction, especially in the Narnian tales (22).
```

COMMENT: This is an acceptable use of source material. The writer is still clearly influenced by the facts of her source, but she has not tried to present Lindskoog's work as her own. The one clear borrowing is appropriately documented.

While one may debate what needs to be acknowledged in a research text, the writer's goal is to document his text in a way that permits his reader to follow up on his research and pursue his own. Of course, one needs not detail the most obvious facts. (The writer above, for instance, need not "prove" that C. S. Lewis was a writer.) But in dealing with any idea or critical opinion that clearly informs one's own ideas and perspectives and may not be easily accessible to the reader, it is both more honest and more helpful to the reader to document them.

How to Document

As I suggested earlier, most fields of study have their own peculiar systems of documentation. In this section, I will be illustrating the documentation process with the Modern Language Association style, which is becoming the standard citation form for research papers and articles in the humanities. It follows closely the logic of many other documentation systems and you will find it easy to adapt to others once you master it.

Until recently, the MLA (and other organizations in the humanities which propose documentation conventions for research) used a "footnote–endnote" system of documentation in which a writer inserted numbers throughout a text which corresponded to notes at the bottom of the page or at the end of the text. These notes contained bibliographical information as well as elaboration or qualification of the points made in the text itself. The sciences, in contrast, have always preferred a "reference list" style of documentation in which minimum bibliographical information (e.g., author's last name; year of publication; page numbers) is inserted parenthetically into the text. This information cues the reader to a reference list at the end of the text which contains the full citation needed to follow up on the writer's research.

The new MLA documentation style is a "reference list" system. Even so, some footnotes or endnotes may be useful to the reader, even though they are not used for documentation purposes. In reference list documentation, the footnote or endnote is used to further explain, elaborate, qualify, or clarify a point made in the text. Footnotes or endnotes should, however, be used sparingly, and only for supplemental information that may be helpful to the reader but which is not essential to an understanding of the point being made in the text itself.

The chief advantage of the reference list style is that it unclutters the actual body of one's paper. Footnotes and endnotes can interrupt the flow of a paper, forcing the reader to flip back and forth from page to page or section to section to locate a particular source. The reference list style is simply more economical and less taxing to use in documenting one's research since in involves fewer "rules" to memorize and employ.

MLA CITATION FORM

The basic logic of documenting your text involves providing the minimum bibliographical information needed to guide your reader to a fuller citation at the end of your text. This usually includes the author's last name and page numbers. If the author is already identified in the passage, the page number may suffice by itself and the name may be omitted. If an author is included more than once in your reference list, you may use a shortened version of the title of the work to identify it in your text. Here are several examples of this parenthetical documentation:

A Work by One Author

Lewis has been described as a "an adult writer with the heart of a child" (Harver 34). This, however, is only partly true.

(Note that there is no punctuation between the author's name and page number.)

A Work by Two or Three Authors;
A Work by More Than Three Authors

The question becomes whether "Lewis was a product of his times" (Klever, Edwards, and Lungstrum 134) or merely "an anachronistic writer whose fairy tales have survived by their sheer novelty" (Alexander et al. 56).

(Note that the Latin abbreviation, "et al., " includes the other authors besides Alexander.)

Works by Different Authors with the Same Last Name

At least one critic believes that Lewis wrote the Narnian tales as a reaction to Britain's industrialization (Joan Ericson 67–70), though that opinion is widely opposed (Gordon Ericson 45–50; Tollman 16–23).

Works by an Author of Two or More Works Cited;
A Work by an Anonymous Author

While Fairbanks contends that Lewis's reputation has not suffered in the 1980's (*Guide to Narnia* 78), elsewhere he has criticized the tendency of some readers to regard Lewis's intent as allegorical (*Lewis: The Critical Image* 145, 147). This paradox seems to trouble critics more than it does regular readers ("Having a Time in Narnia" 23).

Poetry, Drama, and the Bible

When citing lines of poetry or drama, or verses from the Bible, the writer should use the line numbers or verses themselves instead of the page numbers of the edition used. (Of course, the edition and editor of the book should be included in the final bibliography.) Act, scene, and line numbers are separated by periods with no space before or after them. Biblical chapters and verses are cited similarly. Here are some examples of appropriate documentation:

Poetry

> Lewis concludes his tribute to Andrew Marvell with characteristic straightforwardness:
>> Sweetness and strength from regions far
>> Withdrawn and strange you bring,
>> And look no stronger than a star,
>> No graver than the spring. (13–16)

A quotation from poetry that is not set off from the text indicates line breaks with a backward slash (/):

> Lewis's final two lines, "And look no stronger than a star, / No graver than the spring" (15–16), conclude his tribute to Marvell with a characteristic straightforwardness.

Drama

> In *Forgotten Chapter*, Lillian Desmond effectively demolishes the case for capital punishment: "To err is both human and divine. Tell me not that the state can do better than God in meting out justice . . ." (2.1.45–46).

Bible

> Randolph was fond of quoting his favorite verse: "For God so loved the world that he gave his own begotten son that whosoever believeth in him should not perish but have eternal life" (John 3.16).

Punctuation and Mechanics in Documentation

There are only a few punctuation conventions the writer should keep in mind in using parenthetical documentation.

1. Commas are used to separate authors' names and titles: (Lewis, *On Stories*) and to indicate interruptions in a sequence of pages or lines (56, 59).
2. Hyphens are used to indicate continuous sequences of pages (56–59) and lines (3–8).
3. Colons are used only to separate volume and page numbers (*Collected Stories* 2: 167), space following the colon.

   4. Periods separate acts, scenes, and lines in drama (4.1.78–89) and chapters and verses in the Bible (Luke 6.8).

   5. In quotations set off from the text, citations should follow the final punctuation:
      As Clinton Stone has observed,
         Lewis's decision to name the lion ''Aslan,'' after the Turkish word for ''lion,'' was a masterstroke. (45)

Using Footnotes and Endnotes

Even a paper using parenthetical citations may require the use of notes, placed at the bottom of the page (footnotes) or at the end of the text, before the bibliography (endnotes). In such cases, the notes are used to clarify, amplify, or supplement the information given in the text. Here are two examples of notes which may be useful to the reader in a given context:

   [3] For a more detailed account of Lewis's upbringing, see Green and Hooper (19–50).

In this note, the reader is guided to a source that includes more detailed information about the topic the writer has discussed in the text. Note that parenthetical citation is used even in a footnote or endnote. The full citation awaits the reader in the bibliography at the end of the text. Also note that a space is inserted between the raised number and the first word of the citation.

   [5] Lindskoog has argued (1979: 45), however, that *The Lion, the Witch, and the Wardrobe* was, in fact, the first Narnian tale to be composed by Lewis. Whatever their actual order of composition, it is clear Lewis intended *The Magician's Nephew* to be seen as the novel that explains the origin of Narnia.

This note is used to amplify a specific discussion in the text and provides not only further reference material but also supplemental (though nonessential information) that the reader may find interesting.

Integrating Quotations Smoothly in Your Text

A research writer should choose and use quotations judiciously in the text. As I suggested earlier in the chapter, a research paper is not just a string of quotations hanging together by the thin thread of its author's introductions. Direct quotations should be used to illustrate, document, and amplify the points you make and should not be used merely to fill space. Long quotations should be minimized and, where appropriate, should always be analyzed and interpreted in the context of the researcher's thesis and intention. Here is an example of both poor and acceptable quotation use, with commentary:

Original:

The Narnian Chronicles have thrilled millions of young readers. As John Larkin states: ''Few children can escape the power of Lewis's narrative style'' (23). The Narnian tales are also very popular with older adults. Geraldine Carson suggests: ''Despite their appearance, the Narnian tales find a great many readers among adults who 'are only buying them for the kids' '' (67–68).

In this paragraph, the writer has used two quotations abruptly and superficially; in each case, the writer provides little context for the quotations and leaves the reader to guess about the writer's purpose in citing them.

Revised:

Many writers, including John Larkin, have noted that the Narnian chronicles have thrilled millions of young readers: ''Few children can escape the power of Lewis's narrative style'' (23). It would be a mistake, however, to assume that only children read the tales; they are also very popular with older adults. Though the covers of the seven volume series suggest adolescent fare, Geraldine Carson observes that ''Despite their appearance, the Narnian tales find a great many readers among adults who 'are only buying them for the kids.' '' (67–68). Clearly, Lewis's works span generational gaps in popularity.

In this revised version, the writer has successfully integrated the quotations into her discussion, providing both a context and a rationale for their use.

A few of the conventions for using quotations should be cited here. These conventions are illustrated in Sarah's research paper found at the end of this chapter.

1. Quotation marks are always used in pairs.
2. Double quotation marks enclose direct quotations; single quotation marks enclose a quotation within a quotation.
3. Long quotations (usually ten or more lines) are set off from the text itself and do not begin or end with quotation marks.
4. Quotation marks are used to enclose titles of short works (short stories, essays, short poems, songs, articles) and subdivisions of books. Longer works and periodicals (books, newspapers, magazines) are underlined.
5. If the writer uses an ellipsis in quoting a source, the deleted portion should be indicated with three periods. If the deletion comes at the end of the passage being cited, four periods should be used, the last period representing the end punctuation of the passage.
6. Periods and commas are usually placed inside quotation marks. Colons and semicolons are always placed outside of quotation marks. Other punctuation marks (dash, question mark, exclamation point) are placed inside quotation marks only when they apply to the quoted matter; they are placed outside when they apply to the whole sentence or passage.

Activity #6:
Writing a Final Draft
and Documenting Your Sources

As you work through a second or third draft of your research paper, you should note those passages that require documentation or can be amplified with the use of appropriate quotations or paraphrases. If your word processing software permits you to merge files, you may call up the appropriate content file and, using the block copy/block move function, place the quotation in your text proper, deleting extraneous matter. Integrate and insert the appropriate bibliographical information parenthetically into your text.

You should revise your draft using the same strategies you learned elsewhere in *Processing Words*. Save your final editing for the end of your composing process.

CREATING THE FINAL BIBLIOGRAPHY

The bibliography at the end of the research text based upon the new MLA documentation system is called a "Works Cited" list. It includes only the specific sources used in documenting the text. If you have previously entered your bibliographical materials into a file, you should be able to prepare your "Works Cited" list simply by calling up your BIBLIO file and inserting it at the end of your research text. You should, of course, delete irrelevant annotations, and order the remaining sources alphabetically by the author's last name. The proper manuscript form for entering the bibliographical information is to type the first line flush left and to indent subsequent lines five spaces.

A sample "Works Cited" page is found in Sarah's research paper at the end of this chapter. Following are the appropriate forms for the most common kinds of citations. It is possible that you will encounter or use sources that are not covered in the following list. Check your handbook or a research manual in your field of study for the appropriate format. In some cases you may be forced to create your own citation form by analogy with those presented below.

BOOKS

Books with One Author

Lindskoog, Kay. *C. S. Lewis: Mere Christian*. Downers Grove, IL: Inter-Varsity Press, 1981.

Books with Two or Three Authors

Green, Roger Lancelyn and Walter Hooper. *C. S. Lewis: A Biography*. New York: Harcourt, Brace, Jovanovich, 1974.

(Note that only the first author's name is inverted in citations involving more than one author.)

Books with More Than Three Authors

Brown, Leslie T., et al., *The World's First Night: C. S. Lewis and Speculations on Time and Eternity*. New York: Gordon Press, 1981.

Books in Edition Other Than the First

Brown, Leslie T., et al. *The World's First Night: C. S. Lewis and Speculations on Time and Eternity*. 2nd ed., New York: Gordon Press, 1981.

Book in a Series

Faffer, Jane. *C. S. Lewis*. Finchly Essays on British Writers. No. 15, Ed. Gerald Kark. New York: Gordon Press. 1967.

Work in Two or More Volumes

Gaining, Sheryl. *Children's Literature in the 1980's.* 2 vols. New York: Gordon Press, 1982.

Translation

Eco, Umberto. *The Name of the Rose.* Trans. William Weaver. New York: Harcourt, 1983.

Reprinted Book

Lewis, C. S. *Rehabilitations.* 1939. New York: Gordon Press, 1981.

Edited Book

Edwards, Bruce L. ed. *Taste of the Pineapple: Essays on C. S. Lewis.* New York: Gordon Press, 1985.

Anonymous Book

Norse Myths. Trans. Bill Myers. Olso: Dreyers Forlag, 1967.

(Note that anonymous works are listed in a bibliography by the first important word in their titles.)

Unpublished Dissertation

Hart, Dabney. ''C. S. Lewis's Defense of Poesie.'' Diss. Univ. of Wisconsin, 1959.

ARTICLES

Signed Article in Reference Work

Vallon, Catherine. ''C. S. Lewis.'' *Literary Encyclopedia of Britain.* 1976 ed.

Unsigned Article in Reference Work

''C. S. Lewis.'' *Encyclopedia Literaria.* 1978 ed.

Article from Journal with Continuous Pagination

Duncan, Clay. ''Visiting Narnia.'' *Journal of Children's Literature* 13 (1982): 67.

Article from Journal with Each Issue Separately Paginated

Abels, Tim. ''Buying Time in Fiction: The Dilemma of C. S. Lewis and J. R. R. Tolkien.'' *Literary Studies* 34.1 (1985): 34–56.

Article from Weekly Periodical

Klever, Betty. ''Corrupting the World.'' *These Times* 8 Jan. 1985: 25–28.

Article from Monthly Periodical

Green, Brenda. ''The British Invade Children's Literature.'' *London Survey of Books* Dec. 1985: 678+.

(The '' + '' indicates that the article begins on p. 678 but does not continue on consecutive pages.)

Article from Daily Newspaper

Tyler, Becky. ''Sounding the Alarm Against Immorality in Children's Books.'' Wadsworth *Daily Times* 23 July 1977: 44.

Activity #7:
Creating the "Works Cited" List

If you have created a BIBLIO file with bibliographical citations properly ordered and appropriately formatted, creating the "Works Cited" list at the end of your text is simply a matter of merging this file with the file containing your final draft of the text. Unlike the older bibliographical conventions, the new "Works Cited" reference list should contain *only those sources* that you actually have cited in your research text and not those that you merely "consulted."

After you have completed the "Works Cited" portion of your text, you should be ready to examine your text for a final editing, using the strategies you have learned in editing other writing assignments during the term.

SARAH'S FINAL DRAFT

Sarah worked on her research paper for two weeks. In addition to her discovery draft, she wrote two other drafts: an intermediate draft and a final draft. Sarah conceived her research text as an analytical text for an audience somewhat familiar with Lewis and the *Chronicles,* but not especially experienced in literary analysis. Her goal was to write a nontechnical paper that would reveal the essential origins and features of the stories she had loved since she was a young girl.

When she felt sure that her revision of her second draft was appropiately reader-based and ready to be put into final form, she consulted again the style sheet her instructor had given her. The style sheet specified such formatting considerations as length, margins, title page, etc. She produced the paper which follows according to those specifications.

As you read through her paper you will note how Sarah effectively integrated quotations and paraphrases into her paper and successfully documented her text according to the MLA documentation style. At the end of her text, the "Notes" page contains elaborations or further information regarding points she made in her text. Likewise, the "Works Cited"page lists the full bibliographical information for the references Sarah placed in her text.

Sarah Scheinblum
Intermediate Writing
Professor Schreffler
18 November 1987

Imagining Narnia:
How C. S. Lewis Composed
His Never-Never Land

There has never been a more unlikely writer of best-selling children's books than Clive Staples Lewis. Lewis was a British professor of English at both Oxford University and Cambridge University most of his life, a writer of dry tomes about medieval and renaissance literature. He is best known, however, as the author of dozens of influential religious books. In fact, Chad Walsh, one of Lewis's proteges and interpreters, suggests that Lewis "had an impact on American religious thinking and indeed on the American religious imagination which has been rarely, if ever, equalled by any other modern writer" (106). Lewis's theological interests clearly had an impact on the subject matter and emphasis in his most popular fictional work, The Chronicles of Narnia (hereafter Chronicles).

Amidst his teaching and scholarly writing career, he somehow found time to write the seven volumes of Chronicles, a series that has sold more than ten million copies--certainly more than any other set of children's works in the past decade (Reading with the Heart, ix). In addition, it has spawned numerous spin-offs in other media, including a television special, several record albums, countless maps and posters, and even computer software![1]

That any book or set of books should sell thousands of copies year in and year out and that the author in question should be an Oxford don is more than a matter of great curiosity. One is moved to ask, "How and why did an author with no children of his own and no special training as a children's writer go about constructing works that appeal to so many different age groups and kinds of people?" An inquiry into the essential nature and origin of these popular volumes will help us understand better Lewis's

1

achievement and shed some light on the "Narnian phenomenon."

C. S. Lewis wrote the Narnian tales over a period of several years between 1949 and 1952 (The Lion of Judah 12-13), the first volume, The Lion, the Witch, and the Wardrobe, being published in 1950. The remaining six were released at the rate of one per year through 1955, when both The Magician's Nephew and The Last Battle were published. As Walter Hooper, Lewis's personal secretary during the last months of his life, explains, "These seven fairy stories were an instant success with children, for whom they were ostensibly written" (quoted in The Lion of Judah 13). Popular as they were during his lifetime, Lewis did not live to witness the explosion of interest in his work or reap the financial rewards that his books would have brought him in the past two decades.

How does one adequately describe The Chronicles of Narnia? In attempting to classify them, James Como suggests that "The Chronicles seem to be a perfect marriage between form and function, mystical fancy and escapism. . ." (Como 5), while Charles Huttar has said that the only genre of literature that the Chronicles come close to is "scripture" (Schakel, The Longing for a Form 119). The Chronicles comprise a seven-volume set of children's books, though describing them as "children's books" is a little misleading. Manifestly, they appeal to a wide age group: from preschool kids who love to hear them read aloud and teenage fantasy enthusiasts to older adults who are mesmerized by Lewis's narrative skill. Beyond whatever literary appeal and merit they have, the Chronicles also serve as a kind of spiritual guide to the personal faith of some readers, saturated as they are with images of the Christianity to which Lewis converted in his early 30's. Paul Ford is a representative voice of those who read the Chronicles in this way. Speaking of the first time he encountered the Chronicles, he captures, in his book, Companion to Narnia, some of the affection many adult readers feel toward Lewis's tales:

> When I first read the Chronicles as a college student, I knew that I had crossed a frontier. I found in them a world in which I was welcome, in which I was at home. At first they made a strong appeal to my more

apologetic side: they gave explanations of all that I held most dear. But as the years and the re-readings went on, I found myself returning to Narnia at times of crisis, and recommending them to everyone I cared about. (xxix)

It is clear from Ford's testimony and that of many others that the Narnian tales are more than exceptional yarns; they, in fact, inspire the most extreme loyalty and devotion. As Walter Hooper playfully notes, ". . . hard up college students will run up enormous book-bills in order to give copies away" (quoted in The Lion of Judah 13). How does one account for this amazing success that engenders such behavior in the books' readers?

The answer is two-fold, resting both in the quality of the books themselves and in the way Lewis imagined and constructed Narnia. Narnia is a fantastic land of talking beasts, wicked witches, chivalrous boys and girls, swashbuckling adventures, and moral lessons learned under pressure. As such, Lewis's Chronicles almost single-handedly revolutionized the writing of books for children: In the years before The Lion, the Witch, and the Wardrobe, publishers returned the manuscripts of such books with the stereotyped rejection slip: "the modern child is not interested in magic and fantasy" (Green and Hooper 256).

What made the Chronicles different? Part of the answer is the excellent description and characterization Lewis crafted. Margaret Hannay, analyzing the success of the tales, suggests "Lewis is able to make us believe in this world made of pieces of Christian doctrine, Arthurian legend, Norse mythology, and English boarding schools because it is a real world, full of homey detail. We believe in it because we have walked through it" (Hannay 70). The key character in the Chronicles is Aslan, the Great Lion and Son of the Emperor Beyond the Sea; as creator and ruler of Narnia, it is he who is the center and source of the tales. In The Lion, the Witch, and the Wardrobe, the first of the Chronicles and the most popular of the seven volumes, Aslan, in his sacrificial death and resurrection, conquers the evil White Witch and returns Narnia to freedom and joy. The Last Battle, the seventh book in the series, completes the history of Narnia, tying up the loose ends as Aslan breaks the final spell of evil

3

in his kingdom, returning all characters to their homelands beyond Narnia into eternity. Lewis believed that art should teach by delighting, by making the reader enchanted with an ideal (Hannay 59). In Aslan, Lewis created a noble, valiant hero whose appeal to young and old, religious or not, is undeniable and compelling.

Another quality in the Chronicles beyond the carefully crafted characters and description has already been alluded to earlier. Though they were somewhat written with children in mind, Lewis first wrote a book that he himself would enjoy: "People don't write the books I want, so I have to do it for myself" (Green and Hooper 253-254). Clarifying his approach to writing the tales, Lewis explained, "I was therefore writing 'for children' only in the sense that I excluded what I thought they would not like or understand; not in the sense of writing what I intended to be below adult attention" (On Stories 47). Lewis bristled at the use of "adult" as a term of approval, especially among critics; too often, he claimed, such critics were too concerned

> about being grown up, to admire the grown up because it is grown up, to blush at the suspicion of being childish; these things are the marks of childhood and adolescence. . . . When I was ten, I read fairy tales in secret and would have been ashamed if I had been found doing so. Now that I am fifty I read them openly. When I became a man I put away childish things, including the fear of childishness and the desire to be very grown up. (On Stories 34)

In The Chronicles, Lewis treated children--and their imaginations--with respect; Lewis neither condescends to them nor tries to create a false sense of "adulthood" in his narrative style. In writing these stories, Lewis has simply invited all readers, young or old, to join him in Narnia, leaving aside their pretentions and misgivings. The result is a series of stories that may enthrall and entertain anyone looking for adventure, derring-do, and the triumph of noble hearts over fear and danger.

It is possible for some readers at this point to imagine that the Narnian tales are no more than dressed-up religious allegories. In fact, the stories are read and enjoyed on many levels--with or without the reader's

4

cognizance of the religous elements which may undergird the tales. But since there are some Christian parallels in the Narnian tales it might be assumed that Lewis started with a "message" he wanted to get across, and then he simply made up the characters and ideas that would carry this banner. How Lewis escaped this fate is best explained by an inquiry into his composing process. Any author's actual composing process is, of course, a mystery, often to writers themselves. But when an author's testimony is available to us, it should be consulted with interest and respect.

In one sense, Lewis had been imagining and writing the Narnian stories since early childhood. Walter Hooper explains,

> At about the age of six, C. S. Lewis invented the imaginary world of "Animal Land" or "Boxen," as it later came to be called, and over the next few years he wrote numerous stories and histories about "the dressed animals" which inhabited it. Though it is remarkable that a boy could write so well and could sustain a single story over a hundred pages. . . The "Chronicles of Boxen" [were] marred by a conscious effort on the young Lewis's part to make them "grown up"--which to him meant stodgy, prosaic, and political. (quoted in The Lion of Judah 7)

Lewis, the boy, meets Lewis, the adult, in Narnia and the world gains a magical series of books. But the adult Lewis did not view the creation of art as an occasion for writing propaganda. Rather than choosing a "message" and finding a convenient "mold" to pour it in, Lewis contended that "You find out what the moral is by writing the story" (On Stories 145). In reply to an editor's invitation to explain how he wrote the Chronicles, Lewis responded:

> All of my seven Narnian books, and my three science-fiction books, began with seeing pictures in my head. At first they were not a story, just pictures. The Lion all began with a picture of a Faun carrying an umbrella and parcels in a snowy wood. . . . At first I had very little idea how the story would go. But then suddenly Aslan came bounding into it. I think I had been having a good many dreams of lions

5

about that time. Apart from that, I don't know where
the Lion came from or why He came. But once He was
there he pulled the whole story together, and soon He
pulled the other six Narnian stories in after Him.
(On Stories 53)

Authors who are too self-conscious about their
composing processes are more likely to become
propagandists of the kind Lewis disliked, and he was
skeptical of authors who claimed they could explain
everything about how they worked: "I don't believe anyone
knows exactly how he 'makes things up'. Making up is a very
mysterious thing. When you 'have an idea' could you tell
anyone exactly how you thought of it?" (On Stories 54).
Lewis was, in fact, oblivious to many of the details in his
own composing process: "I'm not even sure that all the
others were written in the same order in which they were
published. I never keep notes of that sort of thing and
never remember dates" (Dorsett and Mead 68-69). The
Narnian tales enchant the reader precisely because Lewis
was first concerned with telling a good story based upon
the "pictures" he had seen--and not with an overbearing
lesson or moral he wished his readers to learn.

The final explanation of the success of the Narnian
tales lies in the fact that they help young and old readers
alike see beyond the limits of their experience and to
renew or recapture the imagination and wonder of youth.
Wonder is, in fact, the key to Narnia. Aslan's adventures
and those of the rest of the Narnian citizenry create that
"taste of the other," a tantalizing sense of a never-never
land which Lewis has described elsewhere in this way: "the
scent of a flower we have not found, the echo of a tune we
have not heard, news from a country we have never yet
visited" (The Weight of Glory 5). Those readers who stand
beside Lewis, "imagining" Narnia, enter a delightful land
of wonder and joy that they may never-never have to (or
choose to) leave.

NOTES

¹For a complete survey of the many Narnian "by-
products" see the bibliography in Kathryn Lindskoog's
<u>C</u>. <u>S</u>. <u>Lewis</u>: <u>Mere</u> <u>Christian</u> (236-237).

WORKS CITED

Como, James. "A Look into Narnia" <u>CSL: The Bulletin of the
New York C. S. Lewis Society</u> 15 (1984): 1-6.

Dorsett, Lyle and Margaret L. Mead. <u>C. S. Lewis Letters to
Children</u>. New York: Macmillan Pub. Co., 1985.

Ford, Paul F. <u>Companion to Narnia</u>. San Francisco: Harper
and Row, 1980.

Green, Roger Lancelyn, and Walter Hooper. <u>C. S. Lewis: A
Biography</u>. New York: Harcourt Brace Jovanovich,
1974.

Hannay, Margaret P. <u>C. S. Lewis</u>. New York: Frederick Ungar
Pub. Co., 1981.

Lewis, C. S. <u>On Stories and Other Essays on Literature</u>.
Edited by Walter Hooper. New York: Harcourt Brace
Jovanovich, 1982.

-----------. <u>The Weight of Glory</u>. Grand Rapids: William B.
Eerdmans Pub. Co., 1965.

Lindskoog, Kathryn. <u>C. S. Lewis: Mere Christian</u>. Downers
Grove, Ill.: Inter-Varsity Press, 1981.

-----------. <u>The Lion of Judah in Never-Never Land</u>. Grand
Rapids: William B. Eerdmans Pub. Co., 1973.

Schakel, Peter, ed. <u>The Longing for a Form</u>. Kent, Ohio:
Kent State University Press, 1977.

-----------. <u>Reading with the Heart: The Way into Narnia</u>.
Grand Rapids: William B. Eerdmans Pub. Co., 1979.

Walsh, Chad. "Impact on America." In <u>Light on C. S. Lewis</u>,
ed. Jocelyn Gibb. New York: Harcourt, Brace and
World, 1965.

APPENDIX I

Getting Acquainted with Your Word Processing Software

The tutorial that follows, composed of five sections, will lead you through the steps you need to know to compose with your word processing software. Be sure to have a copy of your computer's appropriate documentation at hand in order to answer the questions in this guide. If you need help in answering any of the following questions, consult your instructor.

UNDERSTANDING KEYBOARD AND VDT FUNCTIONS

Most of the keys on your computer keyboard operate exactly like a typewriter's keys: if you hold the shift key down and press "R," a capital "R" will appear on the monitor, or VDT, as we will refer to it throughout this guide. The entire QWERTY keyboard is present—but look again, there are probably other keys you haven't seen before: directional arrow keys, numbered or lettered function keys, a delete key, a return or enter key, an ESC(ape) key, and a CTRL (control) key. These latter keys serve special functions in operating a word processing program, and you will want to familiarize yourself with their use.

Check your keyboard for each of the following keys. If your keyboard has the key, place a check mark by the term. Determine what the key is used for (either by looking it up in the glossary for your software or by consulting your instructor), then write your answer in the space next to the key's name. The usual use for the key is suggested below in parentheses.

_____ ARROW KEYS _____ (Governs cursor movement by the use of four directional, arrow keys)

_____ BACK SPACE _____ (Controls directional movement backwards or works as a delete key)

_____ CAPS LOCK _____ (Locks capitalization)

_____ CTRL (Control) _____ (Holding it down while pressing another key initiates a special function in the microcomputer)

_____ DEL (Delete) _____ (Deletes text to the left of the cursor)

_____ ENTER/RETURN _____ (Enters a command or inserts a ''hard'' carriage return)

_____ ESC (Escape) _____ (Speeds up certain functions)

_____ HOME _____ (Returns cursor to upper-left corner of screen)

_____ REPT (Repeat) _____ (Holding it down while pressing another key repeats the same function)

_____ RESET _____ (Restarts the program disk presently active in the computer's disk drive[s])

_____ RUN/STOP/BREAK _____ (Interrupts or ends a particular program or function currently in operation)

_____ SHIFT _____ (Works like a shift key on most conventional typewriter keyboards; but, on some computers, is used in combination with other keys to initiate a special function in the microcomputer)

_____ TAB _____ (Works like the tab key on most conventional typewriter keyboards)

The following information will also be useful to know:

1. How do you enter capital letters on your keyboard? By holding down the shift key? By selecting CAPS LOCK? Will certain characters be placed on-screen only when holding down the shift key (or, some other key—for example, CTRL key)?

_____

2. Do all the keys on your keyboard repeat—that is, if you hold them down will they continue to register the same character? Or do only certain ones repeat? To repeat a character, will you need to hold down a special key (for example, a REPT key) while pressing the desired character key?

_____

3. Does your word processing software have a ''word wrap'' feature—that is, when you exceed the right margin on the VDT does the cursor automatically return to the left margin?
_____
If so, you should only hit the carriage return at the end of a line or paragraph in which you want a ''hard'' return. _____

4. What is the maximum number of characters your word processing software can display on one line? Insert number here: _____ (The standard is now eighty, though some inexpensive computers use forty characters. This will affect some of your composing strategies—for instance, visualizing the length of your paragraphs—since the screen does not display the text as it will appear when it is printed.)

5. What is the maximum number of lines your word processing software can display on the screen at one time? Insert maximum number here: _____ (The standard is now twenty-five, depending upon how much space the menu takes up. The menu display is usually something that can be "toggled," or turned off, once you get used to the basic commands of your software.)

BEGINNING A WRITING SESSION

In this part of the guide, you will ascertain what steps and keystrokes you must follow to begin a writing session, enter text, and save text as a file. **Text** refers to the characters and strings of characters you place on the screen during a writing or editing session. **File** contains the text you are working with. Either *before* you begin a session or *while you are saving it,* the file must be given a specific name. If you have two disk drives, you will normally put the word processing software in the "A" drive and your initialized diskette in the "B" drive. Fill in the blanks with the appropriate answers from your word processing software manual:

1. Once the word processing software (WPS) is loaded, what option do you select from the menu to begin a writing or editing session? _____ If you have only one disk drive, will you need to eject or remove the WPS diskette and insert your initialized diskette? _____

2. Do you have to name the file you create *before* you begin the session or *while you are saving the file,* at the end of the session? _____

3. What restrictions are there in naming your files? Are only a certain number of characters permitted? Are only a certain kind of characters permitted? Does your file need to have a three-letter "extension" name, like FIRST.TXT, which desingates the kind of file it is? Explain here:

_____

4. After you have entered the appropriate command for accessing your WPS, what command or keystroke begins an editing session? Enter command here: _____ Does the WPS prompt you for a file name or do you select it in some other way? _____ Will you need to swap diskettes in order to load or open the appropriate file? _____

5. After you have opened or loaded your file, what other menu items are on display? List items here:

_____

How do you enter text? Do you simply begin to type _____, or do you have to select a particular option from the menu _____?

6. After you have entered text, how is cursor movement handled, that is, how do you move the blinking light (an underline character, a special symbol, or a lighted square) from one portion of the screen to another? from one line to another? from one word to another? Note: not all WPS will have each of these features.

Do you use arrow keys _____? Or, a combination of the CTRL key and another key _____?

In the blank, fill in the special keystrokes, if any, which allow you to move from the present cursor position to:

_____   the far-left margin of the line

_____   the far-right margin of the line

_____   one character to the left

_____   one character to the right

_____   one word to the left

_____   one word to the right

_____   the beginning of the next paragraph

_____   the end of the paragraph

_____   the beginning of the text

_____   the end of the text.

What other special keys govern cursor movement in your WPS?

_____

_____

7. How do you end an editing session and save your file? _____ By selecting a SAVE option from the menu? _____ By pressing a certain combination of keystrokes? _____ Do you name your file when you save it, or before? _____

8. After you save your file, does your WPS return you to a special menu, to the computer's operating system, or back to the file itself for further editing? _____

9. Once you have saved your file and want to end the computing session entirely, how do you exit the system?

_____

Trying it Out

Now let's see if the information you've compiled works:

1. Turn the computer and/or monitor on.

2. Insert the appropriate diskette(s) to begin a writing session.

3. Select the appropriate option from the menu to allow you to enter text.

4. Type in the following text, as is:

> The last decade has seen a number of revolutions in technology, not the least of which has been the advent of high-speed data processing equipment. In milliseconds, a business concern in Portland, Maine, can transfer a set of price quotations to its distributors in Portland, Oregon, with the use of these new machines. It will be interesting to see what the next generation of computers will mean to business and to our culture as a whole.

5. Perform the following cursor movements:

> Move the cursor to the beginning of the paragraph.
> Move the cursor to the end of the paragraph.
> Move the cursor to the beginning of the second sentence in the paragraph.
> Move the cursor to the space in front of the word *Maine.*
> Move the cursor to the letter *a* inside the word *Maine.*
> Move the cursor backwards to the beginning of the word *milliseconds.*
> Move the cursor to the beginning of the line you are currently on.
> Move the cursor to the end of the line you are currently on.

6. Save this text by the name DATA (or, if your WPS uses file-name extensions, DATA.TXT).

7. Exit the WPS program and end the computing session with the appropriate keystrokes, the removal of diskettes, and the turning off of the computer and/or monitor.

BASIC EDITING AND REVISING FUNCTIONS

In this section of the guide you will quickly survey the main editing functions of your WPS: scrolling, deleting, inserting, copying/moving, and searching/replacing. Each WPS has its own peculiar way of handling these functions. You will want to carefully review these procedures before entering them in the appropriate blanks in this portion of the guide. The best way to find out how these editing functions work is not by reading about them, however, but by getting your feet wet, performing the sample activities found at the end of this section, and practicing on your own texts.

Scrolling

Scrolling is the function by which you move from line to line, screen to screen, or page to page within your WPS. One way to scroll through a document is to keep pressing the ''down arrow'' if you have directional keys on your keyboard, but this takes a long time, especially if you have a long document. Most software has a set of commands, activated by holding down the CTRL key and pressing another key, which allows you to move quickly through the text without using the cursor movement keys. (Systems which use a "mouse" for scrolling and cursor movement will usually have an on-screen menu to consult for answering these questions.) Investigate your WPS manual and ascertain how to scroll through your text in these ways:

Command/Keystrokes	Action
_____	Move to the beginning of the file.
_____	Move to the end of the file.
_____	Scroll one line up.
_____	Scroll one line down.
_____	Scroll one screenful up.
_____	Scroll one screenful down.
_____	Scroll up continuously, line by line.
_____	Scroll up continuously, screen by screen.
_____	Scroll down continuously, line by line.
_____	Scroll down continuously, screen by screen.

Deleting

Most word processing software (WPS) permits the user not only to delete characters, but to delete from different directions and in large chunks. (The section on moving/copying blocks of text will discuss deleting blocks of text.) In order to use this function, you will want to know whether your backspace key works as a delete key. Survey your WPS manual to determine how it performs these functions:

Command/Keystrokes	Action
_____	Delete character left.
_____	Delete character right.
_____	Delete word left.
_____	Delete word right.
_____	Delete line from right of cursor.
_____	Delete line left of cursor.
_____	Delete entire line.

Inserting and Reforming

One of the key features that all WPS permits is the insertion of characters, words, and large segments of text in the midst of already entered text. Many WPS programs, however, have a "toggle" mode in which the user selects either INSERT or OVERWRITE as the mode for entering text. The INSERT mode allows a writer to add text in the midst of other text by pushing characters to the right. The OVERWRITE mode allows the user to type directly over existing text, thereby deleting it. Normally, you will want to select the INSERT mode; the OVERWRITE mode is useful later in editing for minor typographical and spelling changes.

To insert or add information in the midst of other text, one moves the cursor to the appropriate insertion point and begins typing. Some WPS automatically *reforms* the text between two carriage returns, lining up the left and right margins and altering the spacing if the user has elected a different spacing value (double- instead of single-spacing, for example). However, some require that you perform this function manually by placing the cursor at the beginning of the text and entering specific keystrokes. Check your WPS manual to determine how to perform these functions:

Command/Keystrokes	Action
_____	Select/toggle INSERT MODE
_____	Select/toggle OVERWRITE MODE
_____	Reform text/paragraph

Block Copying, Moving, and Deleting Text

While some writers literally cut and paste their "hard copy" when they are revising, your WPS makes this possible electronically, without scissors or glue. To copy or move text from one location in your text to another, or to delete a large block of text, you must determine how your WPS "marks" or designates the portion of text that will be moved. Most often this is done by entering a special control character at the beginning and at the end of the portion of text to be copied or moved. Other WPS—for instance, those which work with a mouse—require that you press the mouse key at the appropriate beginning and ending locations to select the appropriate block of text.

After the text that you wish to copy, move, or delete is *marked,* your WPS requires that you enter the appropriate keystrokes for performing the function you desire. When copying or moving text, it is important not to accidently delete it, especially if your WPS does not have an UNDELETE or UNDO function! Likewise, remember that unless your WPS automatically reforms a paragraph or section of text after you have copied or moved it, you may have to manually perform the appropriate reforming commands.

Most WPS will not only let you copy and move text within a file, they also permit the user to copy or save a portion of the text in its own file. This is a handy feature, especially when you cannot decide whether you want to delete or relocate a portion of text which may be useful later. Thus instead of deleting it, you can save this text in its own file, making it available for insertion later. Many WPS also permit the user to add or insert an entire file into the "active" file—the one the user is currently working in. See the section in this appendix, Using Template Files, for a discussion of how this may be useful to you.

Examine your WPS to determine how you may perform the following functions:

Command/Keystrokes	Action
_____	Mark the beginning of text to be moved.
_____	Mark the ending of text to be moved.
_____	Move the cursor to locate the new insertion point.
_____	Move the text to the location where you wish to insert it.
_____	Copy the text to the location where you wish to insert it.
_____	Delete the text.
_____	Reform the paragraph or section.
_____	Copy the text in its own file.
_____	Open another file for insertion in text.

Searching for and Replacing Text

In addition to the block copy/block move discussed above, the SEARCH/REPLACE function provides the writer with tremendous advantages in revising a text. This function permits the writer two different options in examining a text: First, the user may simply *search* for specific items, pausing at each occurrence of single characters, strings of characters, whole or partial words, even special control codes and carriage returns. Second, the user may elect to *replace* the item searched for with another item, either globally—throughout the entire file—or in specific instances as the search function scrolls through the text.

A typical session using the SEARCH/REPLACE function might go like this. Judy has completed the first draft of her text but knows that she left several words misspelled, including "separate," which she usually misspells as "seperate." Before saving her file and exiting her WPS, Judy selects the SEARCH/REPLACE function by pressing the CTRL key and the key her WPS requires to elect the option. Here is what her screen looks like:

SEARCH FOR?—

REPLACE WITH?—

OPTIONS—

Options: W = whole word; P = partial word; G = replace in entire file; N = replace next N occurrences; K = replace next occurrence; U = ignore case; B = search backwards

The cursor is automatically placed to the right of the SEARCH FOR prompt, and Judy enters ''seperate.'' She presses the carriage return and the cursor moves to the right of the second REPLACE WITH prompt, where she enters ''separate.'' After another carriage return, she selects one more option: ''G,'' or REPLACE IN ENTIRE FILE. After the next carriage return, the WPS systematically replaces the misspelled word with the correct one. To return to the beginning of her file, Judy keys the appropriate CTRL key combination, and she is ready to check some other possible error.

SEARCH FOR?—seperate

REPLACE WITH?—separate

OPTIONS—G

Options: W = whole word; P = partial word; G = replace in entire file; N = replace next N occurrences; K = replace next occurrence; U = ignore case; B = search backwards

Though each SEARCH/REPLACE function works a little differently, all WPS have in common certain features. Analyze your WPS manual to determine how it handles the following functions:

Command/Keystrokes   **Action**

_____   Elect SEARCH option.

_____   Enter character or string to be searched for.

Selection options within SEARCH function:

_____   Search for whole word.

_____   Search for partial word.

_____   Ignore case (search for upper or lower case).

_____   Search backwards.

_____   Interrupt search.

_____   Elect REPLACE option.

_____   Enter replacement character or string.

Select options within REPLACE function:

      _____   Replace next occurrence of search character or character string.

      _____   Replace throughout file.

      _____   Replace automatically without user interruption.

      _____   Replace "N" (specific number) occurrence of . . .

Other Editing and Page Format Functions

There are a number of important page-design functions, such as margins, tabs, page numbering, centering, and so on that you will want to know how to use. Your WPS is probably one of two kinds. The first kind displays the page as it will appear in print—that is, "what you see is what you get," and the format of the page is directly affected by the commands and keystrokes you use to set margins, to center text, and so forth. The second kind does not display the directions you give about page format; the effects appear only in the printed version as the WPS sends control codes to the printer to set these values.

    Some of these options may be selected after you elect to print, that is, the WPS will prompt you with specific questions. Others will be selected by embedding "commands" within the text itself. Read your WPS manual carefully to see when and how to select these options. In addition to such regular functions as tabbing, spacing, and so on, you will especially want to find out how to use the options for "headers" and "footers," which enable you to place one or more lines of information—your name, the title of your essay, the page number—at the top or bottom margins of your text.

    You should consult your WPS to determine how to set these values and functions:

Command/Keystrokes	**Action**
_____	Set spacing between lines (single, double, etc.).
_____	Set left margin.
_____	Set right margin.
_____	Set top margin.
_____	Set bottom margin.
_____	Center string of characters.
_____	Center block of text.

_____	Set page number.
_____	Elect header option.
_____	Set header margin.
_____	Elect footer option.
_____	Set footer margin.
_____	Set tab.
_____	Set page length (normally sixty-six lines).
_____	Set number of printed lines (normally fifty-five lines).
_____	Start new page (to leave blank spaces on previous page).

Trying it Out

At your microcomputer, follow these directions to practice the commands and keystrokes discussed in this section.

1. Turn the computer and/or monitor on.
2. Insert the appropriate diskette(s) to begin a writing session.
3. Select the appropriate option from the menu to allow you to open the file you earlier saved as DATA (or, DATA.TXT). The saved DATA will appear on the monitor.

The last decade has seen a number of revolutions in technology, not the least of which has been the advent of high-speed data processing equipment. In milliseconds, a business concern in Portland, Maine, can transfer a set of price quotations to its distributors in Portland, Oregon, with the use of these new machines. It will be interesting to see what the next generation of computers will mean to business and to our culture as a whole.

When the DATA file (or DATA.TXT) appears on your VDT, perform the following commands and keystrokes:

Deleting and Inserting

1. Move the cursor to the last line, placing it one character to the right of the word "culture". Delete the word "culture," using the DELETE (or backspace key). At the insertion point, type in the word "society."

2. Move the cursor to the first line, placing one character to the left of the words "a number." Delete the words "a number," and insert the word "several."

3. Move the cursor to the third line, placing it one character to the left of the word "milliseconds." At the insertion point, type these words: "a matter of." Then, reform the paragraph (if your WPS does not automatically do so) with the appropriate keystrokes.

After these changes, the paragraph should appear like this:

The last decade has been **several** revolutions in technology, not the least of which has been the advent of high-speed data processing equipment. In **a matter of** milliseconds, a business concern in Portland, Maine, can transfer a set of price quotations to its distributors in Portland, Oregon, with the use of these new machines. It will be interesting to see what the next generation of computers will mean to business and to our **society** as a whole.

Block Copying, Moving, and Deleting

1. Move the cursor to the first line and mark the beginning of the sentence, "The last decade ...''; next, move to the third line and mark the ending of the sentence, after the word "equipment." This sentence should be ready for movement. Move to the sixth line and place the cursor one space after the period which ends the sentence "... new machines." Perform the appropriate keystroke to move the sentence to this new

location. Reform the paragraph if necessary. The paragraph should now appear on your VDT like this:

In a matter of milliseconds, a business concern in Portland, Maine, can transfer a set of price quotations to its distributors in Portland, Oregon, with the use of these new machines. **The last decade has seen several revolutions in technology, not the least of which has been the advent of high-speed data processing equipment.** It will be interesting to see what the next generation of computers will mean to business and to our society as a whole.

2. Move the cursor appropriately to mark the beginning of the last sentence in the paragraph, ''It will be ... to our society as a whole.'' Place the cursor in the first space after the period ending the sentence, ''In a matter ... new machines.'' Perform the appropriate keystroke to copy this sentence at the new insertion point. Reform the paragraph if necessary. The paragraph should like this on your VDT:

In a matter of milliseconds, a business concern in Portland, Maine, can transfer a set of price quotations to its distributors in Portland, Oregon, with the use of these new machines. **It will be interesting to see what the next generation of computers will mean to business and to our society as a whole.** The last decade has seen several revolutions in technology, not the least of which has been the advent of high-speed data processing equipment. **It will be interesting to see what the next generation of computers will mean to business and to our society as a whole.**

3. Mark the beginning and ending of the last sentence in the paragraph (you just duplicated and moved it to a different location in the paragraph). Perform the appropriate keystrokes for deleting this marked portion of your text. Your paragraph should now appear like this on your VDT:

In a matter of milliseconds, a business concern in Portland, Maine, can transfer a set of price quotations to its distributors in Portland, Oregon, with the use of these new machines. **It will be interesting to see what the next generation of computers will mean to business and to our society as a whole.** The last decade has seen several revolutions in technology, not the least of which has been the advent of high-speed data processing equipment.

Search/Replace Functions

1. With the revised DATA paragraph still on-screen, select the SEARCH option. At the SEARCH FOR prompt, enter ". " (period and space) as the search item you wish to locate. Perform the appropriate keystroke to set this function in operation. Note that the cursor will move to the end of each sentence in the paragraph. (There may be a particular keystroke you must perform on your word processor to move from one item to the next. Check your WPS manual.) Move the cursor back to the beginning of the paragraph.
2. Select the SEARCH/REPLACE option. When the program prompts you with SEARCH FOR, type "advent"; at the REPLACE WITH prompt, type "invention." Perform the appropriate keystroke to set this function in operation. When the cursor is relocated, the WPS may prompt you with a question like, REPLACE Y/N? Select the appropriate option ("Y"): "invention" should replace "advent."

FORMATTING AND PRINTING

Since we have not yet become a completely paperless society, the texts you create on a microcomputer must be produced in hard copy, that is, a paper copy that you can submit to your readers. It is crucial, therefore, that you learn how to print your texts on a printer linked with your microcomputer. In addition to mastering the PRINT capability, you will also want to learn some special formatting functions, such as changing font or pitch;

selecting underlining, and boldfacing; and perhaps inserting superscripts and subscripts in your manuscripts.

If the microcomputer station you are using does not include a printer (or is not in some way "networked" to a printing station), you will most likely have to transport your texts to another computer that *is* linked with a printer. You will need both your word processing software and the diskette(s) which contain your texts in order to print them. Consult your WPS manual to determine how to perform the following formatting and print functions.

Formatting

You may wish to skip this section and go directly to the discussion of printing until you are ready to try some of the formatting options presented here.

Software Commands

Most formatting commands are controlled by the WPS commands inserted within the document or text you are creating. You have already surveyed some of these formatting options in the previous section of this guide. Typically, formatting commands are entered by placing special control characters at the beginning and at the end of the text you wish to format in some special way. Other options may be selected by inserting special commands into the text on the lines above and below the text you wish to format. In other word processing software—for instance, ones that use a mouse—these features may be selected by choosing a particular menu and clicking the mouse key at the appropriate place in your text on-screen. Such formatting considerations as selecting justified or ragged-right margins are also handled within the WPS itself, while you are editing your text.

Consider some changes we want to make in the following example computer display. In one popular word processing program, in order to underline "must always" and to place a superscript (or, footnote number) after "least," one must use two pairs of control characters:

The concerns of minorities ˆSmust alwaysˆ S be kept in mind during any economic crisis. Otherwise, the people who need the most help will get the least. ˆT3ˆ T

The control characters ˆ S and ˆ T are entered on-screen by holding down the CRTL key and pressing ''S'' and ''T'' respectively. The first control character turns the formatting function on, the second one turns it off. When using these paired functions, be sure you have turned the function on and off, otherwise you may find when you print that you have, for instance, *underlined* every word in your text! When the above text is printed, it will look something like this:

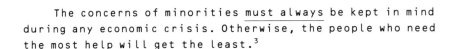

```
    The concerns of minorities must always be kept in mind
during any economic crisis. Otherwise, the people who need
the most help will get the least.³
```

Font and pitch are also controlled by the software. **Font** refers to the typeface one selects, for instance, Roman, Times, Script, Italic, and so on. Some newer microcomputers, like the Apple Macintosh and Commodore Amiga, give the user a wide number of exotic options for selecting a font. Your options in choosing a font may be limited by the kind of computer you have, your WPS, and/or the kind of printer you are using. For instance, if you are using a letter-quality printer—one that works basically like a typewriter with changeable daisy-wheel fonts—you will not have as many options as you might with an ink-jet or dot-matrix printer which forms characters differently.

Pitch refers to the size of the characters you may print. The usual range of sizes is from *pica* (ten characters per inch), to *elite* (twelve characters per inch) to *condensed* (seventeen characters per inch). Some WPS and some printers permit the user to select enlarged or double-width print. Check with your instructor or the printer manual to determine what your options are.

Consult your WPS and printer manuals to determine how to select the following formatting options in your text. At the end of the list are some blanks for you to fill in other features your WPS may support.

Command/Action	Result
_____	Begin/end underline.
_____	Begin/end boldface.
_____	Begin/end double-strike.
_____	Begin/end superscript.
_____	Begin/end subscript.
_____	Begin/end italics.
_____	Begin/end 10 pitch (Pica).
_____	Begin/end 12 pitch (Elite).
_____	Begin/end 17 pitch (Condensed).
_____	Begin/end enlarged or double-width print.
_____	Begin/end justification.
_____	Begin/end flush left margin.
_____	Begin/end flush right margin.
_____	Begin/end centering of text.
_____	Begin/end: other _____.
_____	Begin/end: other _____.
_____	Begin/end: other _____.

Printer Commands

Some printers allow you to change format settings on the printer itself. If the printer you use permits this function, fill in the following blanks. If not, skip to the next section on printing.

Command/Action	Result
_____	Select 10 pitch (Pica).
_____	Select 12 pitch (Elite).
_____	Select 17 pitch (Condensed).
_____	Select enlarged or double-width print.
_____	Select double-strike.
_____	Select boldface.

Printing

Though each WPS program handles printing functions slightly differently, in most cases the user selects the print option from a menu and, when prompted by the WPS, selects the file he or she wishes to print, pressing a carriage return or ENTER key to begin the printing routine. As mentioned earlier, some WPS programs are "screen-oriented," that is, what you see on the screen is what you will get when it is printed; others are "printer-oriented," which means that some of the formatting features you embed in your text are not visible until the text is printed. (There are advantages and disadvantages of both kinds, but we will not go into them here.)

Some WPS permits the user to print from the diskette and the on-line memory, while others require that the user load a file into memory before it can be printed. Check with your instructor or WPS manual to see if this is the case. Consult your WPS manual to determine how to perform the following functions.

1. In order to print, what procedure must you use?

   _____   Load a file into memory first?

   _____   Print directly from your diskette?

2. Once your file is ready to be printed, how do you select the PRINT option from within your WPS?

   _____

3. Once you have selected the PRINT option, what other prompts will you have to answer before the WPS sends your text to be printed?

   _____   Single-sheet or continuous feed paper?

   _____   Number of copies?

   _____   Set page number?

   _____   Set page length?

   _____   Set number of printed lines?

4. After the printing is finished, what do you do to return to the original menu?

---

5. After the printing is finished and you want to end the session, what do you do?

Trying it Out

At your microcomputer, follow these directions to practice the formatting and printing commands discussed in this section.

1. Turn the computer and/or monitor on.

2. Insert the appropriate diskette(s) to begin a writing session.

3. Select the appropriate option from the menu to allow you to open the file you saved as DATA or DATA.TXT, on which you will practice some formatting and printing functions. When this file appears on your VDT, perform the following formatting functions:

> **a.** Enter the appropriate keystrokes to begin underlining at the word *data* and to end after *equipment*.
>
> **b.** Enter the appropriate keystrokes to begin double-strike printing at the words "next generation" and to end after them.

4. After you have entered these keystrokes, either (1) save the file and elect the PRINT option from the menu, specifying the file you wish to print; or (2), if your WPS permits you to print from within an active file, select the appropriate option for printing the file.

5. Examine the hard copy you just printed. Did the formatting options you placed in the text operate correctly? If not, enter the file again and check your manual to see if you chose the right control characters and placed them in the appropriate locations.

USING TEMPLATE FILES

Chapter 1 introduced you to the "template file." This final section of the guide will acquaint you with how to create and use template files as an aid to your composing. Most of the time, you will choose to open the template file within an already active file—providing that your WPS supports this kind of file management. (See your instructor if you have any questions about this.) Using the template file in this way involves what some software calls "file merging," that is, placing in one file the information contained in another. Other WPS may refer to a similar function as "opening another document window." Check your WPS to determine the exact jargon that it uses to describe a similar function. Here are some typical steps in using a template file:

> **1.** Open the file containing the text your are working on and place the cursor at the beginning of the text (or some other appropriate place in the text).

2. Perform the appropriate keystrokes to permit you to open or add another file on-screen at the insertion point you have selected.

3. When the WPS asks which file to insert, type the appropriate name and press the RETURN or ENTER key.

4. When the template file appears, answer the questions it asks, scrolling to specific points in your text if necessary, to get the appropriate information.

5. Decide how you want to use the information that you discovered and whether (1) you want to leave this information in its current location in your text, (2) you wish to save it under another name (using a BLOCK COPY/SAVE command), or (3) you simply want to delete it altogether.

How you use template files will depend upon how your WPS manages files, that is, whether it allows you to open or insert one file in another. Investigate your WPS manual and answer the following questions.

1. After you have opened or loaded one file, does your WPS permit you to *insert* or *add* another file *on-screen* into the text already active? _____ If your answer is "No," skip to question 5 below.

2. Once you have opened one file, what menu option, command, or keystroke must you perform to

  a. locate the cursor in the appropriate place? _____
  b. select the file to open or insert? _____
  c. call up or open the desired file? _____

3. When you have completed the use of the template file, what commands or keystrokes must you perform to

  a. move the template file elsewhere in your file? _____
  b. save the template file under a different name? _____
  c. delete the template file without saving it? _____

4. If your WPS permits you to work on two documents simultaneously, you may want to forego merging the two files and simply open the template file in one "window" while you examine the text itself in the other one. Answer these questions to determine the appropriate steps:

  a. Once you have opened the text you wish to examine, what keystroke or command allows you to open a second window? _____
  b. What keystroke or command allows you to select and open the appropriate template text? _____
  c. What keystroke or command allows you to "toggle" from working in one window to working in the other? _____
  d. When you have completed your use of the template file, what commands or keystrokes must have perform to save the template file under a different name? _____ Close the window containing the template file without saving it? _____

5. If your WPS does not support file merging (or, "windows"), you can still use the template files to great effect in the following way:

    a. Open a template text which you have created.

    b. Using a hard copy of your text, answer the questions on-line that pertain to your text.

    c. Save this template file under a name other than the original name.

    d. Print a hard copy of this newly named template file for later use in evaluating or revising your text.

Congratulations on completing this tutorial. You should now be well on your way to mastering your WPS and using it effectively in your writing tasks.

APPENDIX II

A Computer Glossary

This glossary of computer and word processing terms is not exhaustive. You may want to consult your word processing manual to check definitions of other terms not covered here or to check the specific jargon your particular word processor uses. Most of the terms in this list are referred to in the body of *Processing Words. Please Note:* Many terms cited within definitions have their own definitions in the glossary.

Active File (See also *File*). The file opened and currently in use by the user.

Application Software A program, such as a word processing program, which performs a specific task for the user. Such software "applies" or puts into action the program the user wishes to employ.

Back-up Copy A copy of a file or entire disk which users make to insure that if an original file or disk is lost or destroyed, they will have an extra copy.

Block Copy/Block Move (See also *Mark, Move, Reform*). Within a word processing program, a series of commands which allows the user to mark the beginning and end of a text in order to: (1) move it to another location in the document; (2) copy or duplicate it for insertion elsewhere without removing the marked text from its current location; (3) save it to another file; or (4) delete it from the file entirely.

Boilerplate A text which the user intends to use over and over with little or no modification, such as a name and address, and which is stored in a file, under a specific file name, which the user may insert into an already active file.

Boldface (See also *Double-strike, Format*). A format command which prints characters darker and slightly wider than normal. Most printers create boldface characters by printing each character two or three times, slightly offset from the first printing.

Call Up (See also *Close, Load, Open*). At the beginning of a word processing session, to open a file for use. It may also refer to opening and inserting a file (see Merge) into an already active file.

Carriage Return (CR) An end-of-line keystroke that returns the cursor to the left margin. On a typewriter, the typist presses the carriage return key to return to the left margin. In word processing software that contains the feature *word wrap*, users normally do not press a carriage return unless they wish to end a unit of text (like a paragraph), since the word wrap function *automatically* returns the cursor to the left margin. A carriage return that is intentionally inserted by a user is sometimes called a *hard carriage return*.

Center (See also *Format*). A format command which

centers a line or larger, marked portion of text between the left and right margins.

Character A letter, number, symbol, or diacritical mark which is entered on the VDT with the pressing of a key.

Close (See also *Call Up, Exit, Load, Merge, Open*). To end an editing session with the active file and return to a word processing program's opening menu. This usually occurs after a file has been saved, though some programs give the user the option to end a session without saving the active file.

Command An instruction which users, using one or more keystrokes, give to the computer to perform a specific function. For instance, in one popular word processing program, users open a file by holding down the control key (CTRL) and pressing "d."

Control Code (See also *Boldface, Font, Subscript, Superscript*). Special character(s) inserted into a document which command the printer to print a character, word, or portion of text in a certain way. For instance, some word processing programs require the user to insert a CTRL-T keystroke before and after a number which is to appear as a superscript (as in a footnote).

Control Key (CTRL) A special key on a computer keyboard, usually labelled CTRL, that operates like a shift key, but which generates a special computer function when combined with other keystrokes. Typically, a user holds down the CTRL key while pressing another key to enter a specific command.

Copy (See also *Block Copy*). In a word processing program, *copy* may refer to: (1) making a duplicate of an entire disk; (2) making a duplicate of a particular file; (3) making a duplicate of a particular block of a text which has been marked for insertion elsewhere in the document or in another file.

CPU The central processing unit (CPU) is the brain of the computer, containing circuits that perform the commands of the user and control other units of the computer.

CRT (See *VDT*).

Cursor A blinking light, usually in the shape of an arrow, a rectangle, or an underline, which indicates the next insertion point in a text.

Cursor Movement Key A key which moves the cursor in the direction (up/down, left/right) the user desires. Such keys usually have directional arrows on their keytops. Other word processing software may use a combination of keystrokes or a mouse to govern cursor movement.

Cut and Paste (See also *Block/Copy*). In some word processing programs, for instance, *MacWrite*, the operation identical to block copy/block move.

Data Numerical or textual information stored in a computer's on-line memory or on a diskette.

Database A file or set of files which contains information organized by different categories (fields) and which can be searched, sorted, or ordered in various ways, depending on the needs of the user.

Default The value or setting used by a program when a user does not specify something else. For instance, a word processing program may automatically set the left and right margins or automatically justify all text when opened, unless the user changes these settings.

Delete A word processing operation which removes a character, word, or block of text from the on-line memory of the computer. In some programs, deleted text can be recovered by an UNDO or UNDELETE command, since the word processing program stores it in an on-line, buffer memory; in others, any text deleted is permanently removed from memory and is not recoverable.

Disk Drive A storage device for a microcomputer which allows a user to save and retrieve files. The disk drive works like a tape recorder in that it "records" and "plays back" information stored on the diskettes which are inserted into it. The drive consists of a "read/write" head that creates magnetic dots on a spinning diskette when recording data. When reading data from a diskette, it reverses the process, converting the magnetic dots into electrical pulses which eventually appear as text on the VDT.

Disk/Diskette (See also *Load*). A disk is a small ($3\frac{1}{2}$ inch or $5\frac{1}{4}$ inch) magnetic storage unit which stores saved files. The disk serves as an extension of the computer's memory. Diskettes must be initialized before they are ready to receive information. They are inserted into the disk drive of a microcomputer to enable the user to open, save, or print files that are stored on it. Some computers require the user to turn on the computer before inserting a disk; others require the user to insert the disk before turning it on. Normally, a disk should not be removed from a disk drive while the drive is in operation—usually indicated by a light or a whirring sound.

Document (See also *File, Text*). A text—for instance, a term paper, a letter home, or a set of statistics—which a user is creating or editing on a microcomputer.

Documentation The manual or document which accompanies a microcomputer or an application program and explains how to use it.

DOS (Disk Operating System) Every computer has its own system of program instructions which operate its disk drives. Some computers have a built-in operating system, while others require that the user purchase a special disk which contains an operating system. Operating systems are not necessarily compatible and, therefore, diskettes are not usually interchangeable on different computer systems. For instance, a disk initialized for use on a Commodore computer's disk drive will not be "readable" by an Apple computer's disk drive. You should expect your diskettes normally only to work with the same brand and model of the computer you are using.

Dot-matrix Printer (See also *Ink-jet Printer, Letter-quality Printer, Printer*). A dot-matrix printer is an impact printing device which forms characters on paper by "firing" rows of pins against a ribbon and platen. Dot-matrix printers are usually faster than letter-quality printers, which work much like typewriters, but do not have the same quality of print.

Double-strike (See also *Boldface, Control Codes, Format*). A format command which prints characters twice for emphasis, thus making them darker than normal.

Edit The mode in a *word processing program* which allows the user to create or alter text within a file.

Enter (1) The operation in which a user places text onto the VDT with appropriate keystrokes; (2) a key which serves the same function as a RETURN key.

Erase The operation in which a user discards a file from a disk. Users sometimes must make room on a disk for a file they have created and must erase one or more files. A user may also wish to erase an entire disk to prepare it for receiving fresh data. Some word processing programs permit a user to restore data to a disk or file unintentionally erased.

Exit The operation in which a user leaves or quits a particular program. Exiting a program may return the user to the operating system or to a particular menu, removing the program from the computer's on-line memory. Before exiting a program, a user should be sure that he or she has saved any file important to a particular task.

File (See also *Merge*). A file contains the collection of data or portions of text which are opened or saved during a work session. A file is usually given a file name, either the first time it is created, or after it has been opened, during the saving operation.

File Directory A list of the files currently saved on a particular diskette. A file directory may be called up from an opening menu on most word processing programs.

File Name The name of a file, which the user employs to open it or save it. Some word processing programs specify that a file name can only be a certain number of characters long, or require that it have a three-letter "extension" to indicate the kind of file it is. For instance, a file created by MacWrite for the MacIntosh computer might be named TEXT #1; on the other hand, a file created by Wordstar for an IBM PC might be named DRAFT #1.TXT, in which DRAFT #1 is the name of the file and TXT (standing for "Text") is the extension. Users normally choose a name appropriate to their writing task: MOM.LET (standing for letter to Mom) or LAB REPORT.

Find (See *Search/Replace*).

Flush Left/Right (See also *Format, Justify*). Text that is formatted "flush left" has an even left margin but a ragged-right margin. Likewise, a "flush right" margin has an even right margin but a ragged-left margin. "Flush left" is the normal or default setting in most word processing programs.

Font (See also *Pitch*). A font is a typeface, or particular style of print, which users may choose prior to or during the printing of their file. Some fonts are controlled by the word processing program, while others are controlled by the settings on the printer. Roman, Italic, Manhattan, Dover are names of some different fonts that some programs and printers feature.

Footer (See also *Header*). A line or lines printed at the bottom margin of a text which may indicate page numbers, the title of the text, or any other information the user wishes to appear on each page. Some word processing programs have a default setting for footers which can be altered by the user.

Format (See also *Initialize*). (1) To format a disk is to prepare it to receive information. (2) To format a text is to determine how a page will appear in print, including such matters as margin settings; indenting for paragraphs; whether and where a page number or title should appear on a page; whether to employ underlining, boldfacing, or double-striking for effect; what font and pitch to use in printing the text's characters; and so on. Most word processing programs have default settings for each of these features which can be altered by the user.

Function Keys Some computers have special keys which may be programmed to perform user-defined functions. For instance, a user might program one key to SAVE A FILE, another to REFORM A PARAGRAPH, another to EXIT a particular program.

Global Search/Replace (See *Search/Replace*).

Glossary (See also *Boilerplate*). Some word processing programs permit the user to store frequently used words, phrases, blocks of text, or special printer codes which can be called up with one or more keystrokes and thus save the user some time.

Hard Copy (See also *Soft Copy*). A paper copy of a file or document.

Hardware (See also *Software*). The physical, tangible equipment in a computer system—its circuits, VDT, internal memory, CPU—as distinguished from the software or programs which are created to operate the computer.

Header (See also *Footer, Format*). (1) A line or lines printed in the top margin of a text which may indicate page numbers, the title of the text, or any other information the user wishes to appear on each page. Some word processing programs have a default setting for headers which can be altered by the user. (2) A heading or subheading in a text which indicates to the reader the beginning of a new section. Such a header is usually formatted in boldface or with a change of pitch to draw the reader's attention to it.

Home The upper left-hand corner of a VDT screen. In some computers, the keyboard itself contains a

key which permits the user to move directly to the HOME position.

Indent (1) To print a line of characters a specified number of spaces to the right of the left margin. (2) To print a whole block of text within specified left and right margins, usually set off from the normal left and right margins.

Initialize (See also *DOS, Format*). To prepare a diskette to receive information for a particular disk operating system (DOS). Since not every disk drive is compatible with another, each diskette used must be specially formatted or initialized to enable it to be read by the appropriate disk drive. During the process on some disk operating systems, the disk itself is given a name.

Ink-jet Printer (See also *Dot-matrix Printer, Letter-quality Printer, Printer*). Unlike the dot-matrix process, the ink-jet process does not form characters by hitting a ribbon or platen; instead, the characters are formed by spraying streams of ink through "portholes" at a sheet of paper. Ink-jet printers are often faster than letter-quality printers, and they can equal or exceed the latter's quality of print.

Interactive An interactive program is one which allows the user to "interact"—or ask questions and make specific choices within the program, to which the computer will respond. This is in contrast to a noninteractive program which, once begun, carries through a specified process until completion, without the possibility of user interruption.

Insert (1) A word processing operation in which a user places the cursor within some already entered text to supply additional words, sentences, or whole blocks of text. (2) A file operation in which users place an entire file at the insertion point within the active file they are using. (3) A typing mode in which text is inserted into a document, pushing existing text to the right of the insertion point (See *Overwrite*).

Insertion Point The current location of the cursor, that is, point at which the next character may be entered or inserted.

Justify (See also *Flush Left/Right, Format*). To fit a text within flush-left and flush-right margins. To justify a text, the word processing program inserts spaces between words to fill out a line between specified margins. Justification is usually a TOG-

GLED feature, that is, it may be turned on or off with appropriate keystrokes. Most word processing programs permit a user to justify selected portions of a text or the entire text.

Keystroke Any single pressing of a key is a keystroke. Some word processing operations require that the user use a series or combination of keystrokes to implement a particular command. For instance, in some word processing programs, one must hold down the CTRL key and press ''P'' to print a file.

Letter-quality Printer (See also *Dot-matrix Printer, Ink-jet Printer, Printer*). *Letter-quality printer* usually denotes a printer that uses a more conventional ''typewriter'' printing system to place characters on a sheet of paper. Rotating a daisy-wheel or ball, a letter-quality printer strikes a ribbon and platen to print the characters on the paper. Letter-quality printers usually are substantially slower than dot-matrix or ink-jet printers, but they have a high-quality print resembling that of the typewriter. New technology, however, has developed dot-matrix printers that achieve ''near-letter-quality'' print without sacrificing speed.

Load (See also *Open*). (1) To insert a diskette into a disk drive in order to place a program or text file in operation. (2) To open and place in operation a particular file on a disk which is already placed in a disk drive.

Mainframe Computer (See also *Microcomputer*). A large, nonportable computer system with a substantial memory. Such a system must be accessed by the user through a terminal which is directly wired into the computer system or which may be linked through the phone lines, using a device called a *modem*.

Margin (See also *Format*). The space between the edge of the page and the beginning of text. There are four margins: left, right, top, bottom.

Mark (See also *Block Copy/Block Move*). In order to move, copy, or delete a large block of text, the user must first mark the beginning and ending points of the text to be moved, copied, or deleted. This is usually done by inserting a special character specified by the word processing program at the beginning and ending of the text. In some programs, for instance, *MacWrite*, a block is marked by dragging and clicking the mouse over the block so that it is darkened.

Memory (1) The permanent memory of a computer (ROM: read-only memory) holds instructions on how to store, merge, and arrange data which is entered. Even when the computer is turned off, this information remains safely stored inside. (2) The temporary memory of a computer (RAM: random-access memory) holds the instructions of the user's word processing program and the active file or text that the user is editing. This is sometimes called the ''on-line memory'' or ''work space.'' Once the computer is turned off, any text or file which has not been SAVED TO DISKETTE will be lost.

Menu A list of operations from which the user may select a particular function, such as: OPEN A FILE, PRINT A FILE, ERASE A DISK. Menus may appear within particular word processing programs when the disk is first loaded, or during a particular set of operations within the program. Some word processing programs feature ''pulldown'' menus which allow the user to call up a menu when it is needed and keep it hidden when it is not.

Merge (See also *File*). (1) To combine data from two or more sources into one file or document. This operation may or may not be a feature of a word processing program. Sometimes referred to as ''mail merge,'' this feature allows a user to create custom ''form letters'' which automatically insert names, addresses, product names, and so forth in a document. (2) To open one file while working with another, active file in order to combine portions of text or to use a template file. Some word processing programs permit the user to do this from within a file; others require that the user close an active file first and merge the files with a different process.

Microcomputer (See also *Mainframe Computer*). A small, personal computer containing a programmable processing circuit built upon silicon chips called a *microprocessor*. Microcomputers are ''stand alone,'' self-contained computers with their own internal memory, keyboard, and storage devices (disk drives). When used with a word processing program and linked with a printer, microcomputers may serve as an electronic composing station, superior to and more versatile than electronic typewriters.

Monitor (See *VDT*).

Mouse A manually operated pointing device whose movements on a flat surface correspond to the movement of the cursor on the VDT. A mouse usually features a button which, when pressed or "clicked," sends a special function code to the computer.

Move (See also *Block Copy/Block Move, Mark, Reform*). To relocate a word, sentence, or block of text within a document. This operation typically requires users to mark the beginning and ending of the section of text they wish to move, move the cursor to the new insertion point, and to then perform the appropriate keystrokes (or mouse movement) specified by the word processing program. Some programs automatically reform the paragraph or block of text into which the new text has been moved to align with the margins the user has set; others require that users perform this manually, with specified keystrokes.

Open (See also *Call Up, Close, Load*). At the beginning of a word processing session or at the close of another file, to select a file for use.

Overwrite (See also *Insert*). (1) To replace one file with another by copying or saving a file with the same name. For instance, to replace a file named, Letter.TXT, a user would create a file and save it to a diskette under the name Letter.TXT. The new version would replace the old. (2) A typing mode in which the user types over existing text and thereby replaces it. The default mode of most word processing programs is the insert mode, in which new text is placed in the text at the insertion point, moving existing text to the right. In the overwrite mode, the text is not displaced but deleted by the newly inserted text. The insert mode and overwrite mode are toggle modes on most word processing programs.

Paginate (See also *Format*). To place page numbers in a document. In most word processing programs, page numbering is a function of selecting headers or footers, which place the page number and other information at the top or bottom margins on each (or selected) pages of the document. Pagination then becomes automatic and sequential; users do not (and should not) enter a page number into the text itself.

Pitch (See also *Font, Format*). Most word process-ing programs and printers allow users to select the pitch, or size of typeface, they wish to use. Typically, the pitch is a choice between ten characters per inch (Pica), twelve characters per inch (Elite), or seventeen characters per inch (Condensed). Newer technology is making it possible for users to select *fonts* which have their own range of sizes and shapes, greatly increasing the choice of format by users.

Print A command which orders the microcomputer to send text to a printer for the purpose of making a hard copy of a specified text. Some word processing programs permit the user to print an active file as well as files not currently active but stored on a disk; others require that the user save the file first before it can be printed. Likewise, some programs allow the user to see what a document will look like before it is printed—that is, they will show on the VDT where page breaks occur and how special formatting features such as footers, underlining, and altered margins will appear. Other programs perform these formatting tasks with special characters inserted into the document, whose effects the user cannot see in place until the document is actually printed.

Printer (See also *Dot-matrix Printer, Ink-jet Printer, Letter-quality Printer*). A device which allows the user to print a hard copy of the data within a file or document. Most printers are controlled by the word processing program which the user employs, though a few have features (font, pitch, and so on) which can be selected by programming the printer itself.

Program (See *Application Software*).

Prompt (See also *Menu*). (1) Most microcomputers have a "sign-on" prompt—such as "A >"—indicating it is ready to receive a particular command or open a file; others simply have a blinking light or cursor. The user then types the appropriate command and the computer goes into action. (2) A message from the computer or from a particular program which alerts the user to a problem, a choice, or the next step in a series of operations.

Quit (See *Exit*).

Reform (See also *BlockCopy/Block Move, Move*). After users move or insert text into a location already containing text, they must usually reform the body of the text in order to realign it with existing margins. Some word processing programs perform this automatically; others require users to perform it manually with a series of specified keystrokes.

Replace (See *Search/Replace*).

Retrieve (See *Call Up, Open*).

Return (See *Carriage Return*).

Save (See also *Close, Load, Open*). To place a copy of an active file onto a storage unit (diskette). This operation may include giving the file a name (unless it was named when it was opened); ending the editing session with this particular file and returning to the word processing program's menu; or leaving the word processing program and ending the editing session itself, returning to the operating system of the computer. Saving a file prevents it from being lost when the computer is turned off. Most saving operations displace the version of the file currently on disk. If users wish to preserve both copies of the file—the edited version and the original—they can save the edited version under another file name.

Scroll (See also *Cursor*). The horizontal or vertical movement of the text displayed on a VDT. Scrolling down a document moves text down the VDT so that new lines are added at the top and disappear off the bottom. Scrolling up a text moves the text up the VDT so that new lines are added at the bottom and disappear off the top. Scrolling a text is complementary to, but not the same as, moving the cursor. The cursor moves around the insertion point of the text on the specific screen in view on the VDT. Scrolling is useful for reading through a text and moving quickly from section to section in a document. Most word processing programs allow the user to move quickly to the beginning or end of the document with an appropriate series of keystrokes.

Search/Replace Most word processing programs allow the user to search for a particular character, word, string of words, or command codes in a document and, if desired, replace them with another. This feature becomes indispensible as a tool for finding and replacing problems like misspelled words, locating key concepts and terms, and generally for focusing on particular features of a document users wish to locate or analyze. Sometimes called GLOBAL SEARCH AND REPLACE, the operation usually requires several steps. First,

users select the SEARCH/REPLACE function from the word processor's menu. Second, the program will prompt users to supply the word(s) they wish to search for. Next, if users wish to replace the word(s) specified, the program will prompt them to supply the new word(s) which will be substituted. Finally, users may select from different options the menu presents, such as, REPLACE WITHOUT ASKING, REPLACE THROUGHOUT DOCUMENT, WHOLE WORDS ONLY, IGNORE CASE, and so on.

Select (1) To mark or identify a portion of text for special printing codes, such as underlining or boldfacing. (2) In some computers and word processing programs which employ a mouse for cursor movement, SELECT is the operation for choosing an item from a menu, marking a text for copying, moving, or deleting, or performing other special functions.

Soft Copy (See also *Hard copy*). A copy of a document or file as it exists on a diskette or in the online memory of the computer.

Software (See also *Application Software, Hardware*). The programs or set of instructions which a computer uses to perform selected user functions. A user must employ software in order to use a computer. Most often this means inserting a diskette of programs, like a word processing program, into a disk drive to begin a work session.

Subscript (See also *Format*). A character printed slightly below the other characters on a printed line. Subscripts typically appear in scientific formulas, such as H_2O. Some word processing programs allow users to insert special control codes, letting users print a subscript, but not all programs offer this capability.

Superscript (See also *Format*). A character printed slightly above the other characters on a printed line. Superscripts typically appear in footnotes and in mathematical formulas. Some word processing programs permit users to insert special control codes that let them print a superscript, but not all programs do this.

System Disk (See also *DOS*). Some computers require the user to first insert a special system disk into a disk drive before they can receive any other program disks. Such a disk usually contains the computer's operating system and permits such functions as copying and deleting files, and opening a file directory.

Template File (See also *Call Up, Merge, Open*). In *Processing Words,* "template file" refers to files or texts created by users that lead them through a set of questions or *prompts,* which assist in analyzing the features of a text or in exploring an idea. Depending upon the user's word processing program, the template file may be called up within an active file or opened at the beginning of a new editing session.

Terminal (See also *Mainframe Computer*). A VDT and keyboard which permit a user access to a mainframe computer. A terminal looks much like a stand-alone microcomputer but usually is not linked to a disk drive or printer.

Text (See also *Document, File*). Any series of characters, words, strings of words, or data which a user places in a file. Text is sometimes used synonymously with such terms as document or file.

Toggle (See also *Default*). In a word processing program, a function which allows two settings: on or off. For instance, on most word processing programs, justification is a TOGGLED function; the user may elect to justify a block of text by performing the appropriate keystrokes, then turn off the justification with similar keystrokes. Most TOGGLED features have a default setting when the word processing program is loaded which the user can alter.

Underline (See also *Format*). A formatting function which places a line underneath selected text. The underlining may be continuous (characters and spaces in the selected text are underlined) or discontinuous (only characters, not spaces, are underlined). Some computers permit the user to see underlining on the VDT. On others, underlining is elected by inserted special control codes before and after the selected text, and the user may only see the underlining formatted on the hard copy of the text.

Undo/Undelete (1) To return a document to its original form prior to a particular function, for instance, retrieving a text accidentally deleted. Some word processing programs permit the user to retrieve or *undo* the last function performed in a document with specified keystrokes; others do not permit such retrieval. (2) To recover a file accidentally deleted from a disk. Some disk operating systems and word processing programs allow the user to recover an accidentally deleted file, but not all do.

VDT A video display terminal is a visual display unit, like a television set, especially designed to display characters for a microcomputer. VDT may be used interchangeably with *monitor.*

Word Processing Program The particular text-editing software that a user employs to create, revise, format, and print a document. A computer, in and of itself, usually does not have word processing capability. This must be supplied by the use of a particular word processing program. Some popular programs include, *Bank Street Writer, Wordstar, MacWrite, Quick Brown Fox, Word-Perfect,* and *Microsoft Word.*

Word Wrap Word wrap is a feature of most word processing programs that automatically moves the cursor and insertion point to the left margin after reaching or exceeding the right margin. Word wrap makes unnecessary the inclusion of a carriage return at the end of a line as is customary when typing on a conventional typewriter. When word wrap is in use, carriage returns are used only when the user wishes to insert a hard return, indicating the end of a portion of text, like a paragraph. Word wrap is usually a TOGGLED feature of a program.

Index

297